40 Classic Crude Oil Trades

The day-to-day world of crude oil traders is not usually open to outsiders. Few non-specialists appreciate how oil traders approach the markets, what their backgrounds are and how they make money.

This book brings the oil trading world to vivid life by introducing the reader to 40 real-life trades or strategies that were carried out by named market participants. The 40 chapters cover different geographies and different crude oil markets, providing an unparalleled insight into how crude oil traders work and think. Oil trading developed in its current form in the 1980s and the chapters cover these early beginnings through to the present day. The trades have been grouped in sections that relate to the nature of each trade and its broader use as an example of a successful trading style. Sections cover approaches to arbitrage trading; the impact of geopolitics; logistics and storage plays; short-term versus longer term trading; managing new crude oil grades; trading crude oil derivatives.

The book provides plenty of inspiration for current or prospective crude oil traders or analysts. It will also be valuable for academic researchers, business school case studies, and for anyone wanting to learn more about the individuals that shape the world's most important commodity market.

Owain Johnson is the Global Head of Research of CME Group, and the author of *The Price Reporters: A Guide To PRAs And Commodity Benchmarks*.

Routledge Classic Market Trades

40 Classic Crude Oil Trades
Real-Life Examples of Innovative Trading
Owain Johnson

For more information about this series please visit https://www.routledge.com/Routledge-Classic-Market-Trades/book-series/RMCMT

40 Classic Crude Oil Trades

Real-Life Examples of Innovative Trading

Owain Johnson

LONDON AND NEW YORK

Cover image: © nazarkru / Getty Images

First published 2022
by Routledge
2 Park Square, Milton Park, Abingdon, Oxon OX14 4RN

and by Routledge
605 Third Avenue, New York, NY 10158

Routledge is an imprint of the Taylor & Francis Group, an informa business

British Library Cataloguing-in-Publication Data
A catalogue record for this book is available from the British Library

Library of Congress Cataloging-in-Publication Data
Names: Johnson, Owain, author.
Title: 40 classic crude oil trades : real-life examples of innovative trading / Owain Johnson.
Other titles: Forty classic crude oil trades
Description: Abingdon, Oxon ; New York, NY : Routledge, 2022. | Series: Routledge classic market trades | Includes bibliographical references and index.
Identifiers: LCCN 2021041903 (print) | LCCN 2021041904 (ebook) | ISBN 9780367700409 (paperback) | ISBN 9780367700416 (hardback) | ISBN 9781003144335 (ebook)
Subjects: LCSH: Petroleum industry and trade—Finance. | Petroleum. | Commodity trading advisors. | Commodity exchanges.
Classification: LCC HG6047.P47 J636 2022 (print) | LCC HG6047.P47 (ebook) | DDC 332.63/28—dc23
LC record available at https://lccn.loc.gov/2021041903
LC ebook record available at https://lccn.loc.gov/2021041904

ISBN: 978-0-367-70041-6 (hbk)
ISBN: 978-0-367-70040-9 (pbk)
ISBN: 978-1-003-14433-5 (ebk)

DOI: 10.4324/9781003144335

Typeset in Bembo
by codeMantra

Contents

Acknowledgements

The main pleasure of preparing these accounts of 'classic crude oil trades' has been speaking to so many intelligent and interesting people: some old friends, some new acquaintances.

During the COVID-19 lockdown in the U.K., when we could barely leave the house, it was a great pleasure to remind myself of the wider world out there and to reconnect with people, even if on the phone or online.

My huge gratitude goes out to the 40 people whose stories follow. Thank you for taking the time to talk me through your trades and your strategies. Thank you for being so open about your successes and challenges. It was a genuine pleasure to hear your stories and to record your experiences.

Thanks are also due to the many traders who for various reasons were unable to speak on the record, but who still took the time to provide suggestions and encouragement.

I am also grateful to Daniel Baruch, Daniel Brusstar, James Lear, Matthew Judge and Michelle Zhang for their kind introductions to their friends in the crude oil market.

Kristina Abbotts of Routledge again proved a helpful and positive publisher, and I deeply appreciate her support once more.

Finally, thanks to my wonderful family who are remarkably understanding when I take on interesting projects on top of an extremely busy role at the exchange. I appreciate your patience with me and thanks for taking an interest in what I do.

Most of this book was prepared in the midst of the pandemic and while I was spending a lot of time visiting hospitals. It therefore seems very appropriate to dedicate it to three fantastic doctors: Piet Haers, Sarra Jawad and Alex Cash.

Introduction

The genesis of this book was a conversation on a pleasant summer afternoon in one of Oxford's historic pubs.

Adi Imsirovic and I had stopped off on the way to a dinner at the Oxford Institute for Energy Studies and Adi was telling me about his 'false arbitrage' trade, which he describes in Chapter 4.

It struck me at the time that the oil market generates some very good stories that never get shared beyond pub gardens or high-end restaurants. (An enthusiasm for fine dining seems to be a common trait among oil traders.)

It also struck me that few non-specialists would have any idea about the ingenuity of oil traders and what they do each day to keep crude oil – still the world's most important commodity – flowing profitably around the world.

Despite growing environmental concerns, crude oil continues to underpin our modern economies and personal lifestyles. But few people have any understanding of how crude oil is bought and sold between different companies, and how it flows from the production fields to the refineries that turn it into gasoline, diesel, jet fuel and the other products that we depend upon.

This general lack of awareness is no accident. Oil companies are often a magnet for negative publicity, many times with good reason. As a result, oil traders generally shy away from the spotlight where possible, even though the nature of their job, which relies on interpersonal skills, means that most traders are by temperament open and outgoing.

I have spent a couple of decades talking to oil traders as part of my job, and I can honestly say I have rarely met a boring trader. All are highly intelligent, analytical and motivated. Most are charming, although there are also those who share "a few common traits with psychopaths" as Mohammed Minkara notes in Chapter 17.

The compensation for dealing with even the most intense and unnerving oil traders has been hearing their tales from the frontline.

Oil trading is many things, but it is not a dull profession. I have always enjoyed hearing about different trading strategies and how oil traders employ their considerable ingenuity to try to turn a profit, even in often challenging circumstances.

DOI: 10.4324/9781003144335-1

This book allows the reader to join in with those conversations and to listen in to a group of prominent oil traders reminiscing about their approaches, their strategies and their careers. Hopefully, it provides some insights into what is normally an inaccessible world.

Trader backgrounds

These spotlights on the otherwise mysterious world of oil trading would not have been possible without the willingness of these 40 contributors to talk openly about their experiences, and I remain incredibly grateful for their candour.

The contributors are drawn from different eras, different regions and different backgrounds.

Their disparate backgrounds should be no surprise. A look through the biographies of the contributors shows that there is no standard path to becoming an oil trader. After all, you can't study 'oil trading' as a degree at university.

Of course, many traders enter the industry through the graduate trainee schemes run by the large oil companies and are eventually assigned to a trading desk, but others find their own path.

Academic success can be an advantage – we have a few very impressive PhDs represented here – but temperament and practical skillset are valued just as highly. Trading is a career where results are always more important than background, and a trader is only as good as their recent performance.

In this sense, the profession is a genuine meritocracy: even if connections or good fortune get you through the door, only positive results will see you retained on a trading desk. After all, as Thomas Andersen (Chapter 30) notes, a trader's achievements are shown in his or her profit-and-loss account for all to judge: "every single day at the end of the day, you can see exactly how much you have lost and gained".

Choose your own adventure

I have organized the chapters into sections based broadly on the trading strategy that was employed or the area of focus of the 'classic trade': arbitrages, derivatives, logistic and storage trades, and so on, but the chapters could also be read in a number of different ways.

A chronological reading would show the development of the oil markets from the 1960s when, as Richard Johnstone (Chapter 26) says, the "profession of oil trader didn't exist and neither did the oil markets as we know them today" through to today's high-speed electronic trading.

We hear Bridie Tobin (Chapter 28) describing her experiences after joining Shell in 1963. Then, bringing us near to the present day, Kevin McCormack (Chapter 37), a very experienced trader himself, describes his chart-based approach to the post-pandemic price recovery of 2021.

There are almost four decades between those two points in time. In that time, oil has become more than a product that is produced and then sold to refiners. Crude has become a commodity that is traded between multiple firms, and which underpins a whole financial infrastructure of paper barrels that are bought and sold by hedge funds, pension funds, individual investors and others that have little connection to the original physical market.

This development can be traced in these chapters through the changing nature of the Brent market, which is one of the two great global oil benchmarks, alongside WTI.

Oil was first discovered in the U.K. and Norwegian sectors of the North Sea in the 1970s, and Richard Johnstone marketed the first cargo of Brent crude oil from Sullom Voe in 1978. In the 1980s, Brent then began to underpin an active forward or 'Dated' market, which Liz Bossley describes in Chapter 14.

Dated Brent provides price signals to a large part of the world's oil production to this day, while physical Brent crude oil also came to underpin a highly significant futures market, which attracted Steve Roberts (Chapter 33) to the International Petroleum Exchange (IPE, now ICE) in the early 1990s.

Milan Kratka (Chapter 34) made the first attempt at moving Brent futures trading from the floors of the IPE to its current electronic marketplace in the early 2000s, while Greg Newman (Chapter 35) is one of a new wave of sophisticated traders that are increasingly active in the instruments that surround the core Brent benchmark.

Alternate readings

If a chronological reading does not appeal, then the chapters could also be read with a geographical focus. The Russian chapters, for example, are some of my favourites.

The impact of Russia's transition to a market-based economy on one Russian oil producer is discussed by Trym Nordhus (Chapter 5) and Elena Lobodina (Chapter 15), while Colin Bryce (Chapter 1) and Philippe Khoury (Chapter 2) convey both the opportunities and the challenges that faced western firms in their early engagement with post-Soviet Russia.

The tremendous geographical reach of the oil industry can be seen from the fact that there are 23 different nationalities among the 40 contributors, although the influence of the three key crude oil markets – Brent in London/Geneva, WTI in Houston/New York and Oman/Dubai in Singapore – is reflected in the relatively higher numbers of U.K., U.S. and Singaporean traders.

We could even try for a thematic reading, instead of a chronological or geographical one, since some of the chapters complement each other by illustrating how the same market conditions affected different firms in completely different ways, stimulating a variety of trading approaches.

When the financial crisis hit in 2008–09, for example, it created the opportunity for Gerardo Rodríguez (Chapter 38) to execute a tremendously successful hedging programme on behalf of the government of Mexico.

Meanwhile, in China, Cui Zhenchu (Chapter 9) responded to the financial crisis by banning his traders from speculating on the outright price of oil, thereby sparing Unipec from the losses that some other Chinese firms suffered.

Also at the same time, Justus van der Spuy (Chapter 25) realized that the resultant economic slowdown meant that some governments were holding excess strategic oil stocks, creating an opportunity, while the ongoing impact of the financial crisis forced Anne Devlin (Chapter 10) to manage credit issues at an already challenging time.

What makes a classic crude oil trade?

Each of these responses to the financial crisis was totally different, but all were successful on their own terms. This reflects the tremendous variety of approaches to the oil markets and the fact that 'success' in trading means different things at different times to different firms.

These chapters clearly do not represent the most profitable trades that each participant could recall, although some of the strategies described in the chapters proved to be highly lucrative, and Gerardo Rodríguez may well have implemented the most profitable hedging programme of all time…

Instead of focusing on pure profit, many of the chapters concentrate on those times when the traders demonstrated their ingenuity, often with the result that they succeeded in turning a challenging situation around.

This is trading at its best – using a combination of market expertise and imagination to find a creative solution, which then makes it a 'classic trade'.

Michael Dugdale (Chapter 18) turned what he thought was a fatally weak position into a strength, while Alessandro Liberati (Chapter 13) and Michael Hacking (Chapter 22) both managed to rescue deals by finding creative solutions to the challenges faced by their counterparts.

Then, in possibly my favourite of all the chapters – if I'm allowed to admit to a favourite – John Krus (Chapter 20) saved Texaco a few dollars per barrel armed with nothing more than a burning sense of injustice and a tremendous ability to bluff.

Some of the strategies described in the chapters did not generate immediate profits. Instead, they were 'classic' in the sense that they built relationships or knowledge that ultimately paid significant dividends, financial or otherwise.

Gary King (Chapter 36) cheerfully admits that he never made much money from Tapis and Minas derivatives, but he is clear that the credibility he gained made the project hugely worthwhile.

Similarly, Colin Bryce's adventures in Russia benefited his firm in the longer term, despite the short-term challenges, while the hazards involved in financing crude oil traders in the more laissez-faire 1980s ultimately led

Philippe Cohen (Chapter 12) and other bank lenders to develop better controls and oversight.

What traders share

Having mentioned the massive variety in backgrounds and approaches between the different traders, it seems only right to also look at the elements that unite them.

A few key traits emerged again and again across the chapters. Each reader might spot different patterns, but for me the three most common shared characteristics of the contributors were their restlessness, high energy levels and sociability.

The restlessness stems, I believe, from an innate spirit of inquisitiveness and a desire to shake up and improve the status quo. These are not people who like to stand still or to execute the same trades day after day, and year after year.

"I don't like just accepting how other people have set things up", says Chris Del Vecchio (Chapter 23), while Philippe Khoury says he loves trading because "as a trader you can change the way you do your business almost every day". For Kurt Chapman (Chapter 3), trading was "a constant intellectual challenge" that he relished.

This restlessness and intellectual curiosity mean that even profitable trading strategies were constantly interrogated to see if they could be tweaked to increase their profitability. "Any decent crude oil trader should always be seeking to do something more", says Manosh Saha (Chapter 7).

The restlessness also springs from the high energy levels that most traders seem to possess. Traders often work long hours on their own market as well as handing over with colleagues in different regions and time zones. Traders also spend a lot of time on planes visiting suppliers and customers.

Beyond the heavy workload is often a heavy social life. A working day for Daphne Teo (Chapter 24) regularly stretched to 4am as she checked the U.S. markets from Singapore, frequently after an evening spent with customers or trading counterparts.

Despite the pressure on personal time, the social side of trading is nonetheless the piece that most traders speak of fondly. The nature of their role typically obliges oil traders to spend hours on the phone every day speaking to customers, suppliers, rivals, price reporting agencies, brokers and exchanges. Shy traders or traders with limited communication skills don't last long and for good reason.

"Before you trade oil, you need to trade information. This means you need to build relationships with other traders because people obviously tend to share more if they like you", says Sylvia Low (Chapter 11).

The social nature of trading comes up again and again throughout the chapters, and many traders expressed concern about any reduction in social contact between traders.

For those contributors, apart from being fun, social contact is crucial to developing a sense of what the counterpart needs and wants from the relationship, while also establishing a bond of personal trust that is particularly important in a high-pressure and volatile environment like oil trading.

"We weren't anonymous traders behind screens, we knew our counterparts and our customers, and we socialized together, so being viewed as a trustworthy person who tried to do the right thing was very important to me", says Anne Summers (Chapter 21).

Words of advice

A few recommendations for would-be oil traders are also repeated throughout the chapters.

These could be summed up as follows: develop a technical proficiency in a complementary area; recognize the value of the team around the trading desk; and don't chase short-term profits at the expense of long-term trading relationships.

The recommendation to achieve technical proficiency came up in several different ways. For many of the physical traders, deep knowledge of physical operations via a spell on the 'ops desk' had proved to be highly beneficial. "If you don't know operations properly, then in my opinion you will lack some key expertise when you are trading cargoes", says Daphne Teo.

Other contributors found that their trading had benefited from knowledge they had developed elsewhere, in areas like bank financing or trading technology. Geena Malkani (Chapter 19) learnt customer relations in the "incredibly hard school" of the car industry, while Gary King's years as a petroleum geologist provided him with additional credibility with certain customers.

Perhaps this awareness of the complementary nature of different skillsets explains why so many of the contributors were keen to call out the contribution to their success of other colleagues, whether it was trading mentors, fellow traders, operational staff, technologists, lawyers and so on.

In contrast to the myth of oil trading as a very individual activity, it emerges in these pages as more of a team sport, where an initial strategy or concept developed by a trader is successfully implemented thanks to the collective efforts of a whole group of people, including external financing banks, the need for whose support is repeatedly emphasized.

The final recommendation that comes up again and again was to take a long-term view and to ensure that counterparts also felt happy with the deal in question. "There's sometimes a balancing act that requires us to look beyond an individual transaction and to apply some form of bigger-picture approach to a specific issue", says Rajaraman Jayaraman (Chapter 27).

Many of the contributors describe their satisfaction in finding a trade that worked for both sides.

It was interesting to see just how many traders when asked to think about their 'classic' trade turned immediately to one where they had benefited both parties by solving a particular issue creatively.

"One of the best feelings in trading is when you find a trade that is a genuine win-win both for your company and for your counterparty", says Ralf-Dieter Poth (Chapter 6), while Ilia Bouchouev (Chapter 39) notes that, "it's a great strategy when you make money, but your customer also makes money".

Much of that desire to leave all parties to the trade feeling broadly satisfied comes from the importance of personal reputation in oil trading. Again and again, the contributors emphasized that performing on their trades – doing what they said they would – and not letting their customers or suppliers down was crucial to them.

Counterparts are expected to push as hard as they can during negotiations to maximize their firms' profits, but once a deal is done, they are expected to stick to it. "It's not great to make a losing trade, but you can always come back from a bad trade", says Michael Hacking. "If you lose your reputation, and you do not fulfil your contractual obligations, then you will not be accepted in the market".

What the future holds

Crude oil trading has clearly changed dramatically since the first genuine traded markets emerged in the early 1980s.

We can trace some clear improvements. The institutional sexism that many of the female contributors describe so clearly has diminished, if not disappeared entirely. Traded volumes have also grown each decade, with occasional setbacks, creating more liquidity and making it easier to get deals done.

At the same time, the adoption of risk management tools, such as futures and options, allows participants to manage their positions more easily and reliably than at any time in the past as well as offering them more tools to speculate and to back their beliefs about the market.

The picture is not all rosy, however. As we noted, many of the participants worry about the long-term impact on relationships and on professional ethics if traders meet each other less and retreat behind their screens.

The growing difficulty for smaller and medium-sized firms of obtaining bank finance, so clearly described by Philippe Cohen, is also a threat to the trading ecosystem, which could potentially end up being dominated by the majors, the largest trading houses and state-owned national oil companies.

Pressure to reduce the carbon in the atmosphere is perhaps the greatest challenge to the long-term prospect for the oil markets, and the role of petroleum products as transport fuels is already being contested by the growth in electric vehicle usage.

One possible response to growing environmental awareness has been to offset the carbon content of crude oil with voluntary carbon offsets, as described in Chapter 27 by Rajaraman Jayaraman, which may offer a partial path forward for the industry.

Trading resilience

Despite its environmental impact, crude oil as a traded commodity is unlikely to disappear any time soon. Trading crude oil, whether physical or paper barrels, still remains a significant driver of profits at the largest oil companies and trading houses.

It is significant that some large oil producers, such as Colombia's Ecopetrol (Juan Carlos Fonnegra, Chapter 16), and some of the Middle East national oil companies have moved from being pure sellers to begin actively trading crude oil in recent years.

Oil trading is clearly still in vogue. That is because trading activities can genuinely add value to a firm. Trading often involves speculation, in the sense of taking a view on a market development, but it is not, or at least it is not supposed to be, gambling or a game of chance. It is a way of maximizing opportunities and optimizing a firm's resources.

Hopefully, these 40 chapters will leave you with an impression of creative and resourceful individuals, whose desire to constantly upgrade and improve whatever positions they hold serves to improve the economics of crude oil as a commodity, increasing the overall efficiency of the market.

Trading arbitrages

The arbitrage is perhaps the most common and the most important trading strategy in the crude oil markets.

An arbitrage is when a trader buys a good or asset in one market where the price is lower, while simultaneously selling in another market where the price is higher, thereby locking in a profit.

The following chapters detail some different and innovative types of crude oil arbitrages: the same quality of oil may be priced differently in different regions; crude oil for export may be priced differently from crude oil for domestic usage; physical crude oil may be priced differently from crude oil futures plus financing costs; or there may be opportunities to exchange crude oil for other commodities, or even for goods and services.

The use of arbitrage stops prices from getting too far away from each other since, at least in theory, as soon as an arbitrage emerges between two markets, an alert trader will step in and take advantage of the opportunity, thereby bringing the two markets back into line.

DOI: 10.4324/9781003144335-2

1 Night flight to Siberia

Colin Bryce started his career at British National Oil Corp (BNOC). He worked in the supply, trading and pricing divisions of BNOC and then its privatized successor, Britoil. Colin joined Morgan Stanley in 1987 to help establish the bank's oil trading and risk management practice. Colin stayed with Morgan Stanley for 29 years in increasingly senior positions, including serving as head of EMEA commodities between 1995 and 2006 and co-head of global commodities between 2008 and 2014. During his time at the bank, he also sat on the board of Morgan Stanley and Co International Ltd, was chairman of Morgan Stanley Bank International and was a member of the firm's global management committee. Colin also served as vice chair of the International Petroleum Exchange (IPE) between 1996 and 2000. Since retiring from the bank in 2016, Colin works as a part-time senior advisor with Morgan Stanley and for advisory firm, Energex Partners, which he co-founded.

The view across the River Ob showed nothing but barren, flat and icy tundra. It was also 40 degrees below zero. Back in 1992, not even *National Geographic* had been to Siberia yet, although the mosquitoes seemed to know we were coming.

I was observing the view from a narrow levee just behind the Samotlor Hotel. Calling it a hotel might have been somewhat of a stretch, but it was at least a friendly hostel. For a while, it also served as my company's Siberia branch office.

We were in Nizhnevartovsk, a large oil town of 210,000 people, built to house the workers charged with extracting the riches of the Samotlor oilfield, the largest field in Russia.

Getting to Nizhnevartovsk was a trial in itself. From the U.K., we would fly to Moscow's Sheremetyevo airport and then trek across the city to Domodedovo airport, before wandering around the tarmac trying to find out which domestic flight to board. Then it was a four-hour flight east, all the while hoping you were on the right plane.

We were a group of ten people – investment bankers, oil traders, lawyers, petroleum engineers, analysts and two translators – and we had done a trade that meant we ended up spending most of 1992 in Nizhnevartovsk.

DOI: 10.4324/9781003144335-3

The road to Nizhnevartovsk

It was a chance meeting that had brought us there.

A large deputation of Russian businesspeople had come over to London the previous year, hosted by the International Petroleum Exchange (IPE). The IPE asked my company if we could host the group for a couple of hours and make a presentation on oil markets and derivatives. One of the attendees was Viktor Paliy, the general director of Nizhnevartovskneftegas (NNG) in western Siberia.

At the time, NNG and the other producers in the region were suffering. Production levels in the 9,480 wells of the Samotlor and other fields had long been compromised by indiscriminate water injection and poor maintenance. The Soviet government had set volumetric production targets, and these were prioritized over careful field management.

After the break-up of the Soviet Union, the situation deteriorated further. Almost overnight, flows of oilfield production and well-restoration equipment, primarily from Azerbaijan, to western Siberia virtually ceased.

This declining availability of equipment and services made catastrophic production declines almost inevitable. By the time our group landed in Nizhnevartovsk, year-on-year production falls of 15% were common across the Tyumen region.

The Urals crude oil that the Siberian firms were producing was excellent and was in high demand. But they simply couldn't get hold of the equipment that they needed. No western firm was willing to supply goods and services to deepest western Siberia when they didn't understand the firms' credit profile and they didn't speak the language. Adding to the deterrents for western suppliers, Russia was experiencing a rapid change in official regulations, while some bad actors were emerging, impacting on the country's reputation.

Our meeting with Viktor Paliy in London went well and we went to see NNG to see whether there was anything we could do to assist them, while also generating a decent return for the bank.

Viktor Paliy was one of the storied Siberian oil leaders who ran both their companies and the towns that had been built to support the business. When Viktor rolled up for dinner at the Hotel Samotlor in his incongruous gold Mercedes 500, the everyday fare of tomatoes, beetroot, eggs and apples was replaced by a table heaving with smoked trout, fine cured meats, exotic fruits and Georgian brandy.

Oil swap

The trade that we proposed to NNG was that we would bring engineers to western Siberia on contract to assess their most urgent needs. The bank would then organize international tenders to meet their requirements and would ship the material to Russia. We would be guaranteeing the financial performance ourselves, which would reassure potential suppliers.

In exchange, the bank would receive volumes of Urals crude oil from NNG that we could export, mainly from the Russian port of Novorossiysk and occasionally from Latvia's Ventspils terminal. We would monetize those cargoes through our physical oil trading business, which at the time was a big business for Morgan Stanley.

The revenue from selling the spot oil cargoes would be used to pay for the equipment that we were supplying to NNG. The profits for the bank would come from a fee on the equipment tenders that we were organizing and from those occasions when we were able to sell the Urals cargoes at prices above the benchmark levels that we had agreed with NNG.

The price we paid was based on an open-market benchmark, and we would always hedge our exposure. With fixed equipment costs arising from the tenders, we might make a small loss from time to time on the cargo side, depending on the oil price, but our plan was to be fully hedged, so any losses would be *de minimis*.

Licensing rules

The trade was simple in theory but complex in practice. The paperwork involved was frightening. Even visits to Prime Minister Viktor Chernomyrdin, various ministers and deputy ministers, and even to the chairman of the Central Bank, couldn't seem to help clear the way for payment processes to be developed, export licences to be obtained and the trade model adopted as policy by government.

The export licence was a particular obstacle. The production companies were required to export 80% of their volumes through the official state trader, Soyuznefteexport, later renamed Nafta Moskva.

In practice, this quota system meant that in the case of NNG, only approximately $100 million per year was under their control to spend on equipment and service ventures, equivalent to around 15 cargoes of oil at the day's prices.

A legacy of central control and bureaucracy effectively combined to prevent foreign ventures from assisting with regional development. This was all the more galling as enhanced recovery regulations theoretically permitted the export, for hard currency, of any 'above quota' oil produced by outside foreign companies.

Despite the obstacles, the trade worked well for four or five tenders, and we brought in mud pumps, hydraulic tongs, drill pipes, oil well tubing and other equipment. Our tendering system and our credit guarantee worked wonders and we were receiving offers that were between 15% and 40% cheaper than NNG were able to source on their own account.

Our aim was to prove that this model would work with NNG and then roll it out across other firms in the region. We had already begun outreach to other key oilmen in the region, including Vladimir Bogdanov at Surgutneftegas, who has held the same role since 1993, Sergei Muravlenko at Yuganskneftegas and Anatoly Sivak at Varyoganneftegas.

But soon much of the Russian oil industry fell into the hands of oligarchs, and the operating environment became more problematic.

After the trade had been running for around a year, our revenues were only slightly ahead of costs due to the complexities of meeting all of the various Russian regulations. We were absolutely unwilling to cut corners on the compliance side, and so the bottom line was that it became clear that we would have only a limited ability to execute the trade over the long term.

Moving on

The trade itself was a marvellous value-added concept that would have helped the whole regional oil industry. It's a shame that it didn't take off more than it did. But as the dark arts increasingly took over, we decided to exit the deal in time to protect the small margins we had made and our own good health and reputation. Other foreign firms persevered with different projects, but many lost substantial sums of money along the way.

The opportunity to restore wells, stabilize production, eliminate unnecessary costs and establish transaction track records was lost, and it took several years for the situation to improve and for production to recover. Perhaps, this was predictable in retrospect. A nation proud of its high-quality technical and scientific expertise may well have resented any suggestion of foreign swagger. Culture clashes were inevitable.

The bank did not end up making much money directly from the trade with NNG, but it was still an incredibly valuable project for us. Putting the trade into practice meant that we entered Russia early and we set up an office in Moscow alongside our operation in western Siberia earlier than the other major western banks.

That gave us a head start in Russia from an investment banking standpoint, and we maintained our presence in Moscow throughout the difficult times in the 1990s, even after we departed western Siberia.

Our commitment to Russia and the initiatives that we developed on the commodities side got us known and in front of a lot of senior people. As a result, we received some really good mandates from Russia, including acting as advisors to state oil giant Rosneft.

The western Siberian trade ultimately paid off for the bank. It also taught us that the commodities business in Russia was not without pitfalls, so we were able to avoid the losses that some other investors faced in the 1990s.

Flying home

After spending the best part of a year in Nizhnevartovsk overseeing the implementation of the trade, it was time for our group to head back to London.

Flying in or out of Nizhnevartovsk was always an experience. We had learnt that it was worth hiring our own plane for around $5,000 rather than waiting for scheduled services. But we never knew what type of plane would await us when we travelled between the frozen east and Moscow.

These were not the private jets that you see on the small screen. The sound of Champagne corks popping was a lot less likely than the sound of a hammer being applied to a jammed tail fin.

On one occasion our transport turned out to be a tiny gas pipeline sniffer plane that was unable to fly above 2,000 feet for pressurization reasons, resulting in a long flight following the ups and downs of the terrain, all the way to the other side of the Urals.

On our final trip home, we were shepherded into what was described as the VIP lounge of Nizhnevartovsk Airport, only to be told that our only option for a private flight to Moscow was a 180-seater Ilyushin.

The journey would cost us $25,000, which was a multiple of our normal rate. But this was our final flight, and we didn't really have a choice. At least, we thought, we can turn left at the top of the steps and use the first-class cabin. This we did.

But you can imagine our surprise when, after take-off, we ventured through the curtain, only to find 170 silent Russians hitching a ride to Moscow. We had to laugh. Someone was counting the money for the ticket sales and congratulating themselves on getting one over the westerners for one final time.

2 A sweet deal

After growing up in the Netherlands and Lebanon and studying in Switzerland and the U.S., Philippe Khoury entered the oil industry in Switzerland in the early 1980s. He joined Elf Trading SA in Geneva in 1989 and in 1993 was appointed executive vice president for the former Soviet Union, based in Moscow. Philippe went on to serve as Elf Trading executive vice president for Africa, Latin America and the Caribbean. After Elf's merger with French major Total and Belgium's PetroFina, he was appointed as president and chief executive of Atlantic Trading & Marketing Inc., Total's Houston-based trading and shipping arm for the Americas. In 2011, Philippe joined HSBC as managing director and global head of the alliance between HSBC and Total. In 2015, he became vice chairman of the bank's oil, gas and natural resources group, working from HSBC's offices in Hong Kong and London. Philippe moved to Dubai in 2017 as HSBC's vice chairman of global banking for the Middle East, North Africa and Turkey. The following year, Philippe was appointed executive vice president for sales and trading at the Abu Dhabi National Oil Company (ADNOC) to restructure the marketing and sales activities and set up the new trading and derivative divisions at ADNOC Group.

During my career, I have worked in a number of roles throughout the oil and gas value chain across downstream, upstream and finance. I have to say, though, that the part which I genuinely enjoyed the most was trading.

Trading offers so many opportunities. In other roles, you might perform more or less the same tasks year after year, but as a trader, you can change the way you do your business almost every day. Maybe tomorrow I will decide to buy, sell or price my oil in a different way. Maybe I will swap crude against gasoline, manage an exposure using different regional pricing indexes or swap one grade of crude oil for another.

That's the fun of trading. You can always try something new in a fast-paced and sophisticated environment. You can change the game every day, or rather you can reset the game at any time, if you see a way to improve your business and if you are open to opportunities and willing to embrace change. Of course, you also need to carefully monitor your exposures and have a few stars aligned with you to succeed.

DOI: 10.4324/9781003144335-4

Moscow bound

Bernard de Combret, who was the head of Elf Trading SA in Geneva, brought me in to run the trading feedstock group in the late 1980s. Our trading results were very good, and Bernard wanted to expand our operations. In particular, he was planning to set up a trading office in Moscow as the era of perestroika had come to Russia and the former Soviet Union (FSU) countries, offering a wide range of new opportunities in what was then the largest oil producing country in the world.

Bernard was looking for someone to position in Moscow, so he went first to the most senior member of the team, the head of the crude oil desk. But he turned him down because he thought Russia might be too dangerous at that time. Bernard's next candidate turned him down as well, so he went to the third person on his list, which was me, saying 'take your time, no rush …'.

I talked to my wife that same night, and, well, I came back the next day and told Bernard that we would be willing to take on the challenge and move to Moscow. Bernard's guidance was that I should go there and spend some time looking around before accepting the role. He had an amazing level of trust in his people and was genuinely concerned about their well-being.

When I landed in Moscow towards the end of 1993, it was like going 'back to school'. I literally spent six months analysing how crude oil flows worked in Russia: who owned which logistics, when did the title to oil pass from producers to export terminals, who financed oil in transit, what were the costs. In a nutshell, who was responsible for what across the FSU's oil and gas industry.

At that time, Russia was a bigger producer than either the U.S. or Saudi Arabia. Outsiders just saw a Communist export machine, but when you were inside and asking the right questions, you became aware of just how complex the situation was, with multiple producers and special export vehicles.

One of my first moves was to hire a logistic specialist from Russia's transportation monopoly Transneft. I figured that whether we wanted to export crude oil, produce it or sell it to a refinery, ultimately, we would be dependent on Transneft's pipelines.

We reviewed every detail of the export system, and one element that leapt out was that, although the final exporter of the crude oil was paid in dollars, the Russian producer was paid 90 days later and in roubles, if paid at all. At that time, the rouble was experiencing tremendous volatility and inflation was in double digits.

The crude oil producer was carrying a great amount of risk and cost, both in terms of possible currency fluctuations and time value of money.

Developing prepayment

The prevailing situation in the early 1990s offered tremendous opportunities for Elf Trading to step in and take an active role connecting an old economy to international markets. We would offer to prepay the producers for their crude oil in U.S. dollars, lowering their cost of capital and receiving in exchange a discount on the crude benchmark price.

I floated the idea to one of the Russian producers, and he was immediately convinced. He couldn't understand how we could offer to pay him in dollars before he'd even delivered the oil; it seemed too good to be true after he was used to waiting so long for a rouble payment.

After I saw the enthusiasm, I wrote a report to Bernard back in Geneva. I laid out how I thought Elf Trading could get involved, and I asked Bernard for $10 million to do a trial prepay deal.

Asking for $10 million in those days would be like asking for $100 million today, so I was asking a lot of Bernard. But I felt it was crucial that we could demonstrate to our potential Russian partners that prepaying could work for everyone.

I was either lucky or very convincing. Geneva wired me the money within days, and I prepaid the producer for a cargo of 500,000 barrels. Not only did the producer deliver the cargo as planned, but they also offered to supply us with an additional three export cargoes, just to show how excited they were about this new way of doing business. I had proved the prepay trade could work with Russians.

Elf Trading got this oil at an attractive price – equivalent to something like a 5% discount – because I had paid in advance in U.S. dollars at substantially lower interest rates than the normal domestic cost of capital. It was a great deal not only for us but also for the producer who otherwise had to wait a minimum of 90 days and get paid in roubles.

Sugar coated

Our prepay trade created additional value for all of the participants in the value chain, and I wanted to develop the concept further. A smart trader always needs to think about the next step and how to expand his or her activities.

I was always asking myself if there was a trade to be done on top of the original trade or before it or after it? Could we expand our role within the commodity chain or maybe even link our activity to another value chain altogether?

I started looking at whether the pre-financing concept could fit into other areas. The Communist system had de-monetized a lot of international transactions to reduce exposure to the U.S. dollar, and so the Soviets had developed barter systems with a lot of satellite countries, like Kazakhstan, Uzbekistan or Cuba.

In the case of Cuba, crude oil was bartered for sugar. Russia was sending to Cuba barrels of Russian Export Blend Crude Oil (REBCO, now known as Urals Blend) and was receiving sugar in exchange.

By this point, I knew most of the Russian oil producers and I had also come to know the local representatives in Moscow of Cupet and Cubametales, which were the state-owned companies that bought crude oil and refined products for Cuba and exported other commodities from Cuba.

The more I looked at this barter arrangement, the less it made sense. The Russians were shipping crude oil from Russia to Cuba, despite the enormous distance and the pricing exposures. I said to my Russian friends,

> come on, guys, we can sell your cargoes in Europe for a better price, and I can supply Cuba with oil from Venezuela, or the North Sea or West Africa. Why on earth bring cargoes all the way from Russia to the Caribbean?

But the Russian producers were nervous that unless there was a direct barter, there might be a risk in terms of payment. I asked myself, 'what if Elf just pays them instead?' I spoke to both the Russians and the Cubans and suggested that I could bring in banks to make the process more efficient and reduce value leakages.

In my concept, Elf Trading would take on the performance and payment risks. Both sides were very sceptical at first. I remember one guy saying, 'I don't understand half of what you're proposing, but if you can make it work, then good luck to you, let's try it'.

There were already a few western banks in Moscow that were beginning to open Russian letters of credit (LCs). I went along and told them that my aim was to connect the crude flow from Russia with the sugar flow from Cuba, but that I would need to plug a financing gap of 12–18 months to pre-pay both sides immediately, given that the revenue from the sugar sales would take longer to materialize because of the time it took to grow the crop and then export raw sugar and process it.

We came up with the concept that the Russian exporter would pass the title and risk for the oil cargo to Elf Trading at the export port. The moment Elf Trading received the cargo, we would pay the exporter with a loan from the bank. We paid producers immediately, not on 30 days' terms, and in U.S. dollars, so the Russian side was happy. Then once we sold the crude oil cargo in the market, we repaid the banks.

Meanwhile, we would prepay for the sugar so that the Cuban producers could buy fertilizers and so on. Once sugar cane was harvested, raw sugar was shipped from Cuba to one of the Baltic or Black Sea ports for processing, then taken by rail down to Moscow, and the final payment would come in from the various sugar distributors to repay the bank facilities.

Express delivery

The chain between the loading date of the crude oil and the date when the refined white sugar finally showed up in Russia was normally – depending on the crops – around 8–18 months. By stepping in to ensure that the Russians got paid immediately on export, we were generating a huge amount of value for the producers.

In exchange for the prepayment, the Russian producers were willing to provide us with secured supplies of crude oil flows on a favourable basis. The Russians at that time used to factor in a 10% cost of capital, whereas we could achieve about 4%, hence sharing a spread of about 6% margin with the financial institutions, to fund and carry Russian and Cuban delivery exposures for about a year.

To then take the trade one step further, we needed to bring in partners for the sugar leg of the export deal. Elf Trading was an oil firm, and we had zero experience in sugar, so we started working with a handful of large agricultural traders, like Sucden and Louis Dreyfus.

You can only deliver value and secure a cheap cost of capital if you have strong names on both sides of the chain. These international firms lifted the sugar from Cuba, and their high credit ratings reassured the banks that they were in a position to process the sugar and bring it back to Russia.

Of course, at that time there were no U.S. sanctions on non-U.S. companies doing business with Cuba. I don't think you could replicate that deal as sanctions on Cuba are so much broader today.

Beyond oil

The prepay oil-for-sugar trade performed very well indeed and became quite significant. Between this giant deal and the spot transactions that Elf Trading was doing, I would estimate that in the mid-1990s, around 10% to 12% of Russian crude exports were lifted by our company. All of this from a blank piece of paper when I arrived in Moscow in 1993.

At that time, there was a window of opportunity. My original prepayment deals had all performed well and had built up trust. When you develop a reputation for being reliable, honest, professional and able to deliver, then you often find yourself in a situation where business comes to you.

Oil is not just a product to consume, it is also a currency in its own right. You can trade oil against other commodities, as long as you have a vision and an understanding of how commodities and finance interact, how partnerships work and how to establish proper governance around transactions.

This type of cross-commodity trading requires the capacity to think a deal through from A to Z, to bring in the right partners and to have sufficient determination to get to the end of the process. It is difficult to get it right, but when it does, it can improve tremendously the productivity of a value chain. In this case, we connected two value chains, one for oil and one for sugar, added some financial engineering and optimized two very different and vital commodity markets.

When we started our prepay deals, we struggled for financing. When I left, four years later, we had a syndicate of 20 banks that were prepared to back our trading and I was spending more time structuring deals than trading.

We were able to originate barrels for Elf's trading desk in Geneva with a flow that was predictable, at predefined export locations, with a decent return, offering value to the suppliers, the off-taker and the financial partners.

In those days, most oil majors were opening offices in Moscow. Everyone had hundreds of engineers all trying to access Russian upstream and downstream opportunities. But the last thing the Russians wanted was to share their upstream business with foreign institutions. They didn't particularly need their industrial expertise, what they wanted was someone to help them monetize their production and introduce more financial and commercial efficiency into rigid Soviet value chains.

Professionally addressing the concerns and requirements of partners is something a trader does every day; managing physical flows, financial requirements, pricing exposures or timely deliveries turns you into an 'unavoidable' partner, who can fast track your transformation efforts and safely land you in sophisticated international commodity and financial markets.

I had four people in my Moscow office, while Elf's upstream group had 400, but you can guess who was performing better and who had the better relationships within the FSU. A good international trader still has more value for a Russian producer than yet another upstream company.

When you resolve a problem, people are grateful. Often, it's not so much about the money, it's more that you have taken a headache away from them. As a trader, you have to know which battles you want to pick, but, if you pick the right one, it can be a game changer for everyone involved.

3 Where physical meets paper

Having earned an economics degree from Harvard and served as an infantry officer with the U.S. Marines, Kurt Chapman joined Morgan Stanley's New York commodities division in the late 1980s. He was later transferred to their London office. He left Morgan Stanley to work for Elf Trading, now Total, in Geneva. He was subsequently hired by Sempra Energy. In 2004, two colleagues from Sempra left to form a new trading firm, Mercuria, which has grown to be one of the world's largest commodity trading companies. Kurt reunited with them in 2006 as an equity partner and as global head of crude oil trading, a role he held through to his retirement from Mercuria in 2018. He has since taken on a number of advisory and non-executive roles.

I spent my trading career in the nexus between physical crude oil and the paper derivatives market, often looking to arbitrage one against the other.

The way I approached the market was to try to understand the relationship between the physical barrels and the forward paper, and how those two elements converge.

In theory, as time progresses, the forward market becomes physical, but there are so many complexities in the oil markets that the relationship is not always linear.

Sometimes arbitrage opportunities open up between the financial instruments and the physical crude oil that underpins them. Most of my trading strategies, certainly the successful ones, have come from opportunities presented by the fluctuations in that relationship.

It's not a traditional physical arbitrage where you move oil from Point A to Point B. The arbitrage between physical and financial oil often requires a little more sophistication since you have to be aware of what is happening with both aspects of the market simultaneously.

Financial beginnings

I started out as a trader on the financial side, and my knowledge of the physical side developed later, although I guess it was in my blood because my father had traded physical oil for Unocal in London, which later became part of Chevron.

DOI: 10.4324/9781003144335-5

When I graduated from university, I joined the marines. After I finished my service, all my buddies had gone to Wall Street, so I followed their lead. My first trading job was on the oil derivatives desk with Morgan Stanley.

At the time, Morgan Stanley was known as a 'Wall Street refiner'. We were actively hedging and trading crude oil and refined products on behalf of our customers and the bank.

An opportunity arose for me to move across to the London office. I figured it made sense to be one of five traders on the desk in London rather than one of thirty in New York. Additionally, my family had spent time in London, so the move seemed natural.

The switch to London worked out great. I got to work for and learn from Colin Bryce (see Chapter 1), David Morgan and Frédéric Baule, who were cutting edge traders in oil derivatives.

Learning physical

When Fred left the bank to work for Elf Trading, he took me with him, and it was at Elf that I started to get significant exposure to the physical market. I knew by then that I really enjoyed the oil business, but I was lacking a solid understanding of physical oil. Rex Steed had joined from Cargill and helped me grasp the fundamentals. He was a great mentor and unsurprisingly went on to run the oil trading business for Total.

Elf had production in the Atlantic basin, and so I dealt with physical cargoes, watching what the physical traders were doing and then using my financial background to do hedging and manage basis risk.

I was fantastically lucky with my first two roles. At Morgan Stanley in London, I was exposed to people who profoundly understood markets and risk. That experience helped me develop a passion for the business, while Elf opened my eyes to the world of real physical oil.

My career progressed from there. As a trader, you are always looking for a competitive advantage, and I tried to develop a strong understanding of risk management tools and see how they could be applied to physical crude.

I had learned at Elf Trading how to handle and move physical barrels, whether via shipping or in and out of storage, but I thought that my strength as a trader lay in the ability to take my existing risk management skillset and to apply that to the more traditional physical space.

As a trader, you build your own toolbox over the years, collecting different techniques and skills. Then at the appropriate time, when the market presents an opportunity, you pull those tools out and use them.

Select group

If you want to be a serious global player in crude oil, then you must be active in the Brent benchmark.

There haven't traditionally been many firms involved in the forward Brent market, no more than ten at any one time, but you need to be active in that space in order to arbitrage the physical and financial and capture convergence. That requires a strong balance sheet as you are trading with and against the major oil companies (BP, Shell, Exxon, Total, Statoil) for significant volume.

Marco Dunand and Daniel Jaeggi left Sempra in 2004 to start up Mercuria, transforming J&S into a global trading powerhouse. I stayed on at Sempra to run the international crude book. After two years, Marco and Daniel felt they had the appropriate financial backing and risk management systems to be able to become a player in the North Sea market. They contacted me and said they were ready to trade the front end. Marco and Daniel's unwavering support and guidance allowed me to achieve at the highest levels.

Wolfram Thümmel, formerly BP and Cargill, who had great relationships with all of the North Sea players, and Neil Hitchinson, with his strong analytical skills, completed the team. Wolf's reputation allowed us to start trading with the oil majors straight away. But ultimately, Mercuria had to put up the capital and take on the risk.

Wolf and I worked well together as Wolf is an engineer and a refiner by background. He understood fundamentals and oil molecules. I was more financial, so our skillsets complimented each other. With so many moving pieces, it's very hard to trade successfully on your own. I can't imagine how you can sit in a room by yourself, looking only at a screen and be successful.

Tackling oversold Dated

The North Sea crude oil market was my professional home for the best part of three decades.

The North Sea is the most important oil market globally because it provides the benchmark for all of the business done in the Atlantic basin. For many years, perhaps 70% of the world's crude was priced in relation to Brent, although that began to change in 2015 when the export ban for U.S. barrels was repealed and WTI reconnected with the international market.

The North Sea fortunately suited my trading style because it was, and remains, a highly complex market where there are multiple relationships between physical Dated, referred to as Dated Brent, forward Brent (currently month-ahead BFOET) and the related derivatives markets, such as contracts-for-difference (CFDs), Dated-to-frontline (DFL) and ICE Brent futures.

Obviously, given the complexity of the North Sea, dislocations are bound to arise from time to time. One significant moment occurred in the second half of 2006, when the market was coming under a lot of pressure.

We were in a situation of oversupply, and so there was a great interest from North Sea traders in selling Dated derivatives. Companies that were long physical crude – and a lot of people were long, given the oversupply – were selling Dated as a hedge to their physical position, which was putting further pressure on the Dated benchmark.

As a result, the price of Dated was underperforming, in particular relative to the prompt forward market. Even though the physical market was getting weaker and storage opportunities were starting to present themselves, Dated was undervalued relative to the prompt forward market by over a dollar per barrel.

We knew that this discrepancy couldn't last because at some stage the forward market would have to converge with physical Dated. After all, if you buy a forward contract, at some stage you are going to get a three-day nominated window on a physical cargo in the North Sea, which is a Dated cargo.

You don't know exactly how that process is going to happen. But if there is such a wide discrepancy between Dated and the forward market, then one approaches the other, whether it's the Dated market improving towards the forward level, or the forward market losing value and slipping towards the weaker Dated price.

We were confident that the relationship would have to realign itself, and so we started building up a trading position by accumulating CFDs and selling near-term forward Brent.

Profitable convergence

It took a while for that convergence between physical and forward levels to happen because there was a lot of liquidity that helped to maintain the status quo for the moment.

We believed in our premise nonetheless and we kept on building our position. Our exposure grew to around 30 million barrels, which was getting a little bit tricky, especially with Mercuria being a relatively new player on the block.

It got to the point where we started questioning ourselves and wondering if we had made the right call. Our bosses also started to tap us on the shoulder, and when we got to 30 million barrels, they suggested that we didn't add any more to the position.

But then Dated got a little cheaper again, and we couldn't resist buying some more, so we ended up with 35 million barrels. I think that was the moment when we recognized that we had probably taken on enough risk.

We were looking to reduce our position as we moved towards year end and the market fortunately moved in our favour.

The contango structure of the market made it profitable to store crude. Mercuria had acquired storage at Saldanha Bay in South Africa, and we picked up a very cheap cargo of Oseberg crude oil from Norsk Hydro in the Platts window.

Amazingly, it made sense to ship it all the way down to Saldanha Bay as a single parcel, where it went into storage along with other barrels that we had accumulated.

By buying North Sea oil, we were able to help a convergence between the physical and the paper ourselves, rather than just waiting for it to occur.

The convergence would have likely happened anyway, but by being pro-active meant that we ended up with the bonus of an Oseberg in our tanks.

That Oseberg ended up in storage in Saldanha for about 18 months. Ultimately, we shipped it on a larger vessel with some other crude oil grades and sold it into Asia. That single cargo might be one of only a handful of Osebergs to ever go to Asia.

Our convergence trade proved to be a relatively profitable manoeuvre. The fundamentals had played out in our favour because the market structure, which had led to the Dated dislocation in the first place, allowed us to buy the very oil that started to create the physical convergence that we were expecting.

Reverse engineering

Over the years, Wolf, Neil and I saw recurring market scenarios, and in late 2012, we were able to repeat our convergence trade, only this time trading it the other way round.

In 2006, we had bought cheap Dated and sold the prompt forward to try to capture that convergence. Six years later, when the market was in pretty good shape, the relationship between the Dated market and the forward paper market was tight, and so this time, we did the reverse and we sold Dated and bought forward Brent. Dated was priced at only a slight discount to the forward market, but we felt that the spread was too narrow. Ultimately, if the two instruments are trading at roughly the same level, then you would always prefer to end up with the physical barrels because they give you a significant position in the market. If you are holding physical crude, then end users will likely contact you and provide you with a better understanding of demand. There is also value in cargo tolerance and specific loading windows.

We were very conscious of the strategy we had used successfully in 2006. We kept asking ourselves three key questions: where is Dated valued; where is the prompt forward curve valued; and how are they going to ultimately converge?

In 2012, the market was strong. Traders were out to buy on the basis that Dated would keep rising. They weren't necessarily thinking about the North Sea complex as a whole, and they were paying too much for Dated relative to the forward market.

A directional strategy like that, where traders are just betting on a simple price rise, can get easily derailed. In contrast, we were trading the arbitrage between Dated and forward, which gave us more security because we knew that ultimately the physical and the forward would have to come back into line.

Again, the convergence trade worked well. We actually ended up receiving the majority of the Forties loading programme for December because we had been able to hedge our physical buying at such a reasonable level.

When other traders asked us how we were able to buy an entire month of a key North Sea grade, we were able to reply that 'the market told us to do it'. The arbitrage between physical and paper had opened, and we closed it.

History lessons

Our job was to understand when dislocations occur and to try to take advantage of them from a relative-value perspective.

In 2006, we were able to do that because Dated was at such a discount to the forward market, and we were also able to move a physical cargo on the back of the dislocation in a way which you wouldn't have expected. We repeated the strategy in reverse in 2012, this time leaving us with a month of Forties cargoes.

You need to be intelligent about how you approach markets, and you certainly have to be reactive. There's a lot to be said for experience too. It's like a history lesson: history doesn't always repeat itself, but you can learn by observing and evaluating what has happened before.

I liked the intensity on the desk; it was stressful at times, but there was great satisfaction when you got it right. Obviously, that didn't happen all the time and you had to know when you were wrong, when to get out, when to regroup and when not to trade.

The oil and energy markets are influenced by so many different elements: geopolitics, economic growth, supply, weather, to name a few. That constant intellectual challenge under pressure, as well as the close relationships, is what makes trading hugely rewarding.

4 A false arbitrage

Adi Imsirovic has over 30 years of experience in oil trading. He held a number of senior positions, including global head of oil at Gazprom Marketing & Trading, director of Petraco and head of their Singapore office and regional manager of Texaco Oil Trading for Asia. He was a Fulbright Scholar, and he studied at the Graduate School of Arts and Sciences, Harvard University. Adi also taught economics at Surrey University for several years. He has a PhD in economics and a master's degree in energy economics. Adi has written a number of papers and articles on the topic of oil and gas prices, benchmarks and energy security. He is the author of the book: 'Trading and Price Discovery for Crude Oils: Growth and Development of International Oil Markets', published in August 2021.

I always like a good old-fashioned trade where you actually add value by looking at the fundamentals and then doing something differently, rather than just trying to make money by trading against someone with a different point of view.

Back in 1998, the oil market was on its knees. Demand was very low, and the oil price was terribly weak because the world was just awash with oil. June 1998 saw the lowest prices for a decade, even despite massive cuts in production by OPEC and others.

I was working at Texaco at that time, running their European crude business and supplying our two refineries in Pembroke in the U.K. and in Rotterdam in the Netherlands.

There was a really good policy at Texaco in those days that the refineries had to have a representative on the trading desk, which worked absolutely brilliantly because it meant the refineries were fully involved in all of our trading decisions.

I used to spend a lot of time chatting to the guy who was representing Pembroke. We were always trying to come up with ideas that might boost our trading desk's performance, which wasn't always straightforward when the market was so awful, while also making sure the refinery would also do well.

Draft excluder

One day I must have had a moment of inspiration because I turned to him and asked him why we couldn't bring a very large crude carrier (VLCC) to

DOI: 10.4324/9781003144335-6

unload at Pembroke. After all, the Milford Haven Waterway that connects the refinery to the Irish Sea is pretty deep.

My thought was that if we could bring a vessel as large as a VLCC, which carries up to 2 million barrels of crude oil, to Pembroke, then there would be times when we would be able to benefit from economies of scale in shipping crude oil to the refinery.

My colleague's first thought was that the draft of the waterway would be slightly too shallow to accommodate a fully laden VLCC, but after a series of meetings with the refinery, he came back and said that it could be done, but that the waterway would need to be dredged first, otherwise there was a risk that the VLCC could get stuck.

The cost of dredging was going to be somewhere around $300,000, which was quite a significant upfront investment, and probably explained why no one had seriously considered delivering to Pembroke via a VLCC before.

But the more we looked at it, the more we thought that the concept might work. At the time, the oil market was really weak and so was the freight market. It was not economic to ship oil from Europe to the U.S. at that time, and so there were a lot of VLCCs that were available at very reasonable rates.

In the end, we decided to go for it. As a trading team, we agreed to sponsor the dredging of the waterway on the refinery's behalf. Of course, it made the refinery very happy that we were paying for the improvement works from our account.

Preparing the way

The next step was for our Texaco chartering team to spot a VLCC that we would bring to Pembroke. We managed to find one that appeared to be reasonably cheap, and we began discussions with the owner.

The first stage of chartering an oil tanker is to reach agreement on the broad terms and conditions for the charter with the shipowner. This broad agreement can then be finalized subject to the confirmation of a number of other less important items.

At this stage, the vessel is said in trader jargon to be 'on subs' because, essentially, the tanker is reserved subject to final confirmation.

Now, the oil market, as I've said, was truly awful at that time. All of the North Sea traders were massively short of contracts-for-difference (CFDs), which are the weekly swaps that provide price protection against moves in the Dated Brent benchmark.

The CFD market was just collapsing because the outlook was so weak, and so we knew that any positive sign that demand was improving would lift the market.

News that Texaco had put a VLCC on subs would be a very bullish signal. CFD prices would likely rally because people would assume that we had found a way to take crude oil out of Europe, reducing the overhang of supply that the region was experiencing.

There was really no way for anyone to guess what we were considering. After all, VLCCs are typically used for transporting large quantities of oil over long distances, like from Europe to Asia or to the U.S., because they are normally so expensive to charter. Plus, it was common knowledge that you couldn't take a VLCC to Pembroke.

It was clear that we would need to protect ourselves before the news leaked out that we had put a VLCC on subs, and so we went out and slowly built up an initial position of 4 million barrels of CFDs in the week that we were planning to load our VLCC.

Of course, everyone came to know that we were buying CFDs, and so people started looking at us and asking us what we were doing. All we would say was that we were positive about the market, to which everyone would reply, 'you have to be kidding, how can anyone be positive about this terrible market?'

Well, we kept on buying CFDs for that week. Of course, we had to protect the refineries as well because if our VLCC trade helped to move the Dated Brent benchmark higher, then that would raise the cost of all of the other oil purchases we were making on behalf of our two refineries. We made sure that we bought a significant volume of CFDs to protect the refineries.

Call my bluff

We had managed to buy quite a large amount of CFDs by this point, and so the calls we were getting started to get more intense, as people pushed hard to know what we were up to. Eventually, we told them the truth: 'we are going to lift a VLCC'.

Everyone just laughed at us. They basically told us that there was no buying in the U.S., and so it wasn't economic to ship crude out of Europe by VLCC. It was like a frenzy. People outright refused to believe us.

Then when the news hit the market that we had really put a VLCC on subs, I remember a lot of people saying, 'yeah, right, you are just bluffing'. They thought we must be trying to move North Sea prices higher by giving a false impression of demand from the U.S.

But once we had bought all the swaps that we needed to hedge our physical position, we went ahead and 'lifted the subs' on the VLCC, which means that we had reached agreement on all the minor items with the shipowner and had confirmed the final details of the charter.

Lifting the subs on the vessel provoked an unbelievable reaction. No one in the market could believe it. News of the charter even made the trade press and we had journalists calling up to ask us what on earth was going on.

Of course, when you charter a vessel in the North Sea you agree fees for different destinations and different options, so no one could tell from the charter exactly what we were planning to do with the VLCC.

The biggest question in the market that month was what the hell is Texaco doing and where on the planet could they possibly be taking that oil.

Eventually, we had to admit that we were taking it 'home' to one of our refineries and, of course, after loading the ship did head for Pembroke.

Fortunately, the VLCC did successfully navigate the newly dredged Milford Haven Waterway, which wasn't easy, and the unloading was very smooth.

Taking a bow

Our plan had worked really well. That deal was really celebrated within the company because we had taken advantage of the weak market to get cheap oil for the refinery in a large vessel that massively reduced our average transportation costs.

We had also hedged everything beforehand, so the refinery was happy because, although our buying did push Dated Brent higher, which is something refineries don't normally appreciate, we had expected that and had put the appropriate hedges in place. All of the hedges were in the money, and so there was no negative impact on our refineries' economics.

The only guys who were unhappy were probably the folks on our operation team because they were so nervous about whether the VLCC would actually make it through the waterway to discharge.

We looked into repeating the trade a couple of times, but that was a unique situation. We needed a combination of very cheap oil and very cheap shipping to offset the initial cost of dredging the waterway and that was not something that was going to happen too often.

It was a fun time. It was genuinely a win-win for the firm, the trading desk had added value, and everybody was happy. After all, we effectively pioneered a new trade route!

Thinking economically

Even as a young man, I was fascinated by the energy markets. After I finished my first degree, I got a scholarship to the University of Surrey, which was run at the time by Colin Robinson, who was really ahead of the curve in his thinking on energy economics.

Colin was a big influence on U.K. energy policy at the time and he inspired all of us. Major energy economists like Paul Stevens and Graham Bird were also working on oil-related issues at Surrey too. I knew that a role in energy was the path I wanted to follow, but then my parents moved back to Bosnia, and I went with them. I was supposed to do my national service in the army, but I kept deferring it because I had actually found a job in an oil company in Sarajevo.

I spoke English quite well, and they needed help on the international side because the environment was changing so quickly.

Yugoslavia's leader Marshal Tito had spent a lot of the 1970s doing deals with oil producers in the developing world, under which Yugoslavia would build infrastructure projects like dams and so on and would be paid in oil.

It was a classic socialist way of doing business and of course no one ever would think to include in the agreements any details about the actual pricing of the oil.

It was left to the two oil companies on the export and import side to try to figure things out afterwards, and obviously we would regularly end up in arguments with the suppliers about what the actual market price of the oil should be.

Eventually, the Yugoslavian government cracked because the refineries refused to carry on lifting oil at prices that were well above market levels. In the mid-1980s, just before I moved back to Bosnia, the government allowed refiners to purchase certain volumes independently in the short-term 'spot' market.

Balkan spot

I was only 25 years old at that point, but no one else locally knew any more about spot purchasing than I did, and my time at Surrey had taught me about the various global oil benchmarks, and so my company ended up putting me in charge of spot crude oil purchases for the whole of Bosnia-Herzegovina.

There were a lot of dodgy traders offering to help me buy supplies, as you might imagine, but I didn't want to go down that path. I found a London telephone directory that my parents had brought back with them when we moved back from the U.K. I looked up Shell Trading in the directory and I called them up. Luckily, I spoke pretty good English and eventually I got through to a trader called Jan van Kleef.

Jan asked me what we needed, which at the time was mainly Iraqi Kirkuk, Russian Urals and Iranian Light. Jan had a cargo of Iranian Light about to load at Egypt's Sidi Kerir oil terminal, and so in partnership with Serbian oil company Jugopetrol, we bought the cargo from Shell. That was the first spot cargo of crude oil to be traded in this part of the Balkans.

After that, I did my national service, and I ended up working as a dispatcher for a huge transport park where there were hundreds of trucks and tanks. I was looking after the fuel side, making sure they were supplied and that no one smuggled out any diesel.

When things were quiet with my army job, I started rereading my economics textbooks, and eventually a good friend persuaded me to apply for a Fulbright scholarship to the U.S. I wasn't sure about it, but I couldn't turn down Harvard when they gave me an offer, so I spent a fantastic year there working on an econometric model of the Yugoslavian economy that would show the impact of oil price changes on the broader economy.

After my year in the U.S., the war broke out at home, and it was difficult to go back to Bosnia. I couldn't work in the U.S. because I didn't have a green card, but because I had lived in the U.K. for a long time, I still had a U.K. resident's visa. I started interviewing from the U.S. for jobs in London, and eventually, I received an offer from Texaco, which I accepted.

Beyond trading

After that, I never looked back, and I went on to trade crude oil for more than 30 years, at various firms in London and Singapore. My primary aim was always to generate profits for my employer, but at the same time, I didn't want to be one of those traders that are hidden away behind a trading screen.

I was never one of those traders who are reluctant to give their opinions on market developments or to speak in public. During the war, I helped to set up a Bosnian Information Centre in London, which later became the Bosnian Embassy, and I did a lot of media interviews about the situation in Bosnia, while I was still a junior trader for Texaco.

That experience taught me first-hand about the importance of the media and how hard it can be for journalists, particularly when they are covering sectors that are traditionally very secretive like the oil markets.

Throughout my career, I have always wanted to keep up the free exchange of ideas that I encountered during my early studies, whether by teaching, writing or by discussing the oil markets with a broader audience.

The oil markets are fascinating: you can develop a new way of buying crude in Sarajevo or figure out a new way to supply a refinery in Wales. Oil is still the most important commodity in the world, and the way its market works deserves to be better understood.

5 A Russian arbitrage strategy

Trym Nordhus started his career working in various supply and trading roles for Exxon-Mobil in his native Norway as well as in the U.S. and U.K. He joined the Russian oil firm TNK-BP in 2005 as head of crude oil sales. Trym went on to work for Lukoil's trading arm Litasco as a senior crude oil trader, before returning to Norway to create a new consulting firm, Cap Nord Energy AS, which provides advisory services to oil companies on supply and trading.

When you can sell a ton of oil at 7,900 roubles at the start of the week, buy the same oil back a couple of days later for 8,100 roubles, and yet still make a very healthy profit, then you know that as a trader you are in the right place at the right time.

That time was the mid-2000s and I was in Moscow working as head of crude oil sales at TNK-BP, Russia's third largest oil producer. TNK-BP had been created in 2003 from a merger between assets owned by Russia's AAR Consortium and the Russian assets of British oil major BP.

TNK-BP was a Russian oil producer, but BP introduced an international trading mentality that made TNK-BP stand out from the other Russian producers of that time. We could see opportunities that our competitors couldn't, and we were organized internally in a way that enabled us to take full advantage (see Chapter 15).

Perhaps our most successful trades were those when we took advantage of the regular discrepancies between the international floating-price market for crude oil and the domestic Russian fixed-price market.

In the early 2000s, when I was still working at Exxon, we often used to wonder why the Russian domestic prices were so low, but it was simply that the oil was landlocked, much like WTI was around 2011.

Russian exports

The Russian market was very inefficient in those days. There were many reasons for that inefficiency and a lot of it has to do with the history of the oil industry in Russia, but also the slow move to a market economy after the collapse of the Soviet Union.

DOI: 10.4324/9781003144335-7

Russian oil production fell quite dramatically after perestroika in the 1990s and particularly after the Russian economic crisis of 1998 so there wasn't much investment in increasing Russia's capacity to export its oil internationally. Also, the domestic demand for refined products was low after the crisis, and refineries were running well below capacity. By the early 2000s, Russia was seeing increased production once more, but its capacity to export was still limited.

When I joined TNK-BP in 2005, my job was to find new export routes for oil. Either by rail, by barge, by truck, or maybe horseback – anything! At that point, the key to success was just to get the oil out of the country.

But within a year, the situation changed so much that we weren't thinking any more about rail or barges, except how to get out of expensive transport deals. Russia had invested in massive new pipeline and port infrastructure, which began to come online.

There were developments at the ports of Primorsk and Ust-Luga, and there were new outlets in the Far East. Suddenly, Russia had a lot more export capacity. With higher oil prices, the economy boomed and ever stronger demand for transportation fuel followed.

Unequal transport costs

You have to imagine the different ways of exporting as each having different price tiers – exporting via a pipeline might cost $40 per ton, then you had rail or river barge which might cost $80 per ton. Early on, the least economic sales channel was into domestic refineries.

Naturally, the domestic market price for crude was set at parity with the least economic export outlet. So, in theory, the domestic Russian oil price should be something like the international price less export customs duty and less the $80 per ton needed to pay for rail costs, assuming rail was the marginal export route.

At the same time, the Russian government changed the way it calculated the export duties. The crude oil export duty became a formula based on 65% of the price of crude oil in Europe, with a lag of two months. And equally important, the export duty for products was set at a percentage of crude export duty: 70% for clean products and 40% for dirty products.

This was clearly a government drive to incentivize domestic crude runs, and the president also stated clearly that Russia should keep more of the value upgrading inside Russia, rather than just exporting raw materials.

Taking profit

Two things happened: pipeline export capacity grew significantly, and oil prices rose as well. The spread in export duties between crude and products therefore grew, incentivizing higher domestic refinery runs. The earlier sought-after rail export channels were hit from two sides: there was less need to export crude overall, and there were much cheaper new pipeline routes.

Refining had become the most economic outlet, while pipeline exports had become the marginal export channel.

At TNK-BP, we noticed that domestic prices were moving up towards the pipeline export netback, driving us to reduce rail export as much as possible to sell domestically. But the growth continued, and at some points, we saw domestic prices at $20, $30, or even $40 per ton above parity with pipeline exports.

At that point, as an international company, we started to say that this was clearly ridiculous and so began to just take some of our oil out of the export pipelines and sell it in the domestic market. I think the first trade we did, we made around $40 per ton.

Making $40 per ton was unusual, but $20 per ton was common and we could make that much on 200,000–300,000 tons, and sometimes more each month. We are talking about a potential $5 million per month in profits just from this one trading strategy, and we were able to keep doing this for the best part of two years.

Just to put that in context, at that same time in BP, people would kill for 50 cents per barrel ($3.60 per ton). It was a completely different story. You couldn't approach TNK-BP management with a trading strategy in mind that would make less than $10 per ton, they wouldn't even consider it because it wasn't worth the time spent.

Open arbitrage

In an efficient market, any open arbitrage like this difference between the export and the domestic price should get closed very quickly. And so the key question is, why didn't it normalize, why didn't this arbitrage close quickly?

Part of the reason is because of history – Russia was coming out of a long period of low export capacity and weak domestic demand.

The Russian government gave every company a pro rata pipeline quota and if you didn't use it, you risked losing it. That meant that firms didn't want to risk their export quotas, even if they saw higher prices locally over some time. They were concerned about giving up long-term value in exchange for short-term profit, which is understandable.

The other factor was that for some exporters, switching between exports and domestic sales was not simple. Exporting by rail required longer term infrastructure contracts to keep exclusivity and justify investment by the owners. And some oil producers had tied up exports into finance deals. Jeopardizing such existing deals would be brave.

Trading window

A further constraint on other firms' ability to flip between domestic and exports was the bureaucratic approval processes of distributing monthly oil production. Each firm would hold a big production planning meeting, on around the 20th of the month before delivery, where all the planned production was distributed between refineries, various export channels and for domestic sales. This was probably dictated again by the country's central planning schedule.

That system meant that all of the Russian refineries worked to a monthly schedule, and once the boss had signed off on the plans, there was little room to deviate from these. The domestic crude market then traded at a fixed price in roubles per ton for the next five to seven days. Nobody really paid attention to the movements of the global oil markets during this domestic trading window.

Traders at other Russian companies were all subject to the bureaucracy of their internal rules and mostly reacted to known facts, for instance, confirmed export quotas or fixed export duties.

TNK-BP was different. We started to plan further in advance. It was not hard to forecast our pipeline export capacity, our refinery runs, or the change in export duty well before they were fixed. We could therefore start selling and allocating most of the oil prior to the production planning meeting. I said could – because we were of course formally not allowed to do so...

Even though our company was quite advanced relative to other Russian companies at that time, this change in trading and operational practices provoked some resistance inside the firm.

It would make the guys responsible for logistics question our sanity whenever we told them that we weren't going to use our precious export capacity. They were used to stable plans, and they preferred them, but as traders we wanted to take advantage of the price discrepancies that we saw between the international and domestic markets, and this required flexibility in logistics. In general, though, we were mostly aligned on our strategies and could not have done this without the support from the logistics side.

Beyond a few days

During the five to seven days of the domestic trade cycle, the fixed price trades hardly varied. But, of course, over the same period international prices might be moving dramatically, maybe even by $3–4 per barrel.

There were months where we sold at, for instance, 7,900 roubles one day and then two days later we bought the same oil back for 8,100 roubles and we made good money on what might look like a terrible trade.

We had first diverted the oil away from exports at a profit, but when international prices jumped during those two days, the incentives flipped, and exports became a lot better. So, we bought back the oil and allocated it back into the export market.

Of course, this would not have been profitable without the use of hedging instruments, which I believe we were among the first to use extensively inside Russia.

Trading in and out of the domestic market as global prices fluctuated was one of our key trading strategies, but we would also look for one-way opportunities. At times when the domestic oil price in Russia was $20–40 per ton above the pipeline export netback, we would pull as much as we could from the export market and offer it aggressively into the domestic market.

Our trading strategy drove some of our rival producers insane. At that time, they treated domestic and export markets as completely separate, so they didn't truly understand or appreciate what we were doing.

One of them even alluded to our actions as destructive. This producer used a model to set domestic crude price equal to the refinery gross product worth less a fixed refining margin. Such a concept is still quite common in Russia, that the market price for something should be equal to cost plus a margin, ignoring the fact that both costs and sales prices are fluctuating in a free market. I believe that it was actually illegal to sell anything at a loss at the time!

In fact, when the oil price collapsed in July 2008, the netback price at the field did turn negative: the domestic price was still positive, but it was lower than the mineral extraction tax due to a time lag in calculating export duty (two-month average, with one-month lag).

In response, we sold a lot of oil at export parity plus a strong premium and thought we had made tons of money, while our competitors didn't do anything at all. It turned out that they were right, and we were wrong.

Since the field price was negative, the other firms argued that it was illegal to sell on that basis, and the state subsequently altered the export duty to a much lower number, bringing the export parity level significantly higher and making our fixed-price sales look dirt cheap. It was a good lesson for the 'smart' westerners.

TNK-BP only lasted ten years before it was acquired by Russian state oil firm Rosneft, but in those ten years, we brought a lot of new trading techniques into the Russian market. Today, domestic crude also trades at floating price, so the arbitrage opportunities are long gone.

We were pioneers in optimizing where we placed our crude oil for maximum profit. TNK-BP knew a great deal about prices in both the domestic Russian market and the international export market, for example. But that information wasn't secret – our trading advantage didn't come from information, but from our willingness to move away from the rigid trading structure and bureaucratic planning that dominated our competitors at that time in order to adapt our plans to market conditions.

6 Leveraging local knowledge

Ralf-Dieter Poth began his career in the late 1970s supplying feedstock to the Veba Oel refineries in Germany, which were co-owned by Veba and Venezuela's PDVSA. In the early 1980s, he joined the newly created Veba Oil Supply & Trading, where he held various roles in the refined products and crude oil business areas. Ralf was appointed manager of crude oil supply and trading in 2000. After BP's acquisition of Veba's stake in the German refineries in 2001, he held similar roles within BP's German subsidiary until 2019. Ralf then moved to Rosneft, which had joined BP as co-owner of the original Veba refineries after acquiring PDVSA's stake in 2011. At Rosneft, he worked as coke and residuals sales manager until his retirement in mid-2020. Ralf also served on the Industry Advisory Board of the International Energy Agency, Paris, as the representative of the Association of the German Petroleum Industry (MWV) and as the chairman of the Supply Coordination Group of the German National Emergency Sharing Organisation (NESO).

One of the best feelings in trading is when you find a trade that is a genuine win-win both for your company and for your counterparty. I always enjoyed the relationship side of trading, and it was particularly satisfying that one of our best trading strategies was based on the quality of the relationships that my firm had built up.

In the early 1990s, I was working in Hamburg for Veba Oil International, which was later combined with trading firm Stinnes Interoil, and renamed as Veba Oil Supply & Trading. We were part of one of Germany's giant industrial conglomerates, the Veba Group.

At that time, Veba Oil was part owner of four refineries in Germany, which we had to keep supplied with crude and feedstocks. In addition, we had some equity crude oil production in several parts of the world. Most of our output was from Libya, but we also had some production in the North Sea, Indonesia and a couple of other countries.

My day job was dominated by supplying the refineries and marketing our equity production, but we also had a mandate to take more speculative positions in the international markets. Veba traded Russian pipeline supplies, North Sea, North African and Far East crude oil whenever we saw opportunities in the market.

DOI: 10.4324/9781003144335-8

Of all of the jurisdictions in which we operated, Libya was perhaps the most important to Veba because it was the site of our most important equity production. We enjoyed excellent relations with the local authorities and our counterparts in the national oil company, and we made sure to visit very regularly to keep up our contacts.

At that time, I was a young man, and it was a great adventure for me to visit Libya. At first, I would travel with experienced colleagues who knew the country, before I grew more confident and Veba trusted me to visit with just one other colleague.

I loved my trips to Libya, and we very rarely ran into any issues. In fact, I only remember being nervous on one occasion. We used to take an international flight into Tripoli and then fly to our inland production areas in small company planes that had to land in the middle of the sands. That was usually fine, apart from one time when we were flying over the desert and the general manager decided he wanted to try steering the plane. Let's just say that it was a long few minutes for me after he ordered the pilot to hand over the controls.

Problem solving

Veba's Libyan business was a big success for the company and continued to develop really nicely. We soon came to realize, though, that not every foreign business was finding it quite as easy to operate in Libya.

Spending so much time in the country, we got to know other members of the foreign business community, particularly the German, Swiss and Italian companies that were active there, primarily in the construction business.

These firms were developing motorways, building hotels, that kind of business. You could see their influence everywhere because the motorways in Libya looked like the motorways back home: they were laid out in the same way; they even used the same colours for their signs.

These companies would tell us that they were experiencing enormous difficulties in getting paid for their work in Libya. Their local counterparts were either genuinely struggling to pay them or else the Libyan firms were finding it difficult to access sufficient hard currency to make the payments.

One of the solutions that the Libyans had proposed was that they could instead pay these firms in crude oil rather than hard currency. That made sense in a way because the international firms would at least finally receive a valuable commodity in exchange for their work, but it was a big ask for a Swiss hotel developer to understand what it was supposed to do with a small parcel of Libyan crude oil.

When we heard about this situation, we immediately saw where we could solve some problems. We reached some agreements with the German-speaking business community in Tripoli, and we arranged that we would acquire their oil entitlements from them and co-load it with our own Libyan production.

Sometimes the firms would only receive small volumes and the timing and the quality of oil they received could be quite random. But Veba generally had some flexibility with our shipping from Libya, and so we could generally always absorb their requirements.

Optimizing economics

We soon developed this service arrangement into a successful sideline to Veba's main production, trading and supply businesses. We were solving the serious problems that our German and Swiss counterparts were experiencing by paying them in hard currency for their crude oil entitlements, which allowed them to carry on operating profitably in Libya.

But at the same time, this was a profitable business for Veba. Libyan crude oil was priced in relation to the government's official selling price (OSP). The international firms would receive a calculation from their counterparties in the country of how much oil they were due based on the current OSP. Veba would then take the oil off their hands on the same OSP basis, but we would apply a fixed fee for the service that we were providing.

We started taking small amounts of oil and the business grew from there. Eventually, we were working with a number of different companies, and we were able to pull multiple parcels together. We co-loaded these with our equity production and then made transfers to the foreign firms after the usual 30-day payment terms. Many of them had been waiting for their money for a very long time, so they were delighted to finally get paid.

Apart from the very reasonable fee that we were receiving from the foreign companies, Veba also benefited from the increased supply we were handling, which helped us with our freight economics. Let's say Veba had 500,000 barrels of equity production to lift from Libya, then adding a further 100,000 barrels of third-party entitlements to the loading would allow us to fully fill an Aframax crude vessel, improving our freight economics.

We usually shipped these Libyan volumes to Europe to supply our own refinery system. There were also times when perhaps we didn't need the material due to refinery turnarounds and then we would resell our Libyan cargoes in the market. We usually managed to sell those cargoes at a premium to the Libyan OSP, so in those cases, we would also profit from the premium between our sales price and the OSP that we had used as the purchasing price.

Mixed expansion

Veba really liked this service business, which was fairly steady and reliable as well as generating additional profits. We thought we could apply this service model in other countries where we were operating and where we knew that other international companies might be struggling to get paid for their non-oil activities.

We tried applying the model in Egypt where we also had some small equity production, but it wasn't too successful. We also tried the same thing in West Africa but that was even more difficult. In fact, I think it only worked once because it was too complicated and too many people were trying to cheat us.

The only other country where we really managed to implement the service model was Iraq. Veba didn't have any equity production there, but we had a monthly term supply deal with Iraq's national oil company, so we were able to lift the third-party oil alongside our own entitlement. Again, we were working with some international construction companies who had found that being paid in oil was complicated but was infinitely preferable to not being paid at all.

Applying the service model to Iraq was quite a successful business for us. We didn't usually run our term Iraqi oil in our own system, but we would sell it in the international markets and move it to Europe or to the U.S. We were usually able to achieve a small premium to the OSP, so we could make an additional profit on top of the service fees we charged the international firms for handling their oil.

The service model was a solidly profitable business. We aren't talking about Veba making hundreds of millions of dollars or anything close, but it was good enough for us because our company was not the biggest trading firm out there, and so we were always pleased to identify profitable niche opportunities.

The Iraqi business worked well, and the activity lasted until the invasion of Kuwait led to the First Gulf War in 1991.

After the war, you couldn't even travel to Iraq easily because of the 'no-fly' rules. When we went to Baghdad, we had to take a 1,000-kilometre taxi ride from Amman in Jordan through the desert. One time we were waiting in our taxi at a checkpoint when a truck loaded with gasoline failed to stop. The soldiers came out and fired in the air, but when the truck still didn't stop, a soldier with a machine gun jumped in the passenger seat of our taxi and ordered our driver to follow the truck.

That was a time when I genuinely feared for my life. We were driving alongside the truck with the soldier firing his machine gun in the air out of the front passenger window. Eventually, we overtook the truck. The soldier stopped our cab and we left him standing in the middle of the road holding his machine gun ready to fire at the oncoming truck. I have no idea what happened next because frankly we didn't wait around long enough to find out.

It was clearly a difficult time to operate in Iraq. After the war, we only managed to load a few cargoes before everything came to a halt. A ban was introduced on bringing Iraqi oil to Europe or to the U.S., and so we had to close down our business there.

Local knowledge

The Iraqi service business went away after the First Gulf War, but the Libyan service business lasted from the late 1980s through until the mid-1990s and was very successful for Veba.

There were a few reasons why we were able to develop this business and other firms weren't, even though they might have had a bigger global footprint.

First, we had strong relationships in the producer countries, where Veba had a reputation for fair dealing that meant that the local authorities were comfortable working with us and allowing us to aggregate third-party entitlements.

We also built up good contacts with the international business community in those countries. At first, it was with the big construction companies, who were mainly from Germany, but then also with smaller companies from other countries that were in the same position and had heard that we could offer a solution and that we were prepared to pay a fair price for their entitlements.

It wasn't just that we often had the German language in common, although that clearly helped. We also had the benefit of belonging to a large German conglomerate, which was respected quite a lot within Europe and was known to be well capitalized. That gave people the confidence that they would ultimately get paid.

In short, our reputation was good both with the domestic players and with international firms and that opened the door for us. But once the door was opened, we had to take the initiative. Veba was prepared to develop this service business, which could be complicated and time-consuming, when a lot of other traders wouldn't have looked at it.

From my observations, the oil market has shrunk somewhat since those days in terms of the number of active trading firms and their different models and focuses. There has been much more consolidation into bigger trading firms with economies of scale and larger balance sheets. For example, Veba's energy trading business was eventually absorbed into increasingly larger companies.

I spent my career in the German oil industry, and when I started, there were a large number of firms based here, particularly in Hamburg, which was the heart of German oil. Back then, firms could make decisions from their Hamburg offices, whereas now many of those companies have disappeared or at least their decision makers have moved to London or Switzerland.

I understand the need for consolidation, particularly in challenging times, but it would be a shame if the oil industry were ever to lose the local knowledge, the specialization and the ability to develop niche businesses that comes from the existence of a diverse range of trading firms operating in and from diverse locations.

7 Finding the global optimal

After graduating in chemical engineering from the Indian Institute of Technology, Manosh Saha joined Indian Oil Corporation in New Delhi as a refinery engineer, before switching to the state-owned firm's crude oil trading desk. Manosh then moved to Reliance Industries, where he spent four years in various roles, rising to be a senior crude oil trader in the Mumbai headquarters. He moved to Singapore in 2012, originally to join BrightOil's newly created crude oil desk. He has remained in Singapore, where he has worked as a senior crude oil trader for Repsol, for ZenRock Commodities and for Cathay Petroleum International.

For a trader of physical crude oil, the maths often starts months before any physical possibilities can be proved.

I spend most of my days as a trader living in spreadsheets that give me indications about potential trading arbitrages. Arbitrage trades attempt to profit from the difference in price in two different but related areas, such as between different locations or between different grades of crude oil.

The time that I spend actually trading a physical cargo is just a tiny fraction of the time that I will have spent beforehand working on my spreadsheets and looking at what I call my competitive metrics.

As a trader with an analytical style, I make sure I keep on churning the numbers. I find that if you talk to your numbers, your numbers will talk to you. Then the skill is to connect the dots. A trader's mind should be always wondering about the possibilities that the numbers suggest. Then, ultimately, you have to make a market call and accept the risk that brings.

This urge to review every possibility is a fairly standard mindset for a proprietary trader or for a derivatives trader but it's not always the way that firms think when they come to market their own equity cargoes.

Equity cargoes are made up of the crude oil that a firm receives in proportion to its underlying production from a certain oilfield or fields. Oil producers usually get assigned their equity cargoes on a regular basis, say every month, and it's usually obvious whom the pool of potential buyers might be. That makes it easy for a trader to get into a mindset where you essentially do the same trade over and over without really questioning its basis.

DOI: 10.4324/9781003144335-9

Many times, equity holders don't really think like traders but more like pure marketers. That is an absolutely legitimate approach, but it is always worth reviewing all of the options beforehand in order to reach a very conscious and deliberate decision.

When one team that I was part of applied this approach of questioning everything to some of our Brazilian equity sales, the results were really impressive.

Starting point

The first cargo we had to decide about was a parcel of medium Sapinhoa crude oil. We had a million barrels to sell, which would fit perfectly in a Suezmax oil tanker, which can carry between 800,000 and a million barrels. We would load the Suezmax at La Paloma off the coast of Uruguay, which is not a typical loading terminal but rather a location that is suitable for ship-to-ship (STS) transfers where oil is transferred from smaller to larger vessels.

When we looked at it, the best deal for the Sapinhoa seemed to be selling the cargo from La Paloma to Asia, specifically to the port of Qingdao in China. So we pencilled that million-barrel cargo in to be delivered-ex-ship (DES) Qingdao and we moved onto looking at our next equity cargo.

The next equity cargo from Brazil that we had to market was 600,000 barrels of a heavier crude oil grade called Albacora Leste, which was also going to be delivered to us at La Paloma. Because this second parcel was smaller, we expected to load it into one of the smallest class of crude oil tankers, an Aframax, which can handle up to 600,000 barrels.

We briefly considered whether we could combine these two equity cargoes because they were both loading at the same place, La Paloma, but we quickly rejected the idea because adding them together would have given us a total of 1.6 million barrels, which would have left us in no man's land in terms of the potential crude oil tankers we could use. 1.6 million barrels would be too big to fit into a Suezmax but too small to make the best use of a very large crude carrier (VLCC), which is the next largest class of vessels and which is generally designed to take 1.9–2.2 million barrels.

We decided to treat these two cargoes as separate deals and then embark upon any logistic optimization at a later stage, at least if anything occurred to us.

We were happy with the trade we had planned for the Sapinhoa in the Suezmax, but the prospects for the Albacora Leste looked less favourable, mainly because of the higher cost of using a smaller vessel like an Aframax to ship the oil.

The higher shipping cost for the Albacora Leste basically ruled out longer journey times that would make the oil very uncompetitive, meaning that the best destination for that oil looked likely to be the U.S., probably the Gulf Coast, which is the nearest major refining centre to the east coast of South America.

First revision

Then our calculations changed. The market became more favourable in the sense that demand for relatively heavy grades surged globally. Albacora Leste, which is relatively heavy, was set to benefit from this change in market dynamics and that opened up some new possibilities.

As prices for grades like Albacora Leste rose in Asia, the relative value of sending our cargo to Asia was only a little bit worse than sending it to one of our usual buyers in the U.S., even given the much higher cost of sending a more expensive Aframax vessel all the way to Asia.

We started to watch the netback economics of Asia and the U.S. very carefully – the netback is when you look at the delivered price of a cargo and then subtract your shipping costs to see which option will give you the best price at the loading port.

We even looked again at whether it might make sense to combine the two cargoes and send them both to Asia on a VLCC, but the economics of using the bigger vessel still didn't stack up.

Once it became clear that the netback from selling the cargo to Asia had improved significantly, it struck us that if Asia was an option, then selling to Europe would make even more sense as it was closer. We decided to take the Albacora Leste 'home' to our refining system in Europe.

The first plan was Sapinhoa to China and Albacora Leste to one of our usual U.S. customers. The first revision to that plan was to send the Albacora Leste to one our own refineries in Europe instead. This revision is an example of what we call optimizing the trade – taking a trade that was sensible and might even be very profitable and altering its structure to make it even more efficient and profitable.

Second revision

Everyone seemed to be happy with the current structure. After all, we hadn't just followed our standard operating procedure of selling Albacora Leste to the U.S., we had optimized the cargo and made use of our global network.

But as a team in Singapore, we still didn't feel totally satisfied. We still kept wondering if there was a way to combine the two cargoes and then load them on a VLCC, even though the economics hadn't made sense so far.

I kept asking myself how could we boost the netback value of these two cargoes: was there any way of optimizing the two deals any further and whether we had any other options that we hadn't considered?

It was at that point that we started thinking whether we could bring a third trade into the picture that would be profitable in itself as well as improving the netback value of the previous two trades.

After discussing the idea with our Houston office, we came to hear about an available cargo of Polvo crude oil. Polvo is a heavy grade from Brazil that has a relatively limited pool of buyers because of its high hydrogen sulphide content, which is responsible for its bad smell.

The Polvo parcel size was also only 350,000 barrels, which meant that it wouldn't even fill an Aframax. Having to use a partially filled Aframax for freight would make it very expensive to ship the Polvo far from Brazil, probably limiting its potential pool of buyers to the U.S. refiners in the Gulf Coast who are no more than ten days' sail away.

The Polvo cargo on its own was clearly not a particularly attractive option, but my idea was, in combination with our Houston desk, to buy the Polvo and then load all three cargoes together on a VLCC and bring the crude oil to Asia.

This was an unconventional proposal to say the least, but our global team was ready to consider it and we started to run all of the calculations to check the idea out.

We found that if we could manage to load the Albacora Leste onto a VLCC, then it would be more profitable to take the cargo to Asia than to either the U.S. Gulf or Europe because the cost of the additional days' sailing time was less than the advantage that we would get from using a bigger vessel.

We had already been planning to take our Sapinhoa cargo to Asia anyway, but this new plan would significantly improve that trade as well by reducing shipping costs. At that time, the difference between using a Suezmax to ship oil to Asia and using a VLCC was around 75 cents per barrel, so the cost saving on freight was significant.

The improvement of the economics of our first two cargoes was so significant that we figured that even if it was a slightly lower netback to sell the Polvo to Asia than to the U.S. Gulf, the trade would still be worth doing because it would boost the overall value of the three cargoes.

Full Brazilian

The only possibility that could have derailed the plan would have been if the loading schedule for the three cargoes were too far apart, which could have required us to pay significant sums in 'demurrage' – the cost of having a vessel waiting around between loadings – that might have negatively impacted the overall economics.

Fortunately, the loading timetable worked out and we had to absorb just three or four days of demurrage. I guess that you could argue that we were lucky throughout. The loading times for the Sapinhoa and Albacora Leste at La Paloma were close together, and La Paloma was only one or two days voyage from where we were loading the Polvo.

We were also lucky that we found a buyer of Polvo in Asia who was prepared to pay a relatively good price, even though the grade was very unfamiliar in the region. We were even lucky that the size of the Polvo parcel was a perfect fit for the gap we had to fill in order to charter a VLCC.

The point is, though, that we helped to make our own luck by having the idea in the first place and by our constant analysis of all of the changing variables.

Either way, the calculations all stacked up and we had to pull the overall ticket together. Our various teams had to coordinate all the various parts very carefully. The Houston desk had to buy the Polvo from the supplier, and the next morning I closed with the buyer in Asia. At the same time, our freight desk had arranged to charter a VLCC for a journey between Brazil and Asia.

Finally, the loading period came around. We filled that VLCC with 1 million barrels of Sapinhoa, 650,000 barrels of Albacora Leste and 350,000 barrels of Polvo, and we all breathed a big sigh of relief.

The global optimal

We could never have made a success of this trade if we were a smaller local firm. International arbitrage plays like this need a well-functioning global team to pull them off. We made this trade happen by constantly talking between the various offices, even though sometimes it meant I needed to get up in the middle of the night in Singapore.

Teamwork between the three regions was needed to create a successful trading strategy. The deal for the Polvo was done between Asia and Houston, while the whole trade relied on the European office being supportive when they could have sulked that we were pulling the cargo of Albacora Leste away from the European refinery that they were supplying. Everyone ultimately felt good about the trade because by increasing the netback, we had all contributed to boosting our global trading results.

Another lesson was to avoid the trap of self-censorship – if you worry about sounding unconventional, then you will never propose anything interesting to the global team. I have learnt to always take a deep breath and ask myself, 'what have I got to lose by making a suggestion, compared to what we have to gain, if I'm right'.

The success of the trade also confirmed to me the value of unconventional thinking and of never settling, even when the original plan is sound.

Moving 1 million barrels of Sapinhoa to Asia was a fairly conventional trade. Moving 650,000 barrels of Albacora Leste to Asia was much more rare, given that freight economics wouldn't normally support that, while sending 350,000 barrels of Polvo to Asia was very unusual indeed.

So many decisions had to change in a relatively short period. The Sapinhoa was always destined for Asia, but we first flipped the Albacora Leste from its normal home in the U.S. to Europe and then we flipped it again to Asia, while the Polvo that was supposed to go to the U.S. ended up going to Asia. In the background, we were also flipping between three types of freight: Aframax, Suezmax and VLCC.

Traders should never bind themselves to the conventional. Our job is to think outside the box in order to try to add the last cent onto our netback and into our global book. We could easily have been complacent because everyone was happy with how we were planning to sell our two equity cargoes. We had done our research and had found the best netback price for each.

Every trade was seemingly optimized. But it turned out that there was a further optimal. The question has to be: if we bring all the individual optimals in our book together, do they add up to a global optimal? And in this case, the answer was no.

Each of the first two trades in singularity gave us local optimals. But when we put all three trades together, we reached a global optimal. By definition, that was a better result than the combination of all of these local optimals.

Perspiration and inspiration

Many times, equity holders do not think outside the box. They look at marketing their cargo to the best of their ability, but they don't consider whether they could trade additional barrels alongside their equity to increase their global optimal. As a trader, you should always be considering the potential value of taking on an additional risk.

Often equity holders have an advantage when looking at trading third-party barrels. They can even afford to pay up for additional crude oil because their existing equity cargo can give them a better logistical advantage than anyone else could realize at that time, which is what we saw with our Polvo cargo.

This sort of idea only hits you when you are desperate to improve the bottom line and when you are not satisfied with the obvious trade. Any decent crude oil trader should always be seeking to do something more. You can't sit around and wait for the stars to be aligned because most of the time they won't be.

Instead, you have to be inquisitive, and you have to be restless. You need to keep the global optimal in mind at all times. It's not that you need to sleep badly and be stressed out, but you do need to keep your brain ticking and enjoy the puzzle.

In real life, there's no brilliant light bulb that goes off when you have a good idea. For some reason, I kept wanting to come back to those trades and play with the economics in my spreadsheets. A good trade starts with good analytics and then, if you are lucky, the data will spark something in your imagination.

Macro & micro trading

The price of crude oil is affected by multiple factors, such as fluctuations in geopolitics, the health of the global economy, the relative balance of supply and demand, and financial factors, such as prevailing interest rates and the relative strength of the U.S. dollar.

Some traders develop strategies around analysing these macroeconomic ('macro') factors. They then take positions in the physical or derivative oil markets that are designed to take advantage of how they expect these macro trends to play out.

As we will see in the following chapters, other traders may find that, while they did not set out to trade the macro factors specifically, events – such as a financial crisis, a force majeure or a credit event – end up forcing them to adapt their strategies to take macro factors into account.

The opposite style to macro trading is 'micro' trading, which will be described in detail in Chapter 11. Traders more focused on the micro side argue that macro trends are too hard to predict consistently, and so they prefer to narrow their focus.

Micro traders need to be specialists in their particular market because their strategies depend on noticing smaller indicators, such as changes in participant behaviour, that might signal upcoming changes in market sentiment and direction.

DOI: 10.4324/9781003144335-10

8 Calling a collapse

After graduating from Yale University, Eric Rubenstein spent some time as a consultant, including a stint with Essar Steel's retail steel business. His first role in the energy markets was at Louis Dreyfus Energy, later Louis Dreyfus Highbridge Energy, where he worked as a petroleum products analyst and as a trader from 2006 to 2010. In 2010, Eric joined Citigroup in Houston to establish global crude oil and refined products strategy for the oil trading desk and to simultaneously set up their ability to trade physical barrels. Later in his tenure with the bank, he additionally originated investments and acted as a strategic investor for a portfolio of companies. Eric left the bank in 2021 to found a sustainability focused venture capital fund investing in early-stage companies that capture, reduce, reuse, store or avoid carbon emissions.

What has always attracted me to commodity markets is that at the end of the day with a commodity, there is a physical delivery that has to happen: there is a buyer who needs to take delivery of a particular product and a seller who needs to make that delivery happen.

If you do your homework properly, then you can predict how those exchanges of commodities are going to play out. Perhaps, it won't be so easy for a seller to make a delivery because there isn't enough supply, or perhaps the sellers will be chasing a buyer because there is too much supply.

Once you understand the dynamics behind that final exchange of commodities, you can make some assumptions about how prices are likely to behave and then you can place trades based on your expectations.

The first element to any analysis of the oil market is to understand the balance between supply and demand of physical crude oil, which is referred to in the industry as 'counting barrels'.

Whether or not a barrel of crude has been produced from the ground, whether or not the oil actually exists and is available for sale, is still the most important factor influencing prices. Everything else is secondary to that reality, although other factors are more and more influential.

Counting the barrels means tracking as many data points as possible: production, consumption, imports, exports, inventories and anything else relevant.

Quality data is extremely important, and fortunately every year, the data sources get faster and more accurate. You can count cargoes more easily than

DOI: 10.4324/9781003144335-11

ever before and you can check storage levels by flying airplanes over the facilities or by acquiring satellite data on storage from firms like Ursa Space Systems.

After physical supply and demand, the next key element in any oil market analysis is politics because oil is possibly the most geopolitically sensitive commodity. OPEC is the most important factor here as their decisions to cut or increase supply can have a significant influence on prices.

The third element is positioning and money flows, which are by nature influenced by other markets like foreign exchange, equities and interest rates. There are firms that trade oil as a hedge against inflation or against an equities position, so movements in those markets can influence the oil markets.

Positioning also includes the technical indicators, such as key psychological numbers like $50 or $100 per barrel, moving averages, or trend lines, which are almost like a numerical representation of market psychology.

The barrels themselves were once effectively the only driver of the oil price, but today there is so much money doing so many different things for such different reasons that you need to pay attention to multiple factors on a perpetual basis.

Seeing a shift

There was a time in the second quarter of 2014, when we started to see all three of these elements – supply/demand, geopolitics and money flows – point clearly towards a significant change in the oil market.

First, we started to see signs of the global economy slowing, even though most forecasts had not changed. The International Energy Agency (IEA) was still predicting robust demand growth for 2014, but we were looking at real-time or near real-time data about industrial production around the world, and we felt the slowdown was very noticeable.

The slowdown became very pronounced in June and July 2014, to the point that it became very clear that the global economy was decelerating unexpectedly.

At the same time that demand was under pressure, oil supply was still increasing. Oil prices were well over $100, and as a result, everyone was maximizing their output and their plans for growth. At $100, the market was priming producers to increase output aggressively forever.

When you have a slowing economy, coupled with an extreme growth in production, you can predict that there's going to be a price collapse with a good level of confidence. By July 2014, I started to have conversations internally to make sure that my colleagues agreed with my logic.

As the global strategist on the oil trading desk, my primary responsibility was to our traders, but I also had a dual responsibility to our clients because the firm provided our clients with direct access to the insights from the trading desk itself.

I first spoke about a potential price collapse outside the bank in August 2014. It was in response to a question that was very pointed, and which deserved an honest answer. I told the client that oil was going to drop from above $100 to at least $50, and that the reason it had to go at least to $50 was to stop production growth by making it uneconomic to produce the marginal barrel. With prices below $50, I expected that a lot of production would become uneconomic.

That was quite a radical view because back then whenever people talked about marginal production, it was in terms of how high prices needed to be to stimulate production. The consensus at that time was that $80–90 per barrel led producers to maximize output and growth.

My view was that we were about to flip all the way to the other side of the cost curve. I believed that we were about to see prices that would not just slow down production growth but would actually reverse the trend to growth by halting some production altogether.

The geopolitics was also supportive of that view. The OPEC countries were not prepared to cut production themselves to balance the market. They wanted to see U.S. producers reduce output instead, and they thought the only way to get there would be if prices fell.

I think, in hindsight, people would agree that for once OPEC actually wanted prices to fall, but the market was not convinced at that time or else prices would have been much lower already. OPEC proved their intent in November 2014 when they officially chose not to cut production, even after prices had already started falling.

Customer response

The first customer with whom I discussed my thesis of a major fall was a hedge fund. Typically, the 'fast money', such as hedge funds, gets quite excited about events that are going to change market dynamics and create volatility.

No one is going to (or at least no one should) make a trading decision based on a 30-minute or 1-hour meeting though, particularly when I was suggesting quite a radical proposition. People needed to do their own work to check our analysis.

In July and August 2014, there also weren't a lot of other bearish voices out there. In fact, I'd venture to say there wasn't any other available analysis that suggested a massive fall was about to happen, so customers had to have faith in our thesis and their own view of the numbers.

What encourages people to listen in these situations is the relationship and credibility that we had built up over a period of time. I had known a lot of these firms for years, and I had been right about the markets enough times that many had developed a trust in our analysis.

Talk of a potential price collapse was obviously more problematic for our oil producer clients. I was visiting oil producers almost daily during September and October and warning them that oil prices were going to fall.

Some producers thought about what I had showed them overnight, and the following day, they hedged their entire production. They were then able to continue to produce throughout the low-price era because they were hedged. In a couple of cases, those hedges extended the life of their company by a couple of years.

Other folks I talked to at $100 didn't hedge their production because obviously they liked those prices, but when we dropped to $90 in under a week, some of them started to think, 'OK, maybe something is wrong', and they put in an order to buy hedges.

At the other end of the spectrum, there were firms who refused to hedge, even if they acknowledged that I might be right, on the grounds that they were strong enough to survive any temporary downturn, in part because the economics of their production were better than everyone else's.

Those firms thought that a price fall might knock out a few competitors with higher costs, but they would be fine. Of course, the market smashed straight through everyone's cost levels, proving our thesis that the market would end up shutting in any marginal production.

Many of the producers that didn't hedge had to slash production to manage their economics. Those shutdowns are what ended up finally solving the weak market. Enough production was cut for long enough, while demand finally came back up.

Choppy waters

What made 2014–2015 such a challenging market was that the downtrend we had predicted wasn't always clear. The oil market was falling, but it also had periods of time where it would bounce back, before then falling again.

It was hard to tell where the decline would stop and how quickly we would get to a point where the low price was actually disincentivizing producers from producing.

Markets act faster these days than they did previously, and they acted faster in 2014 than they might have done a decade before. There's just much more money in the markets, and the sheer volume of dollars moves markets quickly, particularly when they are one directional.

A vicious circle can develop. When producers start to see markets fall and don't act, at some point they can't hold on any longer. They are losing so much money that they are forced to sell their oil almost at any cost, just to generate some revenue or protect what value still exists.

On the counter side, some people made a lot of money. Those folks believed in the thesis and went short and stayed short, even during the temporary recoveries. They were willing to sit through any rally because they recognized that the market had a big job to do, and it wasn't done yet.

The big wins were in following the market's broad move down, rather than trying to get cute by trying to time buys and sells perfectly.

Lower for longer

My thesis of a giant sell-off had been proved broadly right, but I was wrong in one aspect: the market went lower than I had expected.

A lot of people thought that the sell-off would stop at $80 because that was the marginal cost level, the lower end of where prices would need to reach in order for there to still be growth.

In contrast, I was absolutely convinced that the market was going to need to get to a point where production was actively hindered. I had thought in terms of $50 as a level that we would need to reach to actually stop production.

I certainly wasn't thinking at the time that going from $100 to $25 was realistic, but that's where we reached within a year and a half. It took that long because the shale industry kept producing, despite lower prices, because investors were rewarding firms at that time for their volume of production and their growth, rather than for their economics.

Prices also had to fall so hard in part because production costs also fell far further than anyone was expecting. As it cost less and less to produce a barrel, the market had to go lower and lower to stop that barrel getting produced.

I remember we had an internal debate about what I could say to clients in my presentations. We agreed that talking about a fall to $50 was too aggressive. There's a risk sometimes that you scare people to the point where they stop listening. You don't want firms to ignore your main thesis because they think you are being too outrageous.

Once we got to $80, it was a lot easier to have those more challenging conversations. It didn't seem quite as shocking to say we will hit $50, once we had already dropped from $100 to $80.

Analysis pays off

It's rare to get a thank you in the oil markets, but a couple of people were appreciative enough to reach out and recognize that the call was correct. There are people that I spoke with back then that still remind me of that period now.

I was never worried I was wrong. The move down was entirely predictable. Anyone that had done the same analysis would have been equally convinced. The supply–demand balance was clear, the politics of OPEC looked supportive of the view, and the timing of the trade depended on getting short before the collapse and staying short through the temporary rallies.

The fall wasn't in doubt, it was more a question of the magnitude. That was a big move by any standard. A lot of times the market just needs a small correction in order to keep supply and demand balanced, but this massive move was something extraordinary, reflecting the extraordinary growth we had been experiencing in U.S. oil production.

We saw similarly huge falls in 2020, but that was a different case. That year, COVID-19 emerged, and there was no way to predict how that totally new external factor was going to play out.

That kind of market is way more nerve-wracking than a market like 2014–2015, which was easier to model. Back then, we did our homework, we believed in what came out of that homework, and we made the right call.

9 Learning from misfortune

Cui Zhenchu initially joined a light industrial company in Beijing, after graduating from Beijing University of International Trade and Economics. In 1993, he joined Unipec, which at the time had just been set up as an energy trading joint venture between two Chinese state-owned firms, Sinochem and Sinopec. Mr Cui held various roles within Unipec. He traded chemicals, refined products, freight and crude oil, as well spending time in the president's office and in an oil-sands project of Sinopec in Canada. Mr Cui was appointed as the general manager of Unipec's crude oil department in 2007, a role he held until early 2014, when he moved to Shanghai to become head of crude oil trading at privately owned energy and finance conglomerate, CEFC China Energy. After leaving CEFC in early 2019, he joined Wintime Group as chairman of their petrochemicals division.

People learn more from difficulties than they do when times are easy, and that is especially true of traders. In fact, that is even true for the world in general. The world changes and develops fastest when countries respond to challenges or catastrophes. In the good times, it is easy to stop learning or to only learn a little. Difficult times teach people the most.

I guess in that sense, I must be lucky because God always gave me some troubles. Maybe he wanted me to upgrade myself by giving me some difficulties. It must have worked because I generally managed to turn any challenges into an opportunity for learning, even though I maybe did not always see the situation so positively at the time.

At first everything went very smoothly in my career. The 1990s was a fascinating time to join the Chinese oil industry. At the start of the decade, China had a single importer and exporter for the oil sector. The China National Chemicals Import and Export Corporation, the predecessor of Sinochem, had been founded in 1950 as essentially the state-owned monopoly for energy.

Then in the early 1990s, China adopted its 'open to the world' policy, and the government began to break up some state company monopolies. In the energy sector, the government's intention was gradually to open the window for more active trading of crude oil and refined products.

Unipec was created in 1993 as a joint venture between Sinochem and Sinopec, the giant refiner and petrochemical firm. In the same year, China Oil

DOI: 10.4324/9781003144335-12

was created as a joint venture between Sinochem and CNPC. Unipec and China Oil were designed to look and feel more like the international trading firms. With their creation, the whole picture changed. The new firms were able to attract good trading talent: the more open policy in China had triggered people's creativity and changed their mentality.

I was fortunate to join Unipec soon after its creation in 1993. I was initially assigned to the chemicals team, and from there, I moved into the refined products group. It was fortunate timing. I arrived on the refined products desk just as the Chinese economy was starting to boom.

The demand for gasoil, in particular, was huge. China simply could not produce enough to meet all the country's needs, and so we were constantly buying in gasoil through till around 1998 when the domestic supply–demand gap started to ease.

My time as a products trader was a great experience for me and raised my profile within the firm, but I was still surprised and proud to be appointed as secretary to the president of Unipec.

This role was a huge opportunity for a young man to get to know how the other departments worked and how the whole entity was structured. My career had reached what you might call the 'middle summit' and I felt comfortable and very pleased with my progress so far.

Time to rebuild

Then the blow fell.

The president of Unipec was suddenly fired in 1999, and I received a severe black mark by association. I was demoted to basic employee status and was moved to a new junior role in the crude oil department.

From being secretary to the president, I became the record keeper of daily information. I spent my days sitting in a chair watching the oil futures prices move on the screen and making written notes about what was happening.

At that time, the crude oil price was somewhere in the low $20s per barrel, and I had to write a report to my bosses every time the market moved by more than 20 cents, whether or not it was 1 am or 3 am in the morning.

This was a very dull job indeed. It was basically a punishment assignment. I did not receive much sympathy from many of my Unipec colleagues. In fact, most people thought that the company had been very merciful because at least the junior role gave me enough income to feed myself and my family. It was a big blow, but in such a situation, you must be prepared to do something that other people are not willing to do.

Looking back more on that period today, this was actually an important position for my development as a trader. Watching the markets move day in and day out, I gained a very intuitive understanding of what was happening. I learnt how the oil market moves and I started to spot some of the traps that can lose firms money.

My luck changed for the better when an opportunity came up on the shipping desk. There was no one else suitable for the position at short notice, so I was offered the job. The freight department was not that prestigious at that time, but it was a clear step up from record keeper.

Within Unipec, crude oil trader was the highest position, with the most prestige and the best pay, followed by refined products trader. Shipping was viewed as an auxiliary operation, but it taught me an enormous amount about physical operations, and it was a way back into the mainstream of Unipec.

During my time in freight, I had the opportunity to travel frequently to Canada to develop the trading and logistics side of an upstream investment that Sinopec, Unipec's parent, had made in an oil-sands block in Canada. The Northern Lights project was a joint venture with Synenco, whose share was later acquired by Total, and was a fascinating experience for me.

Then in October 2007, I changed roles again. This time I was nominated to take over as head of crude oil trading.

Crude awakening

My first day as head of crude oil trading was also my first day as a crude oil trader. I suppose it was inevitable that some of the senior traders on the crude oil team resented my appointment. At first, they did not respect me.

Some traders would try to challenge me and to test me by supposedly asking my advice on a complex crude oil trading matter. Their questions were designed to catch me out.

It might seem strange, but even from my first day, I did not have any doubts about whether I would be able to cope with the challenge of leading the crude oil trading team. I was confident that I knew more than any of my traders about logistics and about partnerships. I also knew that my difficult years making notes on the crude market had taught me about volatility and the risk–reward balance of trading.

When my new colleagues came to test me, I would tell them: 'solve your own problems now, but in six months' time, I will be able to give you even better solutions'. I knew that I would learn and that I would succeed because my bad times had built up my confidence.

On my first day as head of crude oil, the oil price was around $45 per barrel. Prices rose steadily from that moment. In July 2008, oil prices set a record at over $147 per barrel. But within a year or so, the market had collapsed to around $30 per barrel in the wake of the global financial crisis.

It was a challenging period. One of our trading counterparties – Lehman Brothers – collapsed, and many financial firms disappeared, merged or had to turn to their local government for support. Several oil traders also lost substantial sums of money during that period, either as the market moved up or as it crashed back down. The price volatility we saw in crude oil in those years was truly unprecedented.

Key principles

Unipec was one of the few firms that avoided losses during this incredibly difficult time.

I feel very proud of this as a trader and as a manager of traders. Our trading strategy helped us to stay profitable when many of our peers were posting significant losses.

My unusual and challenging path to the crude oil team had taught me two key principles that we immediately implemented when I took over as leader of the trading group: first, we did not permit any speculation on the outright price of crude oil; second, my traders were not allowed to write options.

In late 1990s, Sinopec refineries, through Unipec, used to take big positions on the outright crude oil price. They called it hedging but it was not, it was speculation. After all, did our traders really need to hedge the outright price of crude oil when at that time our government set a fixed retail price for refined products that was not linked to the international oil price?

After I took the lead, we stopped the team taking those risky positions. We needed to be active traders and to take positions on the premiums or differentials of different grades of crude oil, but our strict policy was that we should not be making bets on the outright price of oil.

Our other strict policy was that we must never ever sell options. Traders sometimes like to sell options to make some cents or dollars from the premium. In my view, the risks of selling options are too high. For the relatively small premium you receive from selling an option, you give yourself an open risk that can prove to be extremely expensive. Selling an option gets you a finger but maybe tomorrow you will lose your body.

I was fine if my traders wanted to buy options. As a buyer, you have all the upside and the most that you can lose is the premium you have paid. But if you sell options on crude oil, you risk a big problem. Over the years, some Chinese firms have lost a lot of money from selling options, and there have been quite a few public scandals. I was determined to avoid this situation.

Know thyself

My two rules were derived from my overarching concept of trading: the most important starting point for a trader is to clearly understand the true nature of the company where they work.

Unipec, for example, is the trading arm of Sinopec. Sinopec is a giant industrial group that makes its profit from processing feedstock and selling value-added products. The core role of Unipec within the group is to find the crude oil that delivers the most value to Sinopec's huge refining system. Compared with this significant industrial activity, speculative trading, even if it is very profitable, is worth less than pennies.

Any true understanding of Unipec's place within the broader Sinopec group makes it obvious that as traders we should never take a big position in the flat price. Traders can make some money speculating, for sure, but the oil markets can also generate huge losses: the sort of losses that can kill firms, even big giants.

On my watch, we had some difficulties from time to time, but we never had a big problem. We maybe lost a finger, or even hurt a thumb, but we never lost our whole hand.

You need to understand your mandate. If I had been running crude oil trading at an independent trading house instead of a large major, I would have applied a different mentality. Trading houses make their money by taking on risk. For them, it is a different story: no risk, no profit.

As well as understanding the firm's appetite for risk, a trader also needs to understand his or her capacity to absorb potential losses. I would always tell my guys, 'look, and see if you have deep or narrow pockets before you make a trade'.

It is true that you can make a lot of money in the crude oil markets in a single day, but the market will double-teach you tomorrow. It is my firm view that as a major player, you can never make money consistently from pure speculation.

At the end of the day, if you want to gamble, you should not become a crude oil trader. You had better go to the casino in Macao instead.

Next steps

I suppose it is funny in a way that, although my team traded countless millions of barrels of crude oil during my time running the trading department for Unipec, my greatest contribution to our success was the trades I stopped from happening: flat-price speculation and options writing.

Our ability to pass through the financial crisis relatively unscathed when others were suffering attracted praise, and I was recommended in 2013 for promotion to managing director of Unipec U.K., a role equivalent to vice president level. Sadly, my promotion was denied because my wife and daughter had stayed in Canada and taken Canadian citizenship, which made it too sensitive.

After that experience, I could foresee the end of my career with Unipec, and so I moved on to CEFC, again as head of crude oil trading. I had a lot of positive and interesting experiences at CEFC and in my subsequent role. But I remain most proud of what we achieved at Unipec in those years: in two decades, we built a crude oil trading operation that was the equal of any firm in the world. We also passed through exceptionally challenging market conditions without suffering any significant losses.

By the end of my time at Unipec, the firm had gone from a new creation to a global player with a great reputation. Everywhere we went, we found that other traders respected our company. Although I had some difficult times during my career, I was always proud when I gave people my Unipec business card.

10 Facing a force majeure

Anne Devlin worked for 22 years at BP Oil International, mostly as a crude oil trader and book leader. Since leaving BP in 2018, she has been working as an independent board member and as an investor with a particular focus on energy transition. Anne is a director of Terra Solar II, a utility size solar development company in Ireland, and an investor in Sitigrid, a carbon offset venture. She is also on the board of the Centre for Enterprise, Markets and Ethics (CEME) think tank.

Often when you are trading, it can feel like problems never come singly but always together. A series of events in the early summer of 2015 confirmed to me that Murphy's Law really does exist and that it applies only too well to the physical crude oil markets.

That was the summer when I was well and truly caught out by geopolitics. It was only a combination of good luck, some nimble execution and the strong relationships we had developed that stopped our desk from experiencing some significant losses.

The initial trade I had made was very straightforward in nature. I had agreed to sell a cargo of Iraqi Kirkuk blend crude oil that was loading at the Turkish port of Ceyhan to a Greek refiner.

This was a fairly standard trade for us. At that time, we were loading a couple of Kirkuk cargoes every month. The economics of the trade made a lot of sense to both sides, given that the refiner was located just a few days sailing time from Ceyhan.

It all looked like business as usual, or at least it did until the loadings suddenly came to a halt. While we were waiting for news about why the exports had stopped, tension mounted in the market. Ceyhan is in the Eastern Mediterranean. Given how short the time was between the scheduled loading and the scheduled delivery for most refiners, everybody knew it would be challenging to bring another cargo from a different part of the world to avoid refiners stocking out.

Problems never come alone. Just when I was trying to figure out how to source a replacement to Kirkuk, life got more complicated, thanks to a sudden escalation in the Greek economic crisis. Greek banks were closing down, and my credit department became increasingly nervous about my sale to the Greek refiner.

DOI: 10.4324/9781003144335-13

Geopolitical gyrations

Geopolitical disruptions like the internal politics in Iraq impacting the level of exports can create mayhem in a trading book.

These events are no black swan. Oil has been at the heart of geopolitical tensions for over a century given the economic power the natural resource brings to its owner. The ownership of oil becomes a great prize coveted by many and used to serve national, political and sometimes personal interest. Over an 18-year period, I traded through a PDVSA general strike that paralysed the whole of the Venezuelan oil industry and their assets abroad, the Arab Spring and the Libyan Uprising where several of my vessels were close to the combat zone.

I also worked through the ever-changing regulations linked to the tightening of American and European sanctions against producing countries or trading entities. Discussing with the in-house legal team became a regular feature to work out which trades we could put on without breaking the law!

The particular tension between the Kurdish and the central government in Baghdad was not new. While everybody was aware of the tension building, it was more difficult to forecast when it would come to a head. The Kurdish region resented the centralization of the oil windfall and considered the amount of money redistributed at the regional level both inadequate to the need of the region and not sufficiently reflective of its contribution.

While a revenue-sharing mechanism between the Kurdistan Regional Government (KRG) and the Iraqi government was being negotiated, the KRG concluded that by controlling the export route, they could control the money generated by exports.

By 2013, they had opened a pipeline linking the Kurdish fields of Taq-Taq and Tawke to Fish Khabur at the Turkish border, where it connects with the Kirkuk-Ceyhan pipeline. The new pipeline was built along a route which effectively bypassed portions of the original pipeline controlled by the Iraqi State.

In parallel, the government of the semi-autonomous Kurdish region continued to sign Production Sharing Contracts (PSC) with companies to develop regional fields, openly challenging the prerogative of the central government.

Baghdad was angered by these successful attempts to undermine their authority over the region and by the activity of neighbouring powers: Turkey hosts most of the export pipeline and the terminal infrastructure in Ceyhan, so no seaborne deliveries can happen without their agreement.

Most tragically, all those regional tensions were exacerbated by the ongoing fighting against ISIS in western Iraq and eastern Syria. Most of the Kurdish population, split between Syria, Iraq and Turkey, was at the heart of the combat zone. These dramatic circumstances aggravated the need for means to finance the fighting in order to defend Kurdish territory.

Oil infrastructure became quite literally a battleground, so when exports of Kirkuk were interrupted in June 2015, the trading community knew the problem could last for a while.

Know your exposure

In the meantime, in Ceyhan, the cargoes of Kirkuk were not loading but were not cancelled either. This is an awkward moment since as the owner of the cargo, you still have the contractual duty to present a vessel ready to load.

At that point, the shipowner starts invoicing 'demurrage', which is the daily rate the charterer owes to the shipowner because the latter has fulfilled his contractual obligation by presenting a vessel ready to load on the day you mutually agreed. The fact that the crude is not there to be loaded is not his problem. This can easily cost $60,000 per day, so the cost goes up quite quickly.

In parallel, the final receiver of the cargo started getting nervous as they saw the stock at their refinery depleting fast and were urgently requesting confirmation of the timing of the delivery.

Eventually, SOMO, Iraq's state oil company invoked a force majeure (FM) clause, which provided some basis upon which we could communicate and act.

The concept of FM in English law is reserved for events that are beyond your reasonable control and are not foreseeable. Originally, this concept was limited to Acts of God, such as earthquakes, eruptions and floods. Although strictly speaking, the concept of FM is not formally recognized under English law, so to ensure that it can be relied upon, your contract should contain specific events.

From the moment a party declares FM, the obligation is suspended, not terminated, until the FM is lifted. Usually, if it goes beyond a certain number of months fixed in the contractual clause, the parties can walk away without any obligations on either side.

When you are not back to back on this clause, for example, because you buy a cargo under Iraqi law and sell it delivered under English law, you are exposed. The best strategy in my view is to find a commercial solution and avoid going down the legal route.

It is in these types of circumstances that you usually discover the true nature of the person you have on the other side of the phone line.

As mentioned before, problems never come alone. As I was working on the possibility of delivering another cargo into Greece to avoid stocking out my Kirkuk receiver, the Greek debt crisis reached its climax.

On 29 June 2015, Greece closed its banks and imposed capital controls to prevent financial chaos, after the breakdown of bailout talks with its international creditors. The shutdown of the banks was to last until 6 July, and cash withdrawals were limited to 60 euros per day. Obviously, my credit department was watching the latest development very closely.

Thankfully, I had built a strong relationship with the credit department over the years. They knew I was not the reckless type, but from their point of view, the fact that the obligation to deliver the Kirkuk was simply suspended could imply a possible doubling of the credit exposure if I were to deliver another cargo, and this in the midst of an acute national debt crisis.

Egyptian piece of the puzzle

Tensions can also create opportunities. What can be a challenging cargo to place one day can become a life saver the next.

I received a call from BP Egypt, asking me to handle at short notice the export of a Gulf of Suez Mix equity cargo. The decision to export was part of a wider negotiation between BP Upstream and EGPC, the Egyptian State Oil Company. Reminding a counterparty that you have the ability to export your own oil made a powerful point in a delicate commercial negotiation.

I was instructed to load the Egyptian cargo as soon as I could get a ship to the terminal. The grade had not been seen in the market for a long time. Its falling production meant it was typically refined domestically.

We first had to check that the cargo quality was in line with the specifications we had previously used for this particular crude oil. Refiners would otherwise seek a discount to the crude oil's theoretical value to protect themselves against any adverse yield and sulphur content variation.

Gulf of Suez Mix loads out of a terminal on the southern side of the Suez Canal and therefore is only a couple of days sailing time from the Eastern Mediterranean. At such short notice and with perceived quality risk, it would be a tricky sale at the best of times, but the delay and subsequent cancellation of Kirkuk cargoes from Ceyhan made the prompt timing of this export an asset.

Transparency and goodwill

It is in trying circumstances that you test the strength of your relationships, in trading as in life.

Breaking down the issues was essential for their successful resolution.

On the Iraqi side, our negotiations with SOMO focused on getting some replacement oil somewhere. I acknowledged that Iraq was under attack and that planning exports from the north could be very tricky.

We also needed to mitigate our shipping exposure and recover some, if not all, of the eye-watering shipping bill. Thankfully, we had no pricing exposure yet, and that kept the discussion relatively simple, although lengthy.

On the Greek side, my receiver was facing a very real risk of running out of stocks for her refinery in the midst of a financial crisis that was limiting her company's capacity to react. I had taken years to develop a trusting and respectful relationship with her and I was determined to explore all the avenues available to help mitigate the problem.

To be fair, the sudden availability of the Egyptian cargo from BP Upstream was sheer luck and relieved the biggest risk of running out of oil. Nevertheless, many other aspects of the deal had to be agreed, starting internally with robust discussions about credit exposure. An open and frank exchange followed with my receiver. We were both aware that the legal fallback was best to be avoided and that a commercial solution ought to be found.

After a vigorous negotiation about the price and quality of the Egyptian cargo, the cancellation of the original sale and some strong statements by our counterparty that they had both the ability and the intention to pay us in a timely manner, the deal went ahead.

Into the matrix

One of the keys in ensuring that this replacement trade went smoothly was, I believe, the positive relationship that I had built up over the years with my counterparty at the Greek refiner. While she knew that the FM was not our company's fault, she trusted us to help with a replacement cargo.

We had an open channel of communication throughout the discussions, and I was always open with her about our options.

So many things can go wrong in physical trading: the weather intervenes in loadings, geopolitical disruptions emerge, and shipping delays happen. There are dozens of potential problems and when they do happen, you have to be able to discuss them calmly and productively with your counterpart. I genuinely don't think you can be a successful physical trader in the long term without the ability to develop human relationships.

Physical trading for me is primarily about building a matrix of physical lengths and shorts in different regions. When you do that, you will end up with contracts on different price benchmarks because each company that you negotiate with will be looking to mitigate their own inherent exposure by using the benchmark that best reflects their position.

As you build up a series of commitments of physical lengths and shorts, you can match off the physical requirements and effectively create a matrix where you can trade the price exposure generated through the different ways of pricing the contracts.

The difficulty of that approach is that physical trading is not as liquid as the paper derivatives market because the cargoes tend not to be linked directly to a paper instrument like a future.

Over the years, more and more instruments like contracts for difference (CFDs) have been created to try to capture the value of physical cargo differentials to the more developed futures markets. But there aren't derivatives that directly link to most of the crude oil cargoes that a physical trader will handle.

If you want to trade the spreads between different physical prices and benchmarks, then the only real way to do it most of the time is by physically moving a cargo of crude oil. That means that straight away you have to be prepared to handle big transactions – a physical cargo will likely be anywhere between 600,000 and 2 million barrels.

The mechanics of buying and selling a physical cargo are also complex and time-consuming. It's nothing like the straightforward execution of a trade that you would experience as a paper trader.

And as I saw very clearly that summer, it is all too easy for a simple cargo trade to go seriously wrong.

The essence of a physical deal is its very human basis, primarily the trader's ability to understand what is important to a third party. That sense of understanding and the ability to create the necessary trust between counterparties is crucial in ensuring that physical trades stay on track.

It might sound paradoxical in a market that is highly competitive and highly transactional, but actually, the only way to generate something sustainable and that works in the long term is to build human trust.

11 Trading the micro structure

After graduating from the National University of Singapore, Sylvia Low joined Koch Refining as a mid-office analyst in 1997. She later worked as a fundamental analyst, before being selected to join the crude oil derivatives desk. In 2005, Sylvia joined trading firm Sempra Energy as a crude oil trader, before moving to the Asia subsidiary of Total as crude oil trading manager in 2007. Sylvia moved to Houston in 2009 to join Occidental as vice president, before returning to Singapore with Occidental in 2011. Sylvia was promoted to managing director of Occidental Oil Asia in 2016.

There are as many approaches to oil trading as there are traders because everyone will take a different view of how best to tackle the market.

I have employed quite a few different styles in my time. I've done fundamental trading, where you look at the supply and demand balance, where you identify macro trends and take longer term positions based on your view of the forward market; and more relationship-based trading, where you work closely with the producers, whether internal or external, and refiners to understand their different vantage point and pricing position and to close the gap between the two by structuring deals that would give one optionality to create value.

Probably the most common approach in the physical market is arbitrage trading, where you take a view on the difference in pricing between different oil grades, different regions and different time periods. The physical movement of oil creates fundamental imbalances which allow refiners to optimize and traders to trade around these flows.

All of these approaches have different advantages and disadvantages, and realistically in the more volatile markets we see nowadays, traders need to make use of each strategy at times in order to survive and to make money.

The efficiency of each style changes with time and depends on the nature of the market. I began my career analysing the fundamentals of the oil market. We used to study supply–demand rigorously, counting barrels to try to see where the imbalances were. The idea was to position ourselves to benefit from a trend that we had identified ahead of time by opening a derivative position that would benefit from the changing supply–demand balance.

But I feel that it is increasingly hard for this type of fundamental trading to deliver reliable results. It's so hard now to predict how any imbalances will

DOI: 10.4324/9781003144335-14

evolve when they can switch in a second due to factors that a supply–demand analysis cannot predict, such as a surprise OPEC decision or an event like the COVID-19 pandemic.

You can put a huge amount of effort into fundamental analysis and then one announcement or one new factor can move everything.

Drowning in data

Even the greatest fundamental trader also finds it hard to make her or his mind up nowadays because there is simply so much data out there to consider.

When I began my career, I would spend a lot of time going onto Chinese websites, translating them, and then converting what I had learnt into data that would hopefully tell us something about whether the Chinese were really buying cargoes or how their storage levels were looking.

Nowadays, there are satellites tracking vessels in real time and feeding back intelligence about the height of the tank tops. The amount of data has increased, and there's a lot more churning to do, but I'm not sure that all of this extra information has made me a better trader.

The vast quantities of data have created more noise. There are so many factors to study for a fundamental trader that you can always find some that are bullish and others that are bearish, which makes it difficult to develop sufficient conviction to put on a trading position.

There's so much information out there, it is inevitable that some of it will conflict. Obviously, it's amazing when every factor lines up, and that is the dream scenario for the fundamental trader, but that's incredibly rare.

As an active trader, you don't also always have enough time to consider every fundamental factor. More information is definitely not an advantage when it takes time to make sense of it. So much information is raw data that an analyst needs to process. Often the market moves too fast for you to absorb the data, reach a decision on what it's telling you, and then act in time to make money.

There's clearly a place for fundamental analysis, and obviously it's good to have more information, but if I am going to act, I need data to be my servant and not my master. I prefer to use the analysis we do to verify a hypothesis that we have developed ourselves rather than waiting for the data to provide trading direction.

Going micro

Increasingly, I am drawn to what I would call a more 'micro' trading approach that is based less on long-term trends and more on spotting short-term opportunities and then taking advantage of them.

I am essentially more interested in the fundamentals of the way the market is trading rather than the fundamentals of supply and demand.

A classic trade for me is when I notice something that is not very obvious, and which might not stand out to anyone outside my market, but which tells me a story.

There are a few key indicators of micro market dynamics. One would be the velocity of trades: is the market trading more rapidly than normal or are there more trades going through earlier in the month than normal?

Another example would be when you see an Asian refiner buying a grade that they wouldn't normally take. If a certain refiner is buying a certain cargo, then that makes me wonder what has changed and what is going on.

Once I've seen a purchase that my experience tells me is unusual, my first thought is that I need to check the background to the trade and whether there is more to it than meets the eye. What I am looking for is signals of inflection points – those brief moments where something in the market has changed.

In particular, I am searching for a sign that what I've spotted is the start of something potentially big. Let's say that the Dubai time spreads have already moved up five cents. I need to decide whether or not the market has moved to a point where it can't move any more, or whether I've spotted the beginning of a move that will move the spreads up by another 20 cents.

Whenever you realize that there is more happening than the market has so far realized, that's the time to execute a trade and to put on a position. In micro trading, the profits come from making sense of the detailed information that you can only know if you are deep in the market.

Micro meets macro

That's not to say that you can trade successfully on micro indications and totally ignore the macro picture. I still track the satellite data: the volumes of oil coming to Asia and the volume of Chinese buying.

Those macro elements, and being aware of the imbalances in the market, provide the context, but they don't provide an actual trading signal. It's the micro information that tells me that things are starting to move and so it's time to put on a position.

Obviously, the size of that position will depend on my level of conviction. If you see everything line up, if it feels like a big shift, and that everything will move directionally, then you need to make the call and add some risk.

The most successful trades combine the macro picture – supportive fundamentals – with the micro details of seemingly small moves within the regional market.

The producer as trader

The trading opportunities that come from understanding the micro picture are so important in my opinion because the traditional space in which the crude oil trader operates is shrinking.

The traditional trader sits between the producer and the refiner and tries to make money from both sides. These opportunities are harder and harder to find.

In the past, traders used to be able to buy from producers with a lot of embedded free options that had value. Maybe they had options around the loading date and the pricing date, and they could try to load the cargo on a different date that moves the cargo from one month to the next. It was easy to make money out of cross-month pricing when the producer provided flexibility on load dates. Now the producers understand what the traders are doing so many don't want to give free options to their buyers.

The producers are also much more aware of market dynamics. Many of the Gulf producers now have built or leased storage tanks in Asia so that they have inventory in places where refiners are located. The producers are more responsive: they have supply available at the demand centres, and they can make it available whenever it is needed. They are also able to switch export destinations in a heartbeat.

All of this makes tracking flows from the Middle East to Asia trickier as well as providing more competition for traders. Gulf flows used to be pretty stable and easy to predict, meaning that if you observed an imbalance, you could act upon it with a good level of certainty. But now those imbalances don't occur as frequently or with such certainty as before.

Information trading

The key to trading based on micro indicators is that you can exchange information with other traders in the market to confirm or disprove a hypothesis.

Before you trade oil, you need to trade information. This means you need to build relationships with other traders because people obviously tend to share more if they like you.

My position allows me to have certain insights that I can share. Then hopefully they share with me what they know as well. Or perhaps, I try to understand their needs and then find a way that would meet them while allowing me to meet my goals for the company as well. I always aim for a win-win situation as that is the building block of a long-lasting relationship.

To build a trading strategy, you need the ability to share information with people who are actually right in the heart of the market. Most Asian trades take place two months before the cargo shows up in the satellite or ship-tracking data so if you are in the heart of trading – I mean actively selling and buying – you should always know the information before the statistics emerge.

That micro trading information is so critical that traders are constantly seeking exposure to physical oil to boost their networks and their understanding of the market.

The trading houses have spent countless millions investing in pipelines and tanks because they need to be part of the flow of physical oil in order to be part of the flow of information. It is detailed physical information and strong market knowledge that allows a trader to spot the micro indicators that point to successful trading positions.

12 Financing oil traders

A graduate of the ESCP Business School, Philippe Cohen joined French bank Paribas in 1981 and held various roles in Houston, Paris and London, rising to become head of commodity finance. In 1992, he joined oil trading giant Vitol B.V. in London as chief financial officer. Philippe also served as chief financial officer of Marca Commodities from 1999 to 2001, after which he moved into the mining industry, serving as managing director of Quantic Gold and director of Q Resources and as co-director of ISON Holdings. Between 2013 and 2017, he was finance director of listed African agri-forestry business Obtala Ltd. He then returned to oil trading and financing and as a business developer for amongst others Neptune Cameroon, Optima and Petra Energy and more recently Mocoh in Geneva. Philippe is a natural resources connector and advisor and sits on the board of various entities including the African Energy Chamber's advisory board.

The story of oil trading started in many ways with the story of bank finance. Traditional bank lending allowed oil traders to engage in a lot more activity because the relative abundance of finance made it relatively cheap for them to operate.

There is a very clear linkage between liquidity in finance and in crude oil. The previous willingness of banks to lend to oil traders allowed for an explosion in the number of transactions and in the number of active traders. But now that a lot of banking groups have exited trade finance in recent years, it is getting increasingly harder for the smaller and mid-size players to continue to trade crude.

Financing and trading crude oil involve very large sums of money, and so nowadays you are seeing a more limited pool of participants: the oil majors, the trading giants, the well-capitalized or private-equity backed traders, the Japanese and Chinese, some of the large refiners and those national oil companies that are trying to get more involved in trading.

It's very hard now for smaller firms, by which I mean companies with $50–100 million in equity, to get a credit line to trade crude oil, and it's even harder for anyone smaller.

One consequence of this increased market concentration is that you don't see any more chains of back-to-back transactions, whereby the same cargo

DOI: 10.4324/9781003144335-15

of crude oil is traded backwards and forwards between a number of different participants. You might see a chain with three or four people in it at the most, whereas in the 1980s and 1990s, it was common to see chains for Brent and Dubai cargoes that involved 40 participants.

(Of course, those lengthy chains were fantastic earners for banks as they were making a lot of money financing the same cargo several times over with very limited risk.)

Nowadays, it is much harder and more expensive for a smaller or medium player to get bank finance for back-to-back transactions, while the bigger players tend to employ their equity and different types of finance.

Financing on receivables

When I first started lending to oil traders, almost 40 years ago, senior bankers based their lending decisions on a company's incoming letters of credit and on its receivables from the oil majors in what they called a 'self-liquidating scheme'.

Those documents showed the bank what the trader expected to earn by selling the cargo. If you also knew the price that they had paid to acquire the oil, then you had relatively good certainty about the transaction. After all, the documents proved that there was a willing buyer, and you could understand the potential profit from the deal as hedges were also apportioned to the bank.

As long as you could track the profitability of the cargo or of the book of cargoes, this system allowed banks to provide very large amounts of finance, covering very many cargoes, for people who actually had very little substance themselves.

Back in the 1980s, you had tiny companies consisting of maybe four of five people, often operating under an offshore corporate structure, who had access and usage of credit lines of a couple of billion dollars to trade crude oil.

There are names that no one even remembers nowadays that were major traders at the time. It was the heyday of Marc Rich and of Phibro, and there were a large number of traders out there all wanting to take larger and larger positions.

Profits on individual cargoes were higher in the 1980s, and there was in general a lot more money around in oil trading. People were making fortunes. One of our customers lived permanently in the Hôtel de Paris in Monaco, and the first IP Week party I ever went to was when he hired the Albert Hall to display the Lotus Formula One cars that he was sponsoring. That company lasted about four years in total.

These smaller firms were generally financed by a single bank, who might be financing over a billion dollars to that client at any one time, which gave wings to the industry. The bank would be making good money for a period, though typically those kinds of clients didn't live very long.

Destination uncertainty

The trade that typified that era for me was when we leant money to finance what looked like a very straightforward transaction, whereby a trader would buy North Sea crude from Total in order to sell the cargo in the Mediterranean.

We knew that the buyer was not confirmed – it was what we called a 'non-allocated cargo' or 'unsold' cargo – but that the trader had the intention of selling it to one of the Greek or Italian refineries.

We first realized the situation had changed dramatically when we found out the cargo was actually passing through the Suez Canal. At the time, banks didn't monitor vessels in the same way they do now, where ship-tracking technology allows lenders to follow the voyage in real time.

We spoke to our trading customer, and we were told, 'sorry, we are taking it elsewhere and we are going to find a way to repay you, but it won't be from a sale to a Greek or Italian refiner'.

That obviously made the bank quite nervous. We thought we had financed a simple deal into the Mediterranean, but we soon discovered that our client had actually moved the cargo into the Red Sea and was processing it at the Khartoum refinery in Sudan.

As you can imagine, that news came as a bit of a shock. The refined products that were produced in Khartoum would all get consumed domestically within Sudan, so there was no chance of their sale generating any export revenue to pay us back.

Our customer tried to reassure the bank by telling us that they had other commodity operations in Sudan and that they would be able to repay us from some of their other exports from Sudan, or that they would find some money elsewhere in the group.

We did eventually get our money back, a large part of it came from Sudanese cotton exports, which they bartered for the crude. As it happened, the trader had a separate sister company that was trading soft commodities, so they moved the proceeds from the cotton sales to their oil business.

At the time, Sudan was a large cotton producer, which is no longer the case, and so we had to wait for the cotton to be harvested and exported from Sudan, before the bank got its money back.

That deal was an interesting experience. It certainly made us much more cautious about doing any other business with that trading firm, but then I believe their whole operation collapsed soon afterwards anyway.

Repayment challenge

Banks no longer like to finance a cargo that is not already sold unless the client has substantial equity and allocates a big cash margin against it, aside from hedging the crude. After all, if the deal doesn't go as expected, it can trigger unexpected consequences.

The trader is obviously trying to find the best home for that cargo that doesn't trigger a big loss, but sometimes that means they will arbitrage the cargo for another one. The bank can then be left with an exposure that it was not expecting and that can be very difficult to manage.

That's what happened to me in Sudan. You finance a crude oil cargo and then you suddenly realize that you are going to be dependent on the performance of some random agricultural export because otherwise there's no other way you are going to get repaid.

This issue wasn't all that uncommon in the early 1980s. You might start by financing crude oil but end up holding cotton from the Sudan, grain out of Russia or sugar from Cuba (see Chapter 2). I was involved years later in similar barter transactions where oil would be typically paid for by the Cuban State in nickel or more often sugar exports.

Tightening up

Issues like that forced the bank to tighten up its lending practices and to limit their exposure to smaller firms. In a sense, though, we were lucky. The bank ended up getting repaid, and at least our Sudanese challenges weren't the result of a deliberate fraud.

There were plenty of attempts at fraud at the time, even on transactional finance, but we generally managed to avoid financing any fake or imaginary receivables because when the cargo was allocated, we always knew who the buyer was, and we would always call or get telexes from the counterparty confirming that the business was genuine.

In general, though, oil traders caused a lot of big scares for the banks in that era and frequently cost them a lot of money. In the late 1980s, we experienced, among others, the demise of Gatoil, which must have cost their banks $400–500 million, the forced restructuring of John Deuss' Transworld Oil, and the bankruptcy of AroChem, whose executives served long jail sentences in the U.S.

The biggest of them all, of course, was the failure of Gulf International Holdings, which at over $1.2 billion was so sizeable that it largely caused the 1991 collapse of their primary bank lender, the Luxembourg-based Bank of Credit and Commerce International (BCCI) and its U.K. and U.A.E. satellites.

On some occasions, some of the banks eventually got part of their money back through asset sales and bankruptcy procedures, but in many cases, it took 10–20 years to recoup their losses, and in the meantime, the issues had cost the jobs of a lot of good people on the lending side.

Much of the impetus to reform trade finance came from the challenges that the banks experienced in that era.

One issue had been that the banks weren't talking to each other. That was partly the result of Swiss secrecy laws, which made it very difficult to combine Swiss and non-Swiss operations and to share information.

The traders benefited from that because they ended up with two credit lines: one from headquarters and one from the Swiss subsidiary.

Now, lending is all consolidated worldwide, and if your credit line is used in the U.S. and there's no room left, then you can't use the same line in Singapore, Geneva or Paris.

Some of the frauds reported in 2020–2021 were in part due to the fact that banks have become too rigid and lazy to run transactions individually and preferred to do balance-sheet lending, opening the door to multiple financings of the same title documents and other frauds.

Banks withdraw

The scandals around commodity trade finance certainly didn't help the industry's reputation with lenders, and some major banks continue to withdraw from the market.

When I started my career, Paribas was very dominant, but you also had BNP, which later merged with Paribas in 2000, and Crédit Lyonnais, Chase Manhattan, Bank of America and other U.S. banks, which kept merging, were all major leaders in the early days that are no longer active. UBS was there then and is still around in a modest way.

Nowadays, you have a very limited number of banks that are aggressively pursuing trade finance as a business. Most of the Dutch and half of the French banks retreated from the market from 2015 onwards, leaving a very small number of banks that can actually finance this kind of activity: typically, ING, Société Générale and Natixis, and some minor Swiss-based banks.

Singaporean banks have felt the heat of the collapse of Agritrade, Hin Leong, GP Group and others during the year of COVID-19. Chinese banks' approach to trade finance is quite different: they tend to require companies to pledge assets as security. Chinese companies will pledge real estate and all kinds of things to get the credit lines to trade crude and products. Obviously, you need to be a very wealthy firm to finance a cargo of crude when you are putting up 100% collateral.

Chinese and Russian banks are just setting up Swiss offices, but it is likely they will only be financing trades that have a respective Chinese or Russian client component.

On the other side of the spectrum, you have African and Far Eastern trading companies, who receive what looks like quite expensive finance from local banks, particularly in places like Nigeria, but they can obtain very good terms and conditions regarding the types of security that they have to post.

Financing challenges

The real game changer for the trade finance sector was the 2017 agreement to amend the international banking standards, which are known as the Basel Accords.

The updated regulations, Basel III and Basel IV, which is due to be implemented in January 2023, establish even more stringent rules regarding the adequacy of bank reserves and capital.

The way that funding oil transactions is categorized now requires more capital allocation and therefore does not offer the same return for the bank. All our lending to oil traders in the old days was outside the bank's balance sheet because we were dealing with letters of credit and letters of indemnity that weren't considered to impact on the bank's capital and liquidity ratios – now, that is all history, except for a handful of Nigerian, Mauritius and BRIC banks.

The new regulations have meant that it is not that interesting economically for banks to get involved in trade finance and that there are better uses for the bank's money.

This withdrawal of credit will impact heavily on traders, particularly the smaller and mid-sized players that are looking for finance on a cargo-by-cargo basis. If they can even find a lender that is willing to provide trade finance, they will discover that the finance will become rarer more and more expensive.

The impact will be felt less by the giant trading groups who have huge corporate credit lines because they are worth billions. It feels like the future of trade finance will be in servicing the largest traders while still doing a little bit of business with the smaller firms.

Smaller and mid-sized traders will likely not be able to continue to trade crude oil unless they get backing from big U.S. private equity. Those firms currently in that situation – Freepoint, Hartree, Castleton, etc. – are generally trading and arbitraging vast amounts while avoiding African and other exotic crudes and destinations.

It is hard to see these sources of alternative finance stepping in to fill the gap that the banks are leaving. The amounts of money required to finance crude oil cargoes are simply too vast, and the profit margins are, in general, relatively limited.

Alternative finance works well for relatively small amounts and for people who are making decent margins and who can afford to pay 7 to 10% interest or more to the alternative funds. But the reality is that no firms with small balance sheets can guarantee that level of profit from trading physical crude oil nowadays.

13 Starting from 'why not'

After graduating in economics from the University of Rome, Alessandro Liberati started his career in the oil industry with Italian major ENI in 1987, rising to be appointed managing director of ENI's U.K. subsidiary, AGIP Trading Services, in 2002. In 2005, he became ENI's trading manager for gasoline, middle and heavy distillates, and then in 2009, he took over as trading manager for sweet crude oil. After spending 25 years with ENI, Alessandro left to join privately owned trading house BB Energy Trading Ltd in 2012. At BB Energy, he revamped the crude oil trading desk, which he led as global head of crude oil until his retirement in August 2021.

My personal interpretation of trading is that a trading company is above all a service company. That means you should make yourself almost like a one-stop shop where any potential partner can come along with any problem, and you are able to say 'yes, I can help with that'.

My aim is to provide anything that my counterparties need. That might be standard oil trading, where we are buying or selling cargoes, or it might be something a little bit different like pre-financing, hedging on behalf of companies that can't hedge, inventory repositioning or anything else that anyone needs.

My goal in providing assistance isn't always to make money from the situation, it's more to say, 'I am here and I am happy to help'. My firm wants to be perceived as a reliable, flexible and trustworthy counterparty; someone you would want to call whenever you have a problem.

Essentially, I want to be the kind of guy where someone with a problem thinks to themselves, 'let's see if Alessandro can solve this for me'. If you are nice to people, then the next time that they have an opportunity, maybe you are the person they will call.

In my interpretation of trading, your starting point should always be 'why not?'

If you suggest something out of the ordinary in a major oil company, you will often hear that finance says no, accounting says no or operations says no, so then of course you don't do it.

In a smaller company, where you are more results driven and much more in control of your destiny, you can reverse that conversation. If somebody

DOI: 10.4324/9781003144335-16

asks me why I want to do something, I usually turn that around: 'if my client wants to do it, then tell me why I shouldn't do it?'

Obviously, we don't take huge risks, we aren't silly, but if we can do something then why not try it? After all, fortune favours the bold, and there aren't many situations in trading where doing nothing benefits you.

Libyan ambitions

When I first moved across from the Italian major ENI to join BB Energy, one of the first deals I did as an independent trader was to pick up a spot cargo of Libyan crude oil.

I had traded quite a bit of Libyan crude when I was at ENI, and I thought there were some opportunities in that area. BB Energy has always had very strong links with Libya over the years, and we were well respected there, which obviously helped a lot.

Back in 2012, there wasn't much activity in the Libyan crude oil market. Several of the other trading houses, like Vitol or Glencore, initially wouldn't touch Libya and for me that meant there was an opportunity. After all, you don't want to enter a space that is too crowded, you want to move into an area where you see potential.

The problem was that Libya hadn't been exporting for a while because of all the disruption in the country, and so they hadn't readjusted their official selling prices, which they set in relation to Brent, to take the weaker market conditions into account.

You see this a lot when producer countries are strapped for cash. They don't necessarily issue realistic official selling prices that reflect actual market conditions, they just try to maintain or increase the official price.

There's always a temptation for the sellers to say, 'what if I add on half a dollar more or a dollar more'. That's the best way to kill the long-term value of your crude in the market, but it does give a short-term lift to the country's revenues.

The difference between that artificially high Libyan official selling price and what potential buyers were prepared to pay me for Libyan oil was huge. That cargo I bought for loading in August 2012 proved to be very hard to sell, even at breakeven, and I was looking at losing around $1 per barrel.

Just when I was starting to get very nervous, I received an offer for the cargo from a Mediterranean refiner that was quite reasonable. I was even set to make a little profit, which to be honest was a major relief because the next best offer on the table after that one was quite awful.

Financial flexibility

I was obviously delighted to sell my Libyan cargo at a better level than I had been expecting. But nothing in trading is ever simple. The deal was jeopardized because my refiner customer was experiencing some financial difficulties.

The bank that was financing my operations would not allow us to provide any credit to them, and it looked like the deal might fall apart.

There was no way I was going to let that happen, so I started to try to think of a solution. If you are a creative trader, you always believe that there must be a way. Many companies would just say 'cancel the deal' because they wouldn't be able to take the credit risk of the counterparty, but we tried to think outside the box.

In the end, I proposed that I would sign a legal agreement with the refinery to temporarily rent some tank space in their refinery complex free of charge. I would then discharge my Libyan oil directly into that tank.

Technically and legally, I was renting the tank, and so it was still my crude oil, even though I had unloaded it at the refinery. In theory, I could always reload the oil onto another vessel and sell it to someone else.

Now in reality, the tank was physically located next to the refinery and reloading the oil from the tank would have been quite expensive, but nonetheless I retained legal title to the crude, even after delivery. That structure provided comfort to my financing bank.

The second part of the deal was to agree an in-tank transfer of ownership of the oil. The refinery would formally take title of the oil in my tank, after which my rental agreement for the tank would also simultaneously cease.

In order to sterilize my risk, the refinery would pay me the money for the oil one day before we made the formal legal transfer. The refiner was comfortable about those terms because they would already be able to see my oil in the tank in their refinery.

The way the deal was structured was a win-win for both sides. I had in theory received the money before I transferred the ownership title, but in practice, the refiner had only paid for the oil some days after it was actually delivered to a tank in their refinery, which helped their financial situation.

Management support

I get the most satisfaction in trading when I have done something creative and found a solution to a problem, which is why I still remember this deal with pleasure.

I don't deny there was a certain risk involved in unloading my oil into their tank while still maintaining that it was mine. The operational and legal side of the deal was very safe and well constructed, but it was a little less clear in terms of potential risk/reward.

I had to believe in the good faith of my counterpart, who had the oil in their facility and could potentially have tried to avoid paying me. I was willing to take the chance because we had a strong relationship and because they were so pleased – and quite surprised – that I would go to such lengths to provide supplies at a difficult time for them.

Ultimately, we made the structure work, and it helped me avoid the loss on that Libyan cargo that I would have suffered for sure. In fact, the structure worked so well that we ended up using it some more times.

I have to say my management was amazing. Some people in the operations department started complaining about the complex structure because it was a lot of extra work: as well as the supply deal, we had to agree a storage contract to rent the tank at a zero fee; we had to check whether VAT was applicable; and so on. But the company chief executive just said, 'if Alessandro wants to do it, then try to find a way to make it happen'.

The positive and open attitude that my management displayed during this period was amazing to me, as someone who had spent 25 years working for a major oil company. At a major, when someone asks, 'can I sell this cargo with slightly different payment terms?' then the chances are that someone will say, 'no, you can't' and the conversation is finished. Instead, my new management helped me to try to find a solution.

The major oil companies often have a number of constraints on their trading for whatever reason, and frankly it's good that they do, otherwise there wouldn't be a role for other trading houses who are able to be more flexible.

Let's say that my team isn't comfortable taking on the credit risk of a particular customer directly, well, instead of just not trading with them, we might instead go to the insurance market and insure our risk. For example, I sold a few cargoes in Latin America because the majors didn't want to deal with counterparties there, whereas I was able to do the trades and use insurance to protect myself.

Finance focus

The other side of the coin, though, is that when you move from an oil major that is cash rich to an independent trader that relies on banks for financing, you realize quickly just how important access to finance is in oil trading.

Finance is a huge issue for traders, particularly when you see crude up over $70 per barrel and you know that it can easily move over $100 because we have been there before. Those price levels lead to big invoices for people and make them want to minimize their inventories and worry about their cash flow.

Financial pressure does create opportunities, though, for trading houses that can provide finance to producers by prepaying them for oil or by offering immediate payments. You obviously have an advantage over another trader if you can offer to pay for the oil in advance or one day after loading, rather than after the standard 30 days.

Unfortunately, that strategy requires big money. Even if oil is $50 per barrel, pre-financing a 2-million barrel cargo requires an initial outlay of $100 million. At those price levels, lending someone half a billion dollars in a pre-financing deal gets you just five cargoes.

In the oil market, no producer wants to talk to you unless you can provide at least half a billion dollars in finance, because they know crude oil is big money.

Refined products are a cheaper market in which to operate and that's why there are so many more refined product traders. Cargo sizes for refined products are smaller, and there are many more potential counterparties. A refiner would be happy to do a finance deal for $50 or $100 million, whereas a crude oil producer wouldn't waste their time for $100 million.

The crude oil market is also so competitive that you have to have the ability to provide finance quickly. If an oil producer needs a billion dollars, then a large trader should be able to provide that almost immediately from their funds, before going to the banks the following day to borrow back the money on the basis of the supply guarantees they have just received.

Different pressures

The market is changing though. It's possible that even the cash-rich majors will begin to experience pressure on their ability to finance crude oil deals because of their 'green' ambitions.

In the medium term, I wonder whether the crude oil desk at a major oil company will still get the same access to finance that they are used to, when so many of the biggest companies are trying to move away from hydrocarbons and to use their balance sheet instead to promote decarbonization and the energy transition.

The world is clearly changing. Change always brings opportunities but, as a trader, you have to be clear about which opportunities you can realistically grab and what is an appropriate long-term strategy for success.

I remember one time when I was at ENI, we brought in a consultant and his advice for us was that we should study a U.S. trader called Enron and try to replicate what they were doing. Luckily, we quickly decided that was not the model for us, but it's easy to lose sight of your core competencies.

When you move from a major to a trading house, you become even more aware of the need to have an appropriate strategy and to use your more limited resources wisely. As an independent, you follow the financial side that little bit more closely than you might do when you are at a major, and that helps encourage you to go that little bit further and work that little bit harder.

You also realize quickly that when you don't have a major production division or a major refining system behind you, then you have to go for it. You have to get out into the marketplace every day and help luck to help you.

For me that means doing everything I can to get deals done and to make my counterparties happy with my service. Surprising customers with your creativity and your willingness to help is the most rewarding part of the job.

I was in the oil industry for 35 years, and I enjoyed myself enormously throughout. I guess I was just lucky in life, as are the majority of us that work in this fascinating business.

Spot versus term trading

A 'term' deal refers to a deal between two oil companies that is longer term in nature, perhaps six months, more typically one year, and sometimes even covering multiple years.

A term deal allows traders to lock in a consistent buyer or seller, which assists with planning and scheduling, as well as helping to develop a longer term relationship between the two firms involved, which may potentially lead to other discussions and business.

Before the development of the actively traded oil markets in the early 1980s, firms did virtually all of their business on a term basis, as Chapter 14 describes.

Most state-owned national oil companies still prefer the security of term deals to this day, although some are changing, as Chapter 16 notes. Obtaining a term deal from a national oil company is therefore a major achievement, as we will hear in Chapter 19.

In contrast, spot deals refer to deals that are done 'on the spot' for delivery in the relatively near future. Spot deals are one-off transactions that do not imply any previous or future relationship between the two firms.

Spot deals provide greater flexibility and allow traders to try to maximize value, but they also carry greater risk. If the market is weak, the seller may be forced to discount a cargo, while in a tightly supplied market, a refiner runs the risk of not finding the oil they need to keep running their facility.

As the following chapters demonstrate, the decision about how much oil to trade term and how much to trade spot is a fundamental judgement call for any oil company. That decision then has a profound impact on the strategies that its traders adopt.

DOI: 10.4324/9781003144335-17

14 Publish and circulate

Liz Bossley joined the British National Oil Corporation (BNOC) in 1978 as a graduate and spent seven years working for BNOC, first as an economist and then as an oil trader. Liz then joined Enterprise Oil, where she rose to become head of trading, risk management and shipping offtake operations. She spent 14 years at Enterprise, before leaving in 1999 to found the Consilience Energy Advisory Group (Consilience), where she serves as chief executive. In addition to her advisory work through Consilience, Liz has published extensively on the oil markets and works as an expert witness in legal disputes. She also co-authored the 2011 report on price reporting agencies that led to the development of the IOSCO principles on oil price reporting.

All of my colleagues had gone to our Christmas party and left me working alone in the office. While they were off celebrating, I had urgently to sell six cargoes of North Sea crude oil into a weak market. Not really the ideal way to start the festive season.

It was the early 1980s and I was working as a crude oil trader for the British National Oil Corporation (BNOC), which at that time was the U.K.'s state-owned oil company. As BNOC traders, we were responsible for marketing the government's share of the crude oil produced from the fields that had been discovered a few years earlier in the U.K. section of the North Sea.

BNOC had the responsibility of setting the official selling price (OSP) for U.K. production. We were not allowed to call it an OSP for political, hair-splitting reasons; instead, we had to call it 'the BNOC negotiated price'. But an OSP is really what it was. BNOC had its own equity share of production in many oilfields and was entitled to take government royalty, a tax on production, in kind.

On top of that BNOC had the right to buy a proportion of production from producers, so-called participation oil, and sell that quantity back to the market at the same price. The idea was that, if there was a crisis, BNOC had access to equity, royalty and participation oil and could divert it for the use of the U.K. government in an emergency.

Once every three months, BNOC would negotiate its buying and selling price for participation oil, and all of the government's oil was supposed to be sold at that price. Obviously, market conditions could change a lot in 90

DOI: 10.4324/9781003144335-18

days. Our term sales contracts included a clause that potentially allowed us to have a review between quarters and change prices if the market had made a 'substantial and unforeseen' move. We had to prove that any price move was actually both substantial and unforeseen. Net producers were always pushing us towards higher prices; integrated companies and refiners were always lobbying for lower prices.

Sometimes we would discover that we had set the price too high, or the market moved after prices had been set, and we couldn't easily sell all of the government's cargoes. Or sometimes BNOC would be encouraged by the Treasury deliberately to maintain a high price for political reasons, to ensure that the U.K. did not appear to be undercutting the levels set by OPEC countries. In both those cases, we would still have to move the oil at 'official' prices, so as BNOC traders we had to get creative.

The government understood our dilemma and after my first year at BNOC, we were finally allowed to sell cargoes that were close to their loading date – known as 'spot cargoes' – at whatever price was necessary to clear the market, rather than just selling everything on a long-term basis at the BNOC negotiated price. This ability to also sell on a spot basis gave our trading desk a lot more flexibility, particularly at those times when our negotiated price was uncompetitive compared with other crude oil suppliers.

Festive length

That's how I ended up alone in the office on the night of our Christmas party. BNOC was coming up to the end of the fourth quarter, and the price we had set for those three months was now looking very expensive.

We knew that we would probably have to cut our quarterly prices for the first quarter of next year, but in the meantime, we still had a lot of oil to move.

My job was to sell six North Sea cargoes in a single evening at as high a price as possible. That would only be feasible if the news of just how many cargoes we had left didn't leak out to the market. Otherwise, potential buyers would step back, prices would fall further, and we might not be able to clear our overhang of oil.

I may have felt a bit like Cinderella, while the rest of the BNOC team were acting as the genial hosts of the BNOC Christmas party. But I had volunteered, and my trading buddies were trying to give the impression to our guests that all of our cargoes were sold, and that the oil market was in great shape.

Running down my contacts list in search of potential buyers, I was mostly looking at refiners, but there were dozens of trading houses operating back then – many more than there are nowadays – often taking a punt on the flat price using physical oil because there were no suitable futures contracts yet.

Most of our crude oil sales were made direct to refiners in either the U.S. East Coast or in northern Europe, with occasional cargoes moving to the

Mediterranean. We offered a range of grades from the U.K. North Sea – Brent and Forties would be the best known, but we were also selling grades like Flotta and Beryl and Buchan as well as Ninian, which was later comingled into the Brent stream.

With six cargoes to sell in a few hours, I would need to spread the calls around, and luckily, back in those days, there were always plenty of brokers to help. Nowadays, it is extremely rare to hear of a physical North Sea trade that was arranged by brokers, but back then, it was very common.

Dealing hadn't really got standardized yet – we were in the early days of the 15-day spot Brent market – and there were still a lot of non-standard cargo sizes to deal with. Brokers were very useful in finding customers that could use smaller cargoes as a top up, for example. But with six full cargoes to move in pretty short order, I concentrated my efforts on the new, standardized 15-day Brent market, which today has morphed into the 30-day Brent–Forties–Oseberg–Ekofisk–Troll (BFOET) market.

The brokers were well rewarded for their efforts. In those days, we all paid commissions of three cents per barrel, which was a very decent level compared to today. The brokers appreciated our business and were always very lavish in their entertainment. When I looked around our office that night, it was like the food department of Harrods, we'd had so many hampers sent to the trading desk. We shared them out with our backroom colleagues, but today accepting such gifts would be frowned upon. Those were very different days. I remember with affection the Amerada Hess model gasoline trucks and the PVM chocolate cakes in the shape of oil rigs or tankers.

The money to be made in broking North Sea cargoes was so attractive that it brought more and more participants into the market, to the point that we were inundated with brokers. My colleagues finally had to institute a rule that brokers couldn't call any of us traders before 11 am, just so that we had time to think and to work on finding our own deals without any third-party assistance.

Firm and confirm

That night, though, I was really glad of the brokers' help. Between my own calls and the brokers putting deals together, I managed to move all six of my outstanding cargoes before anyone clocked just how many cargoes I had moved. Importantly, all the deals were at prices with which I was pretty pleased as being reflective of the market at that point in time but below the BNOC negotiated term price level.

Six cargo deals in an evening represented very swift business by our standards. Before 15-day Brent, typically, the way our physical spot deals worked was that we would phone someone and suggest they bought a cargo from us at, say, $30 per barrel. The other side might say that $29.75 seemed fairer, and we would agree to disagree. After that, we would keep calling around and offering at $30, until the cargo delivery date was getting closer, at which point we might phone someone and suggest $29.90 instead. They would then counter with $29.80 and so on.

Every round of discussions might take days, and because every deal was agreed on a fixed-price basis, such as $29.85, it often took weeks before you reached a price level that suited both sides.

Everything changed when we moved to formula pricing based on averages of Platts or Argus prices. After that you didn't worry as much about the flat price because it was based on a floating index that could be hedged by both sides in the 15-day Brent market or later, with futures in NYMEX WTI and later still the IPE Brent market. Instead, the grade price differential became the much more important focus of attention.

Once it became easier to hedge and to manage prices, a lot of the friction went out of the process of selling a cargo. But when I first started, if you agreed $29.90, then that was it. That was the final price of the cargo, and there were no second chances.

Agreeing six fixed-price deals in an evening was quite an unusual achievement. The next step was to confirm all of the deals. In those days, calls weren't recorded, and so the way to confirm the deal and avoid misunderstandings was to send a confirmation straight away by telex. We had a team of telex operators to handle that. The poor lady on duty that night, Madge Meir, also had to stay late while I was getting the trades done.

Oil leaks

Every deal I had done was on an entirely private and confidential (P&C) basis so that news wouldn't leak out and torpedo my chances of moving my other cargoes.

Secrecy was a big part of the North Sea market then. Even the loading programmes for the grades were supposed to be secret. There was nothing like the transparency that we take for granted nowadays, although inevitably information still leaked out.

Even so, I was pretty shocked to find out that, by the time I got to our party, the whole room seemed to know that I had sold six cargoes. Even the details of the individual deals seemed to somehow have ended up in the public domain. P&C came to be known, ironically, as 'publish and circulate'.

It was interesting, though, that people didn't seem terribly upset that BNOC had just sold multiple cargoes ahead of a likely price cut. Nowadays, that would be considered very bad form and might even be considered as insider trading.

The market then was more phlegmatic. Essentially, they knew that BNOC was a state-owned oil company. We were an arm of the U.K. government.

In any case, there wasn't much recourse for BNOC's customers other than to walk away down what was likely to be a one-way street, at the next contract renewal date.

If the buyer disagreed with our proposed price changes, we would appoint an independent expert to review our prices. It was quite unusual for anyone to invoke the expert clause, but even then, I don't recall a single instance where the expert ever found against the government, given that BNOC's prices had all been approved by the Treasury before release.

That all changed in 1985 when the Treasury came under political pressure from OPEC to support their OSPs at a level that was unsustainable. BNOC had to buy participation oil at an artificially inflated price but could not find customers to buy it back at that same price. BNOC was haemorrhaging money, and, in March 1985, Mrs Thatcher wound it up as 'yet another loss-making state enterprise'. This was probably the intention all along when the Treasury forced BNOC to keep its prices above a market-clearing level, very much against its will.

Hitting the spot

When I first moved from the economics department of BNOC, which was based in Glasgow, down to London to join the oil trading team, I went on a training course that covered market fundamentals. The statistic that I still remember from that course was that spot trading of oil accounted for around 10% of global oil production, with the other 90% all sold on a longer-term basis.

By the time of my busy Christmas evening, that was already beginning to change and firms like BNOC were making full use of the nascent 15-day Brent market to move excess spot cargoes.

The move from fixed- to floating-price deals, which came later, and the introduction of swaps and futures made trading on a spot basis much simpler than it had ever been before, and spot deals became ever more common.

A virtuous circle developed. More spot deals led to greater transparency in the physical oil market, which engendered greater confidence among traders and therefore more spot deals.

In the North Sea, the winding up of BNOC and the privatization of BNOC's equity producing arm, Britoil, which was later acquired by BP, took the U.K. government out of the oil trading business and allowed the market to develop further along purely commercial lines.

Nowadays, the size of the spot market for crude oil is a multiple of global production with many cargoes changing hands many times before final refining. Derivatives are a key part of most traders' armoury, and the price reporting agencies provide reams of data to analyse.

Comparing my pre-Christmas rush of sales with today's market might seem a bit like looking the Stone Age of oil trading, but in reality, this was an incredibly innovative period: we were developing spot sales and the 15-day Brent market, WTI and Brent futures were being launched and we were standardizing trading terms and conditions. The progress that the market has made since in terms of transparency and sophistication is all founded on the developments that were pioneered in the early 1980s.

15 Bringing indexation to Russia

Elena Lobodina has held a number of senior management positions in commodity trading firms, after coming to prominence as the head of the sales, trading and business development teams in Moscow at Russian oil producer TNK-BP. Elena went on to become head of origination and business development for Gazprom Marketing & Trading in London. Elena then moved to Switzerland to become chief executive of NLMK Trading, which manages the export business of Russian metals producer NMLK Group. Elena graduated from Moscow State University and holds a master's degree from INSEAD Business School.

In order to achieve anything in trading, you have to have not only the right mentality but also the right structure. When I first joined the Russian oil producer TNK-BP in 2005, it was clear that we weren't set up for trading success.

Then in 2005–2006, we worked hard on our organizational set up to get everyone working together as one team with one benchmark. We benefited a lot from the experience that our vice president Jonathan Kollek brought with him from his previous senior international trading roles, including working alongside Marc Rich.

We first changed the organizational structure, next we changed the way our traders were incentivized and then finally we shifted the culture from a marketing focus towards a trading mindset.

The main issue was that there was a clear division between the traders who worked on the domestic market and those who worked on the export market. Even though the two groups were sitting next to each other, they barely spoke to each other.

Of course, there were language issues: the Russian team didn't speak much English and most of the international traders didn't speak any Russian. But more than that, it was a question of the way the firm was structured.

Even though TNK-BP was a merger between a domestic Russian oil producer and the Russian assets of British oil major BP, at first we still had the traditional mentality that domestic Russian activity and international activity were two separate businesses and should be kept apart.

DOI: 10.4324/9781003144335-19

When I took over as commercial manager, the vision was to get past this separation so that each trader should look to maximize the overall profitability of TNK-BP by making the most profitable trades, whether or not those were domestic or international.

The first thing we had to address was the issue of incentives. The traders on the domestic market were measured against domestic benchmarks and that's how their bonuses were calculated, while the performance of the international traders was monitored against international benchmarks.

No one was looking at the relative profitability of the two teams. Sometimes the situation was quite ridiculous: you had people fighting for crude oil to market because they could sell domestically at $5 per barrel above the domestic benchmark, while the international traders didn't want additional volumes because they would have to sell them below benchmark, even though the international prices they would achieve might be significantly higher in absolute terms.

That reorganization was the key to our trading success at TNK-BP. I think what made it possible was that that through BP's part ownership we were international. We had management from Australia, the U.K. and the U.S. and a commitment from the Russian shareholders to implement international best practices.

This transformation could never have happened at another Russian producer at that time.

Trading mindset

The traders caught onto the idea quickly, so combining the teams inside the trading department was relatively straightforward because, at the end of the day, traders will respond to changes in the bonus structure.

But the harder part was to think how to incentivize the retail and refining teams because there was also a huge inefficiency in the downstream. We wanted to introduce BP's mentality of looking at every activity through the lens of overall profits. Everyone needs to be working towards that end.

The head of refining remains a good friend of mine and he often reminds me of our conversations at that time. Initially, he was absolutely focused on maximizing refinery runs and then I came along and told him that there were times when we shouldn't run at full capacity because we could make an additional $20 of EBITDA by reselling our crude oil instead of refined products. 'You used to make my brain hurt, Lena', he still tells me.

Then with the retail team we had to adjust their strategy from just maximizing their sales to retail stations. These guys were holding huge volumes in storage ready to be pushed out to retail, but there were times when the domestic market was weak, especially in the Russian winter when no one is going anywhere, and it made more sense to take their volumes to the export market.

Explaining to the marketing and retail guys why we should do things differently took a lot of time. We also had to change our whole system of performance management and benchmarking to get everyone aligned. But, ultimately, that investment of time and effort was absolutely worth it because our trading profits became so significant.

At that time, TNK-BP was the only company where you could earn serious money by developing trading ideas and making improvements that led to an actual contribution to the EBITDA. In all of the other Russian companies, you would receive a general salary without any bonuses, except for maybe 10% of your yearly salary. Of course, in that environment a lot of the smartest people will end up leaving the company.

Floating price

Once we had the right trading mentality in place across the organization, we were able to innovate much more easily. One of our most significant trading successes was the introduction of floating prices to the Russian oil markets.

Floating-price or formula contracts are where the price of the oil is based on a variable benchmark, like the price of Brent crude oil. Using floating prices was standard in the international markets, but within Russia, oil sales were still tied to fixed-price contracts, where the buyer and seller agreed a fixed price of so many roubles per ton of crude oil.

TNK-BP was the first firm to agree term deals on a floating-price basis in the Russian domestic market. We offered people a formula for their crude oil supply where the price they paid would be linked to international crude oil prices.

This appealed to some of the more forward-thinking Russian refiners because they started to realize that the profit margins on their refined products were also linked to the international market. Even if they only sold their gasoline and diesel domestically and on a fixed-price basis, their prices would still inevitably reflect the international market, albeit with some lag.

The refiners basically felt, 'OK, it makes sense that, if my margin is moving with international prices, then I should also buy on international prices'. In fact, they were even willing to pay TNK-BP a premium for floating-price deals linked to export parity.

When I joined the firm in 2005, everything was fixed price. By 2007, we had introduced some floating-price term deals. Then within a few years everything had moved to floating price. We introduced the concept at just the right time. The global financial crisis of 2008 caused oil prices to collapse, and there was so much uncertainty about everything. Producers started to reduce production, consumer demand fell, and it was a crisis.

A lot of refiners in Russia are dependent on exports and at that period the export market was incredibly volatile. They were selling a big proportion of their products to the export market but were buying their crude on a fixed price, and they were very exposed.

The refiners realized that it wasn't really a sustainable business plan to say, 'I'm going to buy crude today at a fixed price of 2,000 roubles per ton but I'm going to sell my products next month at some floating price set in Rotterdam'. The refiners woke up to the benefit for everyone in buying on a floating basis, which is the most efficient tool for everyone.

For us at TNK-BP, selling our crude oil on a fixed-price basis had been very profitable because we could often play the arbitrage between the domestic and international markets (see Chapter 5), but moving to floating-price sales definitely reduced our risk, particularly once we started hedging our exposure with derivatives.

Hedging sales

The crude oil team started to do some big deals on a floating price, and they turned out to be successful. We probably got lucky in some sense because at the time, prices were pretty stable, so there wasn't so much risk in us continuing to sell part of the volume using fixed prices.

By 2007, though, it was clear that the market was getting too volatile to sell on a fixed-price basis without hedging. The international price had embarked on its dramatic run up to above $140 per barrel, and the markets were moving very quickly.

We started to develop a story around the need for risk management internally. We got good support from the finance and tax teams, but the issue at first was that Russian legislation was not supportive of hedging. We were told initially that hedging could only be viewed as gambling. There were tax reasons too: at that time in Russia, you could not offset physical profits against paper losses, even if they were part of the same trade.

We were fortunate that TNK-BP eventually received support from the Russian authorities, who changed the legislation, which then allowed us to offset losses against future profits. We became able to roll hedging losses forward for several years, offsetting them against future profit from hedging.

We started a risk management programme in 2007, and by the time of the global financial crisis in 2008/2009, we already had everything in place to hedge all of our fixed-price supply deals and to secure our profit margins.

Fixed versus floating

TNK-BP definitely made more money in the period where we only sold on a fixed-price basis and where we were able to take full advantage of market inefficiencies. We had to make a conscious decision to bring greater efficiency to the Russian domestic market, even though it might reduce our own profit margins.

Our calculation was that profit margins might be smaller in a floating-price world, but they would be fixed and more reliable. We also calculated correctly that Russian refiners would be willing to pay TNK-BP a premium to buy their crude on a formula basis.

Perhaps, the most important consideration, though, was that we thought that change was inevitable and that, when that is the case, it is always best to make yourself the agent of change.

The move to floating price would have developed at some point anyway. Our competitors would have innovated, and people would have learnt from international best practice.

The important part to us was that TNK-BP should be the first mover. When you have such a huge market inefficiency, you will always get the biggest share of the upside if you move first. We came in with a market-oriented view, whereas our competitors were remnants of the Soviet Union with five-year plans that told them what to do.

The situation would have changed at some point anyway, but TNK-BP was the catalyst. That first floating-price term deal altered the whole market dynamic in Russia. Of course, the trade made money for our company, but its significance went far beyond short-term profits.

The best trades are often years in the making. Throughout my career, I have been interested in developing the structures, systems and incentives that create the environment where traders can make good trades. That process can take time, but it is always worth it.

Preparing for floating-price trading required us to change the way our whole company operated, and then once we made the first trade, it changed the way the whole Russian oil industry operated. After that deal, there was really no way anyone could go back to the status quo.

16 Updating the NOC model

A civil engineer by training, Juan Carlos Fonnegra spent the first part of his career working as an engineer and then manager on projects around the world for Veolia Water. In July 2012, he switched to the energy sector, joining BP in Chicago as a supply analyst. Juan Carlos later moved to BP's U.K. operations, where he worked as a product supply negotiator and then as a crude refinery trader, before returning to Chicago in 2016 as a commercial developer. In 2018, Juan Carlos left BP to return to his native Colombia, where he joined state-owned producer Ecopetrol as head of crude oil marketing and trading.

I moved home to Colombia in 2018 to join our national oil company (NOC) Ecopetrol as head of crude oil marketing and trading. I have had a lot of interesting jobs in my career, but so far, this has been by far my most challenging but also my most rewarding experience.

My boss Pedro Manrique, who is our commercial vice president, describes me as an 'agent of change' – that's the reason that he brought me here. Ecopetrol has been changing quite a bit in recent years, and my role is to build on and accelerate the development in crude oil trading.

The changes on the commercial side really began in 2017 when my boss joined from Chevron. His goal was to transform the way that Ecopetrol handles its commercial activity by applying his experience of how international companies operate.

Ecopetrol hired an advisory consultancy and started a very robust transformation process to promote change and to build a process around where we want to go. The final model that we agreed upon was that we want to be an asset-backed trader (ABT) rather than just a producer and marketer of crude oil.

In terms of mentality, trading was not part of Ecopetrol's traditional DNA. To turn that vision into reality, Mr Manrique needed to bring in people from outside who had significant external experience.

That's where I came in. I joined Ecopetrol in October 2018. My formal job title is head of crude oil trading and marketing, but my broader task is to make sure that our evolution to asset-backed trading really takes place as planned.

DOI: 10.4324/9781003144335-20

The company has started to look and feel different quite quickly, and we were fortunate that our commercial results were also good in 2019 and 2020, which confirmed that we were on the right path.

The transformation has already been a huge success, but changing people, a mentality and a culture doesn't just happen overnight. After a few years of intense work, we are entering the execution phase where we make our aspirations a reality.

Going direct

Three years ago, Ecopetrol's primary role was to market its equity crude. Almost all of our exports go through the Caribbean port of Coveñas, and we sold everything on a free-on-board (fob) basis at the terminal. The clients would just show up with their vessels and load from us.

We didn't worry too much about a few cents here and there in those days. As long as our results were slightly better than the company had built into the annual budget, then 'trading' was considered to be performing well.

I say 'trading' rather than real trading because in reality our crude oil traders were actually really acting as marketers. All of the real optimization of value and any profits from efficiency savings were left in the hands of the client and sometimes also of middlemen like international traders.

We sold around 30% of our crude oil exports to traders in those days, and they were the ones that really profited from those transactions. The trading houses would come in, buy on an export basis from us and then sell our crude to other parts of the region. They used all of their efficiencies in logistics and risk management to capture any additional value.

Clearly, if we were serious about becoming asset-backed traders ourselves, we had to cut out the middlemen. Our new trading strategy is that we want to go directly to the refiner and make use of the great relationships that Ecopetrol has developed over decades with the end-users of our crude oil.

We have decided we will only sell to trading houses if it is absolutely necessary. Instead, we want to change the conversation with our clients. We want to understand their refining system, and to understand what their needs are in terms of crude supply, so that we can make sure that we provide the most reliable and sustainable crude supply.

Offering flexibility

Obviously, if we want to sell directly to refiners, then we had to be able to match the same flexible approach as the traders are able to provide.

As I mentioned, traditionally all of our exports were sold on a simple fob basis at Coveñas. Now we offer our customers the option of using multiple different benchmarks: we are happy selling on the basis of Brent, WTI or Dubai. We are also happy selling on a delivered basis, in fact that accounts for around 20% of our sales now, mostly to Asia.

Depending on the customer, Ecopetrol can handle the freight, the time spreads and even the risk management side. We wouldn't have considered those kind of arrangements a few years ago, but now we are trying to offer maximum flexibility, while also catching some of the inefficiencies and opportunities that the market brings, both from a risk management and from a logistics standpoint.

Framework contracts

One of the trading strategies that has worked really well for us is moving all of our sales to a spot basis, where we agree the sale of all of our exports on a month-to-month basis two months ahead of their actual physical loading.

But we understood that some of our customers like the security of a longer-term arrangement with an oil producer, so we have introduced the concept of 'framework contract holders' into our sales strategy, which we think offers the best of both worlds.

When we sign a one-year or two-year framework contract with our customers, it means that for the next 12–24 months, we will sit down every month and show that customer the barrels that we have available for export.

Our framework contract holders are the first people who will see our availability, and they will have the first chance to discuss supply with us before we start marketing those cargoes in the spot market.

So far, the concept of a framework contract has worked really well. It's not an absolute commitment like a traditional term supply deal because either side can always walk away from a negotiation on a monthly basis, but it does build solid relationships and provide a level of security that is helpful for some of our clients.

I guess around 60% of our sales are covered by the framework contract mechanism. I'm not sure if this is an approach that is used widely outside Ecopetrol, but it has worked really well for us.

The framework means that our relationship with our buyers is not a full-blown marriage, which in turn means that there's no need for a painful divorce if something doesn't go well. We have clearly entered a relationship together, but not one that might force our buyers to take oil they don't want at a price level that they just don't see, and which might hurt their economics.

The framework contracts are intended to be a win-win contract that gives refiners a form of supply security but allows both sides to agree prices every month that are suitable for each party.

Ensuring quality

We want to be sure that we are constantly finding efficiencies and optimizing our performance, all the way from the well head to Coveñas and from there to the refiner.

Part of our decision to sell direct was based on our need to understand exactly where our crude is going. Traders are fantastic liquidity providers whose role is to connect supply and demand, and they have every right to make a profit. But if a trader lifts a cargo from Coveñas, takes it somewhere else in the Caribbean and then blends it with other types of crude oil before selling the oil to Asia, then we face a potential reputational issue that might affect all of our exports and ultimately damage Ecopetrol.

Our strategy of going direct to the refiner has a double purpose: capturing some of the extra profits that the traders were making, but also making sure that when people around the world buy crude oil from Ecopetrol, then they get the actual genuine cargo. It's all about protecting the brand.

Of course, the other side of that commitment is that we need to do our part to make sure that every cargo that leaves Coveñas has the same quality. A major focus in recent years has been connecting the upstream, the midstream and the downstream to make sure that the whole value chain cares about quality, with the end result that quality stability and reliability has improved a lot in the last couple of years.

Behaving like a major

The Norwegian state-owned producer Equinor, which was formerly known as Statoil, is probably the best reference point for the journey that we began with the launch of our commercial transformation back in 2018.

Equinor went through that same journey, but maybe a decade before us. They were originally set up similarly to Ecopetrol, but now they are extremely sophisticated, and Equinor can compete on equal terms with the international oil majors like Chevron, Shell and BP.

Perhaps, the biggest change in our mindset is trying not to think like an NOC but rather like an international oil company (IOC). It's a question of with whom do we want to compare ourselves? Essentially, like Equinor, we want to be an NOC that behaves like a major.

I came from BP, as did our president Felipe Bayón, while my boss came from Chevron, so we have a lot of influence from the outside, and we are starting to feel more and more like an oil major.

Among the NOCs in our region, some are better than others from an efficiency and from a financial standpoint, but Ecopetrol stands out from the rest in terms of its mentality and vision.

We are thinking so much about value creation, commercials and trading because that's where the additional value comes from at the end of the day. Other firms in our region don't necessarily have the same perspective at this point, although I would encourage others to follow our path because we are definitely on the right trajectory.

Next steps

It's important to understand our necessary constraints though. We are developing asset-backed trading, rather than pure speculative trading. You will not see Ecopetrol go crazy and speculate massively on paper derivatives.

After all, we are a state-owned company – it's fundamental that we protect our cash flow rather than jeopardizing it with excessive risk because, after all, it's in part the nation's cash flow we are talking about.

Ecopetrol is the biggest company in Colombia. The state owns 89% of Ecopetrol shares and 50% of company revenue comes from crude export sales, so our trading strategy can really make a difference to the whole country, which is one of the main satisfactions of my job.

That extra money that we are earning by making better trading decisions goes straight back to benefit the nation. That's huge, and it makes a real difference to the way we think about our roles; it's what keeps us going as a group.

Clearly, we have already plucked quite a lot of the low-hanging fruit. We weren't the most sophisticated player in the market when we started the transformation process, so we were able to grab quickly some low-hanging fruit and squeeze it as hard as possible.

Now we are learning more, and we have become a bit more experienced and sophisticated, we can start to look at other opportunities and how we might reach other new levels.

One of the next steps, which we are already doing, is to be more aggressive on third-party trading. We are working with some of the smaller Colombian producers that do not have a commercial operation and are more focused on the exploration and production side of the business.

Ecopetrol steps in and buy their crude, either for our international trading activities or to feed and optimize our refineries. Some of the international traders are getting quite anxious about that because we are taking quite a bit of market share in Colombia, but that's part of the game.

We are also considering whether we should open some offices overseas. We want to be more international and that comes with having a presence in those markets that you care about. Back in 2016, our equity sales to Asia were 16–20% of exports, but in 2020, that rose to 50% and that trend will continue to grow.

If half of my exports end up in Asia, and mostly in China, then that market is hugely important for us, and we should try to get as close as possible to the customer. Growing our international footprint is going to provide the next big opportunity for Ecopetrol. In fact, I just wrote to my human resources department to let them know that I need myself and my crude traders to take basic Mandarin classes.

Joining Ecopetrol was one of those rare opportunities that present themselves at the right time and which had the right people involved.

Obviously, not everything has been rosy all of the time since I came back to Colombia. When you come from the private sector and from a firm like BP and then you join a state-owned company, the culture will clearly be different. But the organization is making a huge effort to transition and to become an energy company that is international and can be compared with other majors.

That vision and that strategy requires a change in culture and that comes from the inside. It takes time, and it's not easy. You have to be passionate and to want to drive change.

That effort is already paying off: the shift to flexible sales and the use of multiple benchmarks, whether fob or delivered, as well as the strategy of framework contracts and the renewed focus on quality are already generating significant benefits, not only for Ecopetrol but also for our customers as well.

17 Flexibility of supply

A graduate of the Georgia Institute and Technology with a bachelor's and master's degree in mechanical engineering and a master's in finance from the University of Houston, Mohammed Minkara joined Texaco in 1997. After a stint as a risk manager, he became a crude oil and refined products trader for Texaco in Houston. Following Texaco's merger with Chevron, Mohammed stayed on as a trader at the combined firm, before joining the Dow Chemical Company as a crude oil and refined products trader in 2005, based in Switzerland. He then later moved to the Middle East, where he holds a senior crude oil marketing role.

I can still remember the exact moment that I fell in love with trading. In 1996, I was travelling from the U.S. to visit my parents in the Middle East. I was flying with Austrian Airlines, and I had a stopover in Vienna. That gave me the chance to visit one of my childhood friends who was living there and working as a foreign exchange trader.

He took me to see his office and he showed me his trading desk. When I saw all those screens flashing up numbers and graphs, I was immediately hooked. You could say that it was love at first sight. My friend talked me through some trading concepts and areas like technical analysis and options, and my eyes just opened up.

I am a very mathematically and mechanically inclined person by nature, and so I knew straight away that trading was where I wanted to be. I felt like a kid in a candy store.

I was already working for Texaco at that point. I was raised in the Middle East and back then Texaco was the biggest brand name in the region – kind of like Google and Amazon are nowadays. I had done well in college, and I pursued Texaco after graduating until I landed a job with them.

After that visit home, I went back to work, but I was still obsessed. I must have applied to every trading position that Texaco had going.

I still remember the call I got from Rebecca Dwyer, who was the head of risk management at Texaco. She called me up and said,

> Mohammed, I am tired of seeing you apply for every single trader role that I have. I won't hire you as a trader, but if you want to come and interview, I have an entry analyst job that might suit you.

DOI: 10.4324/9781003144335-21

Rebecca Dwyer gave me my first break, and so I moved to Texaco's headquarters in White Plains, New York. Then after a year, Texaco needed a trader in Houston, so they moved me down there. They gave me very limited trading authority because I was inexperienced, and we were starting to grow the book. I was a smart-ass then and thought I knew everything, so I wanted to do everything immediately.

I loved trading and I loved options, in particular. I was good at my job but, frankly, I was very restless. I was a hard worker, I was smart, I understood things quickly, but my corporate savviness wasn't on a par with where I was technically.

In retrospect, it must have been frustrating managing me, but I was lucky that Rebecca and Michael Murphy, the senior trader, had big hearts and were able to channel my energy in the right way and I became one of their better traders.

Term to spot

The training I received at Texaco was second to none and stood me in good stead when I made the move to join the Dow Chemical Company, based in Switzerland.

I was trading on behalf of the refinery that Dow co-owned with French major Total at Vlissingen in the Netherlands, which was a facility that could process around 150,000 barrels per day of crude oil. The concept was that Total and Dow would each bring their own crude supplies and then each firm would lift their respective share of the refined products.

Dow had invested in the refinery in part as a way of meeting their need for naphtha and LPG in Europe, which they used as feedstocks, along with condensate, for the crackers they operated to produce petrochemical products.

The refinery originally bought its sour crude on a term contract basis, but Dow took the decision to move from term contracts to buying all of our crude oil on a one-off or 'spot' basis.

At first look, it might appear that this move would increase the refinery's supply risk. After all, the refinery typically required sour crude and the easiest way to secure that was by taking oil under term contracts.

But Dow had spotted that with the growing development of exports of Russian Urals Blend from the Baltic Sea, there was a ready availability of sour crude that had a much shorter sailing time.

Dow's bet was that we could switch away from term contracts to spot purchases, and that this would help us acquire cheaper feedstock without jeopardizing the refinery operations.

The timing was perfect. Urals trading was not as developed as it is nowadays, and our refining calculation for Urals was always slightly higher than the discounted levels we saw in the market in 2005/2006.

The arbitrage sale of Urals to the East was still not fully developed, so there was often an overhang of Russian supplies in Europe, dragging down levels to the point that even President Vladimir Putin complained at the time about the deep discount of Urals prices versus Brent.

There were times when Urals would go to a $7 per barrel discount versus its fair value in our model. Now maybe we valued Urals higher than a normal refinery would have because of the way we were configured, but that Urals price combined with our refinery configuration made the refinery a lot of money.

Getting sweeter

Moving to a spot basis for our sour crude supplies proved to be very profitable, but we decided to develop our crude oil strategy one step further and to buy the occasional sweet crude cargo as well.

We started to watch for any temporary disconnects in the sweet market. For example, a sweet Norwegian grade like Draugen might be available at a discounted rate or Brent might be selling lower for some reason. These disconnects in the sweet market would only last for a day or two, but we would jump on any distressed cargoes.

There were some real bargains to be had. Draugen used to trade at Dated Brent +80/90 cents in those days, but sometimes we would get a cargo +5 or +10 because we were prepared to be so opportunistic.

We could switch from sour to sweet crude on a dime, and we were willing to switch our diet from sour to sweet for just one single cargo. That flexibility ensured that the feedstock supply for the refinery became extremely competitive.

Vacuum gasoil go

The ability to add sweet crude to our menu required some foresight. If we were running sweet rather than sour crude, we wouldn't be producing enough vacuum gasoil (VGO) to feed the refinery's hydrocracker unit that enabled us to turn low-quality VGO into high-quality middle distillates.

The hydrocracker at Vlissingen could process anything up to 65,000 barrels per day. For a small refinery that was oversized, although it's a small unit compared with those at the new refineries being built here in the Middle East.

That hydrocracker was the jewel in our crown. It was incredibly profitable, particularly when the price of gasoil surged in 2006. There were times when the hydrocracker was effectively printing money.

The need to keep the hydrocracker running meant that whenever we wanted to switch our crude purchasing from sour to sweet, we would need to go simultaneously to the market to procure VGO as part of the deal.

That was typically not a problem. At that time, given the configuration of the Russian refining system, the Russians were usually exporting good quality VGO, and we were able to procure cargoes.

When we had maintenance and were not sure of our VGO requirement, we would go out to the small Netherlands VGO traders and agree to stand-by contracts. I would tell them,

> Look, I may need a certain amount of VGO from you, I will need it in barges and over a specific period. I can't tell you when I'm going to need it, but when I call you, you will need to deliver.

That's what we would do, and generally the market was sufficiently well supplied to be there for us.

Flexibility fans

The Dow guys were the shrewdest operators – they knew how to negotiate and how to extract value from assets. Above all, they always looked to ensure maximum flexibility.

Every morning we would walk into the office and run the linear programming (LP) model for the refinery to see what our ideal crude purchases would look like and then we would look in the market to see if we could find any distressed cargoes out there that might match our needs at advantageous prices.

We were always optimizing. If we saw something better than a cargo that we had already booked, then we would look to see if we could swap them. People came to know that we were always there for a bargain.

Although I wanted to buy a distressed cargo whenever possible, we would make a point of not destroying our sellers by squeezing every last cent from them. The relationship between buyer and seller should be a long-term one because when they need me, I should be there for them, and when I need them, they should be there for me.

A lot of the time just being honest about your position in the market goes a long way. I mean things like being straight about whether you are really there to buy or not and not messing people around.

Feed the beast

Our strategy to focus on the very short term worked so well for us because we were a relatively small player, we were nimble and we were in the right place. Your trading strategy has to depend on your situation.

If you are a giant refiner like ExxonMobil and you need to buy a dozen plus cargoes of Urals every month, well, then obviously you need to have the security of long-term supply. Imagine Exxon traders each trying to buy every distressed cargo out there every day. It would be the definition of a riot.

But for me it was different – I needed four or five cargoes of crude oil per month, so I could afford to take the chance on spot purchase supply. And, importantly, the asset was in the perfect place. Our refinery was located in the Netherlands, where we had North Sea and Russian barrels right next door to us. There was a huge refining centre nearby, and so there was always crude available.

That availability of flow gave us the confidence to build a very opportunistic and short-term trading strategy. That obviously brought its own pressures. Number one, you have to make sure you always have the crude and the feedstock in place to keep the facility operating. Don't forget, a trader will lose his job for running his refinery dry.

Number two, you have to make sure that feedstock is there at the right price to make the maximum revenue for the refinery. Oil traders get paid well for a good reason. They have to make decisions quickly and those decisions come with implications for the profit and loss not only of their own book, but of the whole refinery or company.

Emotional toll

The biggest challenge for any trader is to manage their emotions. I think that's why many of the most successful traders have a few common traits with psychopaths: they don't feel pain or fear, they are very detached.

After experiencing the markets for so long, I truly believe that. I am a good trader, but the very best traders I have seen, they have those traits. They just don't feel the pain, and as a result, they perform better than the rest of us. After all, the worst thing as a trader is starting to second-guess yourself because you have a pain memory from past mistakes.

When you are a couple of days away from the facility being dry as a bone and you have to pay up for a cargo, it's only natural that you will start to doubt yourself. Trust me, the worst feeling in the world is when you feel that cold sweat start to break out on the palm of your hands.

It's at those times when you need to get back on track, that you need to draw on all of your training and experience. You also really see the value of a good team and a good manager. I truly believe that for a company to succeed, they have to have the right talent and be able to manage all of their assets appropriately to maximize their value.

I have been very lucky in my career to work for some great people that realized this and were able to develop an environment that was conducive to risk-taking and high performance. At its best, trading is a job where you wake up in the morning, you look forward to your day and you have fun. That's when traders can really flourish and excel.

18 Turning weakness into strength

Michael Dugdale started his career as an accountant with Dixon Wilson and J.P. Morgan Chase before transitioning into the energy industry. He went on to spend over 14 years at Chevron in a variety of trading and supply roles in London, San Francisco and Houston. After leaving Chevron, Mike worked as a trader for Ineos Refining and as European business development manager for independent trader BrightOil. In 2013, Mike became a director of commodity inspection firm Veritek Global Solutions. He also works as an independent advisor to the energy industry.

Looking back, the trade that I am most pleased about came out of a situation that at the time my colleagues and I thought was going to be extremely difficult.

It was 2007 and I was working for Ineos Refining. This was a new firm that Jim Ratcliffe had formed as part of his Ineos group. Ratcliffe was building Ineos into a major player in petrochemicals by picking up assets that other firms no longer wanted. One of his biggest deals was to take over BP's Innovene subsidiary, which included two BP refineries that had large petrochemical plants attached: the 210,000 barrels per day (b/d) Grangemouth refinery in Scotland and the 210,000 b/d Lavera refinery, located near Marseille in southern France.

I originally left Chevron to join Innovene when it was still owned by BP, although it was already a separate entity. Then the deal with Ineos happened, and I found myself working for Ineos Refining. But it was a transitional period. We still sat in BP's offices and Ineos had agreed that BP would carry on doing all of the trading and supply for the two refineries.

This trading and supply agreement was a two-year deal that was set to end at the end of 2007. Frankly, it was a great deal for BP, the old parent, because it meant they could trade as if the two refineries were still part of their refining system, but they didn't have any exposure to refining margins or to operational issues at the refineries.

Asset trader

The way that BP and Ineos had set up their trading and procurement system was to have market-facing traders from BP liaising with asset traders

DOI: 10.4324/9781003144335-22

from Ineos. At that point, I was the asset trader, and I was representing the Grangemouth refinery.

My job was to look at the monthly refinery plan and the linear programme that told us which refined product slate to produce and which blends of crude oil to purchase. I then went to my BP colleague and told him which grades of crude oil we wanted to buy. As a market-facing trader, he or she would then go out into the market and try to satisfy our requirements.

At that point, the asset traders were supposed to fade into the background and let the market-facing traders get on with their job.

The Grangemouth refinery sits at the end of the Forties pipeline that brings the Forties blend of crude oil to the Grangemouth terminal from the Forties oilfield platforms around 100 miles offshore in the North Sea.

As a result, the Grangemouth refinery was designed to primarily process Forties crude oil. Processing Forties made such good sense for us because the oil came to us straight down the pipeline, and so there were no additional freight costs. The economics of running Forties was really what made Grangemouth attractive as a refinery.

After the acquisition, Ineos had arranged that BP would continue to supply us with Forties crude down the pipeline, and we had agreed to pay a premium to the Dated Brent benchmark price for the oil. At that point, we were probably buying an average of six Forties cargoes a month, equivalent to around 3 million barrels every month or 120,000 b/d.

Let's say that if Grangemouth was processing around 200,000 b/d of crude oil, maybe 120,000 b/d of that would come from Forties. The rest of the refinery's diet would come from a variety of smaller North Sea grades, such as Troll, with occasional heavier cargoes from Latin America or West Africa that we blended in with the light sweet North Sea grades to increase our output of middle distillates.

The big question

As the end of 2007 loomed, myself and my colleagues at Ineos Refining were getting increasingly nervous. Our two-year supply deal with BP was about to come to an end, and we were expecting them to put up their prices substantially from the original agreement.

No one at Ineos wanted to pay higher prices for the same supply deal, but at the same time, we were wondering how on earth we could replace the Forties that BP was supplying us and which we relied upon.

I came from Chevron where we had operated a North Sea crude oil desk, so I was very familiar with the North Sea market. It was clear that if we weren't going to renew our supply deal with BP, then we would have to go out into the market and bid for individual Forties cargoes, with no guarantees of success, or else we were going to have to do the rounds of the small Forties producers and pick up 10,000 b/d here and 30,000 b/d there on a term basis.

But those small producers were all being courted by the major oil firms, like our partners BP, who were also trying to pull together significant supplies of Forties. It really wasn't obvious that we would get enough Forties and without enough supply of Forties, it wasn't clear how the refinery could be particularly profitable.

No one had fully appreciated the impact of our dependence on Forties when Ineos took over the Innovene assets, so I remember a lot of concern as the final date of the BP–Ineos supply agreement came closer.

There were a lot of internal conversations about the size of our short position, which is how traders refer to a need for supply. We were all mulling the situation over, basically thinking it might be too much for us to handle and that we might have to renew with BP, even on much worse terms.

I probably felt the worst of anyone on the team. After all I was supposed to be the asset trader for Grangemouth, so ultimately the supply to the refinery – filling the short – was my responsibility.

The big answer

Just when I was beginning to despair of our prospects, I went to an industry function in London. I was having a drink with a much older trader from the U.S. refiner Valero, who was one of the most knowledgeable people in the market.

He was one of those guys who seemed to know everything, every problem or opportunity that a trader was facing, almost as if he had been sitting at your desk all day.

I guess that I'd had a drink and wanted to unburden myself to someone sympathetic, so I was telling him all about my problem and how I wasn't sure I would be able to find enough replacement supply when I had such a big short to fill.

He understood my situation immediately, and still to this day, I remember him dropping his bombshell.

'Mike', he said. 'You just said it yourself. You're the biggest short in Europe and that means you don't need to chase around after people. In fact, every supplier in the region is going to be scrambling to supply you'.

The moment he made that comment, it felt like a light bulb went on in my head. What we had perceived as a weakness was actually our strength. At Ineos, we had been thinking that we were in a bad strategic position because we were so short of crude, but that was precisely what would make us so attractive to suppliers.

The penny had well and truly dropped.

I went back to the office with a new strategy already in mind. My boss was quick to understand the advantage we now realized we had. We decided that we would go and visit all of the big boys – the oil majors like Shell, Total and ExxonMobil, as well as the large independent traders like Phibro – and test their interest levels and their capacity to supply us with what we needed.

We ended up seeing them all over the next few weeks. And we started every meeting by basically saying to them, 'here we are, we are the biggest buyer of Forties, so what can you do for us?'

It quickly became clear in our meetings that our new thinking was correct. As such a huge short, we were actually a highly attractive proposition to the suppliers and traders in the North Sea market.

Of course, this new strategy did not go down well with BP, who were very dismayed at the idea that they might have to compete for our business rather than us being more or less a hostage to them.

In the end and towards the end of 2007, we decided to organize a formal bidding process to supply the Grangemouth refinery.

We were looking to secure a certain amount of volume but with some optionality over cargoes, so each month we would plan to take six Forties cargoes of 600,000 barrels, but some months we might request five or seven with an adequate notice period. This would be a five-year supply deal, and so it was a massive undertaking for both sides, with tens of millions of barrels of Forties at stake.

For a while, the French major Total looked like it would be the most likely winner, but then at the last moment, we had an even more competitive bid from Shell, to whom we awarded the supply deal.

The levels that we agreed with Shell were a good distance below what BP had been proposing in order to renew our supply agreement with them. I would estimate that changing suppliers probably saved Ineos Refining around $25 million over the life of the agreement. Ineos was still making money on that deal long after I'd left the company!

The big short

One of the lessons I took from this episode, which still stands out as the best trading decision I've made, was that in the oil markets you can never assume someone is dependent on you. They nearly always have alternatives.

BP assumed that Ineos was dependent on them. They were used to the asset trader sitting meekly in the background, while they did all the communication with the market, but I had been a frontline trader myself at Chevron, and so I knew how the North Sea worked and who to talk to.

I think the BP traders came to realize quickly that they had blown a big opportunity by taking Ineos so much for granted. Once the two-year supply deal ended, it was much harder for them to trade without those two refineries in their portfolio.

When I was at Chevron and had refinery assets, I saw just how much more optionality owning refineries gives you when you are trading. Your counterparts never know if you are bluffing when you say you might use a particular cargo for your own refinery unless they show you a more attractive price. If you don't have refineries, then the potential buyer knows you will ultimately have to sell.

In fact, a little later on Morgan Stanley came in and did a deal with Ineos Refining to provide them with offices, trading expertise and working capital, purely because they wanted access to our big short – the refineries of Grangemouth and Lavera. Morgan Stanley effectively paid Ineos a lot of money, just to have the right to trade around that big short.

The loss of access to Grangemouth and Lavera must have been an uncomfortable change for BP. I'm sure they came to regret the mindset that they could charge whatever they wanted, and we would meekly accept.

Switching mindset

The other lesson I took from this episode was about my own mindset. I really remember asking myself how I could have failed to appreciate what a great position I was in sitting on with such a big short.

It was eye-opening for me to realize just how important it can be as a trader to review the way you are thinking. A simple change of perspective made all the difference.

When I look back at it now, it all seems obvious, but when you go into a trade and you think you are beholden or trapped in some way, then it's very hard to change your attitude. Sometimes it's important as a trader that you stop and take a deep breath and look at a potential or current trade from a different angle.

In this case, one throwaway comment from someone at a party was the pivot point that we needed to change our mindset. That set us on a path where we managed to turn what we thought was a weak trading position into one that generated a tremendous amount of value.

19 The value of persistence

Before moving into the energy markets, Geena Malkani held senior roles in Ghana's automotive and health sectors. She was head of sales for Ghana's Accad Group of Companies and was the sales and contracts manager for Nissan, VW and Porsche. Geena also served as the regional sales and marketing manager for PHC Motors in Ghana and was also the head of business development for Wellness Labs. In 2011, Geena joined the Springfield Group of Companies, which is one of the leading energy and natural resource development and trading businesses in West Africa. Geena is a partner in Springfield and serves as a director and as chief operating officer.

Springfield was created in 2006 when the founder, Kevin Okyere, identified a shortage of storage for refined products near Ghana's Tema oil refinery. Kevin decided to invest some of the capital he had generated as an entrepreneur in the telecoms sector into building a tank farm.

Springfield had also received a petroleum product import license from the government of Ghana, and in 2008, we began importing refined products into Ghana. The import business went well for us, and we also traded some crude oil cargoes successfully. Our success in Ghana led us to expand our trading operations into neighbouring countries, like Burkina Faso and Mali.

But, although things were going well for us, Kevin and I had this dream of taking the firm to the next level. For a West African firm like ours, that meant developing a business in Nigeria, which is the regional superpower and Africa's biggest oil producer.

We finally took the plunge in 2011 and began to have some very initial conversations with the Nigerian National Petroleum Corporation (NNPC) about how we could work with them and add value. The officials we met were always very friendly – in general, I have always found Nigerians to be very friendly people – but it was clear that their courtesy was not going to translate quickly into the level of trust and confidence in our abilities that we would need if NNPC was going to work with us.

It was therefore a significant breakthrough for Springfield when we signed a crude oil marketing agreement with the NNPC in 2014. We were the first Ghanaian firm to enter into a crude oil marketing agreement with NNPC

DOI: 10.4324/9781003144335-23

and, as a relatively unknown firm in Nigeria, a lot of people wondered where we had come from.

After our name was announced as a trading partner of NNPC, some people called us an overnight success. That was funny to me. They clearly had no idea of the huge amount of effort that we had put in to get to that point.

The hard yards

We had decided that the only way we could build a relationship with NNPC was with regular face-to-face meetings and by creating a physical office presence in Nigeria. That might seem an obvious approach, but we took the concept to the next level, and we committed to ourselves that we would fly to Nigeria every single week.

Our plan was to meet as many people as we could to build relations and to create a familiarity between us and them. We would tell them what we were already doing and why they should work with us, and we did that week after week.

We cultivated those relationships and networks for three full years. And finally, after three years of visits, we secured our first contract with NNPC.

We had earned respect with our persistence and with the experience we had acquired from operating in Ghana and elsewhere in West Africa. Maybe it was also a question of the survival of the fittest. If Springfield managed to keep up a physical presence in Nigeria for three years, then NNPC had to think that we were serious. Most people would have given up long before because three years without a contract represents a significant commitment of money and time.

Luckily, before entering into Nigeria, our business in Ghana was already structured, and so our duties could be performed remotely from wherever we were, even though it meant that we were living on our mobile phones.

It certainly wasn't easy to get that deal in place; it was an extremely difficult challenge that we had decided to set ourselves. After one year into the game, we were like 'well, we've already done a year, it can't take that much longer'. Then another year into the game, we thought, 'well, we've already spent money for two years coming in and out, so we can't let that money go to waste'.

So, we kept going and eventually we got the deal. That's why it made me smile when I heard Springfield described as an overnight success. I would remember that every Monday morning for three years we were on our way to the airport at 4.30 am.

Performance anxiety

Persistence can clearly pay off, at least if you are confident in your strategy. But getting our first crude oil deal in place was only the start, obviously.

Now Springfield had to perform and to show NNPC that they had made the right choice.

We understood the importance of performing well on this first contract, so we could secure subsequent contracts. The Nigerian crude oil trading market is highly competitive and requires performance. As most of the players on that scene are traditionally A-list international oil traders, some people were not sure we would be able to match the performance of the A-list international oil traders. Of course, our performance exceeded their expectations.

Our experience in the markets had shown us that sometimes when oil traders make a commitment, your first job is to try to understand exactly how far you can rely on that commitment. One of the reasons we had such a great relationship with BP was because they always delivered on their commitments. We were determined that Springfield would also deliver and, if possible, would outperform.

The core element to our approach was a focus on customer service. A lot of people in the oil markets might like to say that they are customer centric, but I came from the car industry, which is an incredibly hard school, and I brought what I learnt there to my role in oil.

The culture in our company is that you either have to work for the client or you can't work for us. I'd argue that this is the driver behind Springfield's success. We think of everything we could possibly do and then we set out to do more than that.

When we started trading oil in Ghana, we grew our market share to 12.5% within two years. Before we entered the market, there were only three companies operating, and when competition is low and everyone needs your oil, then there's very little you need to do to sell your oil: people will just come to you to buy it.

When we entered the market, along with some other firms, suddenly the competition started. Springfield focused on improving customer relations and we implemented what we called a 'people strategy'. Our management went personally to see every single distributor of oil in the area. After that, we went to visit every single one of their retail stations.

When you have worked in the car industry, trust me, you know how to build relationships and you can sell anything to anyone. I'm not sure if that level of customer engagement is more typical elsewhere but it certainly wasn't the way that things had been done here.

Our strategy was the same once we entered into the Nigerian market. We had worked incredibly hard to persuade the Nigerians of our merits, and now the key was to hold up our end of the bargain.

Whenever you make commitments, you need to deliver on them. If you say you can lift a cargo of crude and pay on time – or even before time – then you need to make sure you do that, no matter what happens.

Our crude oil contract required us to make payment to NNPC within 30 days of lifting a cargo from them. We made a point of wiring our payment across on day 28. The Nigerians were incredibly surprised that one of their smallest partners was outperforming on payment terms.

We even had a phone call from NNPC trying to understand why we were consistently paying them in full and early. They couldn't figure out why the first Ghanaian company to lift crude oil from Nigeria could pay them earlier than other firms. They wanted to understand what we were doing differently.

Onwards and upwards

Everything flowed from that first trade. We were performing so well on our crude oil contract that NNPC's faith in Springfield grew.

Our success on the crude oil side led us to other partnerships in Nigeria on gasoil, LPG and particularly on condensate, where we were given the responsibility of marketing a new stream of condensate. At the time, the stream was called 'the lightest condensate in the world', and it was produced from an offshore field operated by Chevron in partnership with NNPC.

From the trading and marketing deals, Springfield has moved into the upstream side of the business with the establishment of a new oil production division.

We ventured into the upstream sector to secure private Ghanaian involvement in upstream exploration and production opportunities primarily in Ghana and regional West Africa. We were awarded our first asset – West Cape Three Points Block 2 – by the government of Ghana in 2016. The award was ratified in March 2016 and became effective in July 2016. Springfield is the operator and majority interest holder of the block, with the Ghana National Petroleum Corporation and its exploration company (Explorco) holding a minority interest.

Adding an upstream side to our business means that we will produce our own barrels in West Africa, and we will trade that oil globally ourselves. It is very gratifying to see that we will come full circle as a company but with the added advantage of owning our own barrels. We are proud to have become one of the leading vertically integrated energy and natural resources companies in Africa.

My partner and I intend to build a company that outlives us. A key strategy for this is to build strong long term, global relationships and partnerships as relationships are a huge part of business success in any sector.

Another of our core strategies in building for the long term is ensuring consistent local capacity building and knowledge transfer in our operations. In this vein, we believe that our employees are our greatest assets. We are committed to ensuring that all employees believe in our vision and share the group's core values. When we are hiring for Springfield, we understand that while every employee is different, we all have to share that determined nature and that desire to outperform the customer's expectations.

The key question for any candidate is do you accept that we are going to break all the barriers and all of the glass ceilings, and that we are going to do things that no one has ever dreamt that an African can do?

I'm a people person, and I most often do not accept 'no' for an answer. Neither do I accept limits on what is achievable.

If our firm can expand into Nigeria, successfully lift and sell crude oil on the international market and then own a majority interest in a deep water oil block, then what else can we do?

We have grown rapidly since our inception, positioning ourselves as a firm with a highly efficient team that possesses integrity and exceptional management skills. Those qualities have enabled us to achieve impressive growth through strong relationships and partnerships with suppliers, buyers and end-users. It is this spirit of partnerships and community that drives our work towards a vision of a powered, innovative African continent.

Logistics and storage trading

Most crude oil is transported either by pipeline or by sea in dedicated vessels, but rail and road transport are also used at times. Managing the economics of transporting crude oil between different locations – such as from its production well to the refinery where it will be processed – is obviously crucial to traders.

An innovative approach to logistics can drive down the delivered cost of crude oil, potentially creating a profitable trade that others might not have spotted. Equally, expensive freight arrangements or an expensive pipeline commitment can dramatically eat into traders' profits.

Crude oil can be stored in tanks, caverns or even onboard anchored oil tankers ('floating storage'), and many national governments store crude oil as an insurance policy against disruption in their supplies.

As we will see, traders tend to think about storage more opportunistically.

In particular, traders aim to take advantage of times when the current price of oil is lower than the future delivery price, a market structure known as 'contango'. These market conditions can make it very profitable for traders to buy oil and hold it in storage until prices recover, even accounting for the cost of finance and of renting storage.

DOI: 10.4324/9781003144335-24

20 Preserving pipeline economics

John Krus has held a number of senior positions in the U.S. oil markets. After graduating from the University of Houston, he joined Texaco as an originator, before moving to Western Crude Oil, which merged with Reserve Oil and Gas, which then later merged with Getty Oil, where he rose to become vice president of crude marketing. John took over as Texaco's vice president of trading and transportation when Getty was acquired by Texaco in 1984. In 2001, he joined Shell, after Shell and Texaco merged their midstream businesses. John also served on the launch committee of the NYMEX WTI crude oil futures contract and was one of its first backers. John currently works as a consultant to the U.S. energy industry via his Texas-based advisory service, JSK Holdings.

My belief is that as long as you understand people and you deal with them fairly, then they'll generally treat you the same way. From time to time, there will always be exceptions, but for the most part that philosophy holds true in the U.S. domestic crude oil business. It's changing a little bit these days, but historically that has always been the case.

Let me put it this way, I was a vice president for 40 years, and I was only ever involved in a single lawsuit in all of those 40 years. When you consider we were agreeing in the order of 500–750 contracts a month, then I wouldn't call that a bad record.

But sometimes you do have to take steps to keep people honest. When I took over domestic trading and transportation at Texaco one of my first jobs was to review all of the prices that Texaco was getting paid for their crude oil production around the U.S. We did that by putting ourselves in the shoes of the buyer and thinking, 'well, if we were going to buy that production, what would we offer?'

One of the assets we looked at was around 12,000 barrels per day of crude production that we had down in South Texas that we were selling to a gathering and marketing company that had a pipeline. This was the only pipeline in the area, so basically all of the production nearby, including Texaco's and that of the other majors and independent producers, was hooked onto that pipeline because it was the only way to move the oil out of the area without taking it out in trucks.

DOI: 10.4324/9781003144335-25

When we saw the price that Texaco had been receiving, I straight away thought, 'well, we need to go and talk to the buyer because I don't think we are getting a fair price'. The buyer was getting a great deal. The pipeline went directly into their refinery, but they weren't paying a price that was in any way competitive with the crude oil that they were bringing in from other parts of the country or with foreign alternatives.

We went over and we renegotiated the price with them, and the sums all added up. After that, we were happy and pleased to stay linked to their pipeline.

Changing economics

Everything was running smoothly, or at least it was until about two years later. A new manager joined the pipeline firm, and we suddenly received a notification that they were cancelling our contract subject to renegotiation. When they did make us a new offer, they showed us an indication that that they were going to decrease their purchase price by over $2 per barrel.

I have to say I was pretty upset. If they'd called me and said, 'let's go to lunch and talk about prices', then I might have reacted differently. But instead the cancellation subject to renegotiation showed up in the fax mailbox of one of my lease reps and they brought it in and showed it to me.

I was also thinking, 'well, if they're going to decrease me by over $2 per barrel, I can't imagine what they are going to do to the independent producers locally who have a lot less production to sell'.

My theory was that they thought that they had everyone wrapped up because there weren't any alternatives to move oil out of the area, and so everyone was operating on their pipeline.

I was vice president of marketing, but Texaco Pipelines also coordinated with me. I understood that there were times when pipelines want or need to raise their tariffs, but the kind of increases that I was used to were fairly nominal, like 25 cents per barrel or something like that. Even then, if you felt the increase was out of line, you could usually go and sit down and talk to the people and work something out or ask them to delay the implementation.

I had never seen anything as aggressive as $2 per barrel, particularly on a pipeline that was already completely paid for. You have to bear in mind that the oil price was around $12 per barrel at that time or maybe even less, so a decrease of $2 per barrel was going to be awful for us.

Get mad, get even

It took me two days to figure out what I was going to do.

I called my guys together and told them that I was going to build a new pipeline. I remember people looking at me like I was a little crazy. They asked me, 'John, where are you going to take this pipeline to?' and I said we would take it anywhere really.

I also called the field people and I told them to start rounding up enough trucks to move 10,000 barrels per day of crude oil by road. I didn't know how far we were going to have to truck it to get it to a new buyer, but it didn't make any difference. I told them we were going to have to start moving trucks from all over the country into South Texas because we had about 40 days before we were going to begin trucking all of our production.

Meanwhile, I called some of our pipeline people and said, 'go and stick some right-of-way signs along the highway'. I wanted to make sure everyone could see these flags. The pipeline guys were a little bemused. They said, 'John, you know we don't have any permits, right?' And I said, 'look, guys, I didn't tell you that we were definitely going to build a pipeline, but we're certainly going to look like we are'.

Saying that, I was dead serious that I wasn't going to let another barrel go down that pipeline, if they were going to pay me $2 less per barrel. I kept on making my alternative arrangements.

I was lining up trucks to move 10,000 barrels per day. We were the largest truck transporter in the U.S. at the time, so we could have done it. Carrying 10,000 barrels per day in trucks would have hurt us in other areas and made the transportation market tight, but I was prepared to take that risk.

I was already sending out word internally to gather a fleet of trucks and start fitting them with double seats because we would be bringing them to South Texas for a period of time. I also told my upstream guys to expect a visit from some of our field people who would fit the right size of hoses and connections so that we could load trucks from the fields and take the oil out.

I knew that if I started a trucking operation, then regardless of economics some of the other producers in the area would come with me because we were all so upset.

I also made a provisional deal with another refinery in the area, or at least I negotiated a possible price. That meant that I knew exactly what our economics would be using truck transport. It was a loser for sure to use the trucks, but we could have lived with it while we got on with developing our own pipeline.

The big bluff

I figured I had to make the other side sure that we were serious.

As well as the right-of-way flags along the highway, I made sure that they would see that we were bringing in trucks by parking five or six of them in places where you couldn't really miss them. We made it pretty clear to the whole world that were up to something and were going to go down a different path.

Well, it took about a week and a half of this before I received a phone call.

The guy on the other end of the line asked me, 'John, are you building a pipeline in south Texas?' So I said, 'we're a big firm and we are building pipelines all over the country. It could be that one of them might be in south Texas. In fact, we might even build two of them down there'.

'We noticed your stakes', he said. 'And they are parallel to part of our line'. I said, 'well, we haven't come to a definitive agreement on how our pipeline is going to look and where it's going to be laid, but it wouldn't surprise me if we would run parallel in some parts'.

'John', he said. 'Are you sure you aren't just upset because of the $2 decrease in price we sent over to you guys?' So I said, 'no, I'm not upset, but it just made us re-evaluate a few things and we realized that maybe going into the South Texas pipeline business might be productive for us'.

I think that must have been the end of that call.

Reaching agreement

Within two weeks of the first cancellation, they were back renegotiating with us.

They called me up again and said, 'John, we need to have lunch and talk about South Texas'. I said that I wasn't sure that we would have much to talk about. But we had lunch anyway and we discussed prices.

Not only did they withdraw the $2 decrease, but they also actually offered to raise my price. I accepted the new offer and asked them if they wanted to sign a 30-day evergreen contract, a six-month one or a one-year one. They wanted two years, and I said I wouldn't give them two years, but I would give them one year plus a 30-day evergreen.

In just a few weeks, we were able to turn a potentially huge reduction in income into a price increase. The outlay had been pretty minimal. We had not done any engineering work, the only thing we had done was put some pipeline stakes out as if we were going to build a pipeline, as well as moving a handful of trucks down to South Texas.

For me, this was a great example of how a firm can get comfortable in their own environment and think that they can control an area.

Once the other side realized that those stakes were ours and then they saw our trucks, they figured out that we were going to truck our oil temporarily, until we got a pipeline built and then we were going to go after all of the barrels on their line. That is exactly what would have happened if they hadn't called me to renegotiate. Quite honestly, it would have taken me several months to assemble enough trucks to permanently transport all of the oil from that area. But the one thing that I was sure about was that those barrels were not going to go to their refinery.

Keeping straight

While this was all going on, my bosses warned me that the other side was a big boy too and that they wouldn't just sit back and let me take all of their pipeline business, but I reassured them that I didn't really have any intention of building the line, although I would have, if it had come to that.

Something told me we wouldn't have to go to that extreme though.

Apart from the measures I was taking in South Texas, I also made sure I had another hedge in place. I knew they had a hold over us down there and that they could come after us at any time, so I intentionally sold them some other Texaco crude that was convenient to another one of their refineries, and that they really wouldn't want to lose.

This ensured that they knew that if they took advantage of me in South Texas, then I was going to take advantage of them somewhere else. I think the new guy figured out fast that if he wanted to play tit for tat, then I was holding more cards than he was.

I'm convinced that he had been thinking, 'well, here's an opportunity where we can do pretty much what we want'. At least, someone there thought they had everybody locked down, but we were big enough and motivated enough to do something about it. We used good logical process thinking to evaluate our alternatives and then we made them clear to the whole world.

Today, I can laugh about the whole situation, but I'm not so sure I thought it was funny back when it was going on. I was just so provoked about how it had happened, and I was somewhat hurt by the amount that they had suggested.

The bottom line is that it was a good reminder to me that in business even honest people need to be kept honest sometimes. We just did it in a creative way.

21 A U.S. pipeline frenzy

Anne Summers began her career as an operations coordinator, first with an independent trading company that was purchased by Cargill/Tradax and then for Cargill's petrochemical business. She went on to work as a crude oil operator for Cargill and then as a crude oil trader. Anne joined Morgan Stanley in New York in 1986 and spent the next 30 years working for the bank in a variety of oil trading and supply roles. She traded physical and paper crude oil and worked on refinery supply from cargoes and from pipelines as well as developing hedging, trading and supply programmes on behalf of the bank's customers. After leaving Morgan Stanley in 2016, Anne became a maritime arbitrator with the SMA New York, as well as joining boutique energy firm Citizens Resources LLC in 2018 as business development manager.

The oil markets changed a whole lot during my career. But in my opinion, none of the changes, even including the development of future markets, came close to matching the impact of the development of U.S. shale oil in the early 2010s.

That was a gigantic transformation because U.S. oil production had been steadily falling since the 1980s, and the decline was widely believed to be irreversible. That view quickly changed when U.S. exploration and production firms discovered new and more economic techniques to fracture shale rock formations to unlock the oil that lies within.

The 'shale revolution' was incredibly fast and incredibly prolific. U.S. oil production surged from 5 to 6 million barrels per day in the 2000s to breach the 10 million barrel mark by November 2017, which was a level of U.S. output that we hadn't seen since 1970.

I have been in the business long enough to experience several commodity cycles and multiple major events, but I can't recall any other single development that has had such a profound impact on the oil market.

Shale made North America so much less dependent on other sources of oil; it led to an explosion in the number of firms operating in the U.S.; it threatened the dominance of OPEC over the direction of oil prices; and it changed every aspect of the way the U.S. oil industry does business, from drilling to transportation to hedging.

DOI: 10.4324/9781003144335-26

Many of the other events I experienced that seemed huge at the time ended up having much less of a long-term impact.

When the Iran–Iraq war broke out in 1980, some traders did really well and others didn't, but the market was only dramatically impacted for a short period.

Then the Iraqi invasion of Kuwait in 1990, followed by the Desert Storm campaign, and the 2003 U.S. invasion of Iraq and overthrow of Saddam Hussein were, again, significant in terms of their immediate impact on the oil price, but that effect was surprisingly short lived in oil market terms – the volatility actually settled down pretty quickly.

In contrast, the economics of shale oil continue to change behaviour and drive price calculations in the oil markets more than a decade after shale's first emergence.

Trading shale

The shale revolution took my trading role at the bank to a different level. The hedging needs of the new producers and end-users grew exponentially, and as we were a market maker, we were busier than we had ever been.

The swaps market for different grades like WTI Midland and WTI Houston exploded as participants looked to hedge the prices of the domestic grades relative to WTI futures at Cushing. Trading and making markets in the swaps became a major business for us, particularly once the swaps were cleared on CME as block trades.

Beyond the paper side, we were fortunate in our physical trading because we had agreed to supply a Midwest refinery with crude oil in 2010, just as shale oil was really coming into play.

We had done a few refinery supply deals before that, using our global network to help refineries source oil at economic levels, but this was one of the bigger deals we'd done so far, and it lasted for approximately five years.

The timing for that deal was pretty unbelievable. U.S. production was growing, but the domestic pipeline system hadn't kept pace with the rapid development of shale oil. There simply wasn't enough pipeline capacity to transport all of the new crude oil to the different demand centres, so massive discrepancies in price developed between different grades and between regions, such as the Midwest and the Gulf Coast.

For the first time, the price of different grades was more influenced by access to pipeline infrastructure than by issues like relative quality. For example, WTI Midland in west Texas developed a significant discount to WTI at Cushing. The price spread between the two markets reached as high as $15–20 per barrel, which was gigantic and absolutely unprecedented.

As a consequence of all of these infrastructure dislocations in the U.S. domestic market, there were plenty of buying opportunities, which enabled us to supply the refinery with extremely economic crude. This was also a period before U.S. exports developed, and domestic storage was also experiencing a huge buildout.

Pipeline development

Our timing was definitely ideal when we agreed that refinery supply deal, and it worked out very well, both for us and for our customer. But we quickly realized that the scale of the price differences between different U.S. domestic markets wouldn't be sustainable in the long term.

Given the size of the price differences between grades and regions, there was a very clear incentive for developers to build new pipelines to connect up all of the different markets and to alleviate the crunch in transport capacity.

It was amazing to watch the infrastructure buildout. The growth was remarkable, and of course, everyone was scrambling to get space on the pipelines.

It became almost a mania among crude traders at the time. It was as if you couldn't hold your head up among the other guys unless you had pipeline space. We looked at taking capacity on some of the new developments, but walking away was one of the smartest things we ever did.

We took the view that the shortage of capacity was a short-term issue. It just didn't make sense for us to take on an expensive long-term commitment when so many new pipelines were being built – the whole rush to lock in capacity felt a bit like the dot-com bubble.

Bubbles develop when everyone wants to make the same trade. That's exactly what happened here. Everyone was reacting in the same way to the price discrepancies that had opened up between the different U.S. domestic markets, but when everyone wants to trade in the same direction, it usually ends badly.

Overcapacity develops

As traders grew desperate to get capacity, they chased the price of pipeline capacity to an unsustainable level. When I saw people were paying up to get five- or ten-year deals on the reversal of the Seaway Pipeline, I just thought, 'good luck to them'.

We decided that we wouldn't do it. I recall numerous discussions when it seemed like the macho thing to do was to take term space. But not taking pipeline space was perhaps the best decision we made during the first years of the shale boom.

People were paying a lot of money for term transportation, like over $5 per barrel for term pipeline space, and sometimes even more for spot space. Many of the companies were justifying it as a sunk cost. At times, that might have made sense, but not in the long term.

I remember one company took capacity and then after so much more pipeline space got built out, they ended up selling their remaining term pipeline space allocation to another firm for something like 25 cents per barrel, just to have some cash flow coming in.

It's a different story if you can't operate your core business without a certain commodity or service. But I genuinely couldn't see why it was so essential for oil traders to have pipeline capacity in order to run their businesses.

The growth in the midstream sector was huge, with many of the major oil companies spinning off their production units and adding midstream companies, plus a lot of new producers stepped into the marketplace. But sometimes you just need to sit back when there's a popular trade in the market and question whether you really want to be following the herd.

I know we might have missed opportunities at times by not having capacity, but I believe that overall we made the right decision.

It took a few years for all those new pipelines to get built, but in the overall context of the oil industry, the development was incredibly swift. Within a few years, you could see that we were passing from shortage to overdevelopment.

The investment in new infrastructure could be justified, more or less, while U.S. production was still growing hugely, but by 2018–2019, it was clear that output growth was slowing once more. Then, in 2020, the demand destruction caused by the COVID-19 virus led to a dramatic fall in shale and conventional oil production and revealed that the U.S. had massively overbuilt in terms of new crude oil pipelines.

There might be a few bottlenecks up in Canada but that was about the only part of North America where there were any constraints left.

Positive and negative

Our two major trading decisions had paid off for the bank: the first to pursue a long-term refinery supply deal; the second to stand back from the rush to acquire pipeline capacity.

Both calls involved more than just the front-line traders, like myself. The supply deal wouldn't have happened without the support of the legal team, management, the structured products team and the contract group. It literally took a village to put that deal together. Most of the really good deals that traders like to tell each other about are actually not solo efforts but take a huge amount of group effort.

Maybe one of the reasons female traders are less prominent in the oil markets is because they are more willing to acknowledge that truth and to share the glory with the wider team. Perhaps, we don't have the same ego that some of our male colleagues might have.

As a female, I feel I got 'shorted' in a lot of ways. I'm sure you've heard the stories before, and a lot of the stories were true. Strip clubs and men's clubs were very popular. Not the most comfortable place for us 'girls', if we decided to go along. And, also not very comfortable for the men for a number of reasons.

Some of it was more subtle, like not getting invited to the golf course, where the male traders were buddying up and getting mentoring from the bosses. The lack of an in-house mentor for me was one of the hardest parts of being a female on the trading desk.

But trading culture changed totally during my career. Management stepped in and curbed the excesses and tried to be more inclusive of women. A lot of the rules that came into play were good, but it was maybe a little overdone and by flipping to the other extreme, we damaged some of the camaraderie on the floor.

The trading floor became very proper, the football was no longer tossed around and we had to be guarded with everything we said. We could barely look at each other or laugh together any more. We went from strippers coming onto the floor for birthdays in the mid- to late 1980s, to a time where you couldn't even receive a joke in your email.

Cultural shifts

Some of the trading culture that I experienced early on in my career was kind of disgusting and some of it was great. The sexism could be truly dispiriting, but the positive part of the culture was the social side.

So long as you could be strong and stand up for yourself, it was fine. I remember an issue with a trade, where we were discussing backwardation, and the boss from my counterparty got on the call and said, 'you are just a girl, you don't know what you are talking about'. But then he equally insulted my British senior colleague saying, 'and just because you talk fancy doesn't mean you know what you are talking about either'.

But I was a people person and that was one of the attributes that stood me in good stead. In fact, not long after that conversation, we actually became friendly, despite my being a 'girl' in the oil business.

I really liked people, talking to them and getting out with them. I loved all of the parties and there were a lot of them.

When I first started out in the industry, I was making $6,000 a year, kind of hard to believe in retrospect. But every night I would come home in a limousine from a party or from some fancy dinner.

My boss used to take me along to help him remember all of the deals he'd done because, back then, everything was agreed verbally and sealed with a handshake over plenty of drinks.

The doorman of my apartment building was quite disappointed at Christmas time. He'd see me arriving in limos at all hours, and he'd stand there probably thinking I was making a bunch of money, when I was thinking, 'buddy, if only you knew the truth'. That was early on, and my compensation certainly improved. Despite 'salary differences', I lived well, and it was a lot of fun, for many years.

Social side

Trading oil was social, global, always a challenge, never boring. My early expectations in life were to get married, have kids and maybe I'd work, but I didn't expect the career I had or that I would be the sole supporter of my four kids (for the most part).

Business trips for working moms were often considered a vacation. But that meant having good help in my house. I recall one amazing evening early on in my career, taking an Amtrak train to Washington, D.C.

The hosts rented an entire Amtrak car, hired butlers and held a private party while the train ran from New York to Washington and then after a dinner in D.C. and clubbing in Georgetown, we returned to New York by Amtrak again, like regular people, except exhausted.

It was fun as hell; it was out there, it was insane. In general, as an industry, we drank a lot and we swore horribly. As I mentioned, I have four kids at home, and I could not bring my swearing under control, which wasn't very ladylike. That's a trading desk for you.

For all of the downsides, I couldn't help but get into the culture. The incredibly social nature of business and trading in those days meant we spent a lot of time with customers, we listened to them and we made sure they got what they wanted.

My boyfriend always teases me when I say that 'I was an honest banker' because he says there's no such thing. But we weren't anonymous traders behind screens, we knew our counterparts and our customers and we socialized together, so being viewed as a trustworthy person who tried to do the right thing was very important to me.

Trading culture evolved so much and so quickly during my career. That was obviously for the better in terms of equality, but it would be a shame if the social side of the business disappeared altogether.

Spending time with people helps you to understand what is really happening in the market, and that's how you spot opportunities and avoid costly mistakes like buying into a bubble.

I loved the physical cargo business, which covered my first 25–30 years; I loved the physical pipeline trading; and I'm only sorry I missed the onset of U.S. exports. I probably would have really enjoyed the physical trading of exports.

22 Finding interesting niches

A graduate of the University of Cape Town and of IMD Business School, Michael Hacking joined Cargill in January 1978 and then went to London to join Vanol International in 1982, rising to the position of managing director. In 1993, he was appointed chief executive of the international division of the South African oil group, Engen Petroleum. In 1998, Michael founded Mocoh Energy Ltd to develop energy opportunities, and in 2004, he founded Mocoh SA in Geneva, where he serves as chief executive. Mocoh trades globally, but its focus is sourcing and delivering crude oil and finished products, mainly within and out of Africa. Mocoh acquired Engen's retail distribution sites in Ghana and previously had an interest in an oil exploration block in Madagascar. In 2016, Michael started the mc2h Foundation as an outlet for Mocoh's charitable activities in Africa.

When you are a smaller trading house, you can't easily compete for the plain vanilla trades or take on the big boys at their game. You have to look for the trade that is a little bit different.

Building a business in the niches of the oil market makes for some quite interesting experiences and it requires initiative, deep thought and a spirit of enterprise.

Albanian crude oil definitely qualifies as one of those niche markets. Not many people even know that Albania produces crude oil, but in 2006, we were approached to see if Mocoh could assist with marketing the entirety of Albania's production.

A Canadian company had bought into a field and were looking for a partner to help them market the oil, ideally at a better price than it had been achieving previously.

We spent a considerable time looking at the project and wondered how we could improve the returns. The challenges were obvious. The first hurdle was the quality. This was not one of the world's more attractive grades.

At 9.8° API, the Albanian oil was so heavy that you could stand a spade in it. Most people in the industry have never even seen a 9.8° API crude oil, let alone expressed any interest in buying some.

The second hurdle was the logistics in Albania, which were very complicated indeed. Trains and trucks transported the oil from the fields to the

DOI: 10.4324/9781003144335-27

harbour, but the harbour only had limited storage of 21,000 cubic meters and had a limited draft.

The maximum you could load in any single vessel was 19–20,000 tons. The vessel also had to present its notice of readiness (NOR) within a very specific two-day window. Otherwise, the lack of storage capacity at the port meant that the trains would be unable to discharge, thereby accruing demurrage charges, which are payable when you fail to load or discharge within an agreed time.

Thinking creatively

Given these challenges, there was traditionally only a very limited market for the crude, which was generally sold to Spain for use in bitumen manufacturing.

The Spanish buyers had relatively low freight costs and therefore were able to negotiate aggressively. Given the quality of the crude oil and its lower value, it would not have made economic sense to ship parcels of 20,000 tons any further afield than the Mediterranean.

We quickly realized that if we were going to achieve higher prices for the oil, we would have to create a new market and to look beyond Spain.

The key would be to improve the logistics.

Our solution was to charter a larger 80,000-ton vessel, which we anchored off the coast of Malta. Then instead of sending the smaller 20,000-ton parcels to Spain, we sent them to Malta and transferred their oil into the larger vessel.

The journey between Albania and Malta was only about two days' sailing time, which meant that we could manage four deliveries per month using the smaller vessel. The scheduling of the loading and discharge programmes between Albania and Malta were critical.

Once we had filled up the 80,000-ton mother ship with four deliveries from the smaller daughter vessel, the economies of scale for the larger tanker allowed us to take the oil outside of the Mediterranean for the first time.

We started reaching out to customers all over the world, and we began selling Albanian crude into the U.S., to India and even to the Far East. Our newfound ability to search globally for the best prices meant that our deals obviously worked out significantly better than when the oil had been effectively restricted to a single destination in the Mediterranean.

The Canadian company was delighted that Mocoh had managed to boost the value of what was a very unloved and extremely complicated crude. We had effectively created a new market for Albanian oil, which made for a very good story for us.

Kurdish issues

Our experience in Albania of successfully trading a difficult crude grade meant that when in 2010 the Kurdish Regional Government (KRG) announced a tender for its Shaikan crude, we were keen to participate.

Shaikan was another heavy grade – 18–19° API – and this was the first time KRG were tendering for this crude. Many companies participated in the tender, and we ended up winning it. We had put in an aggressive number based on the molecular value of the grade, whereas most of the other participants had figured out that it would be very complicated to market an unknown grade and so had discounted their bids by up to $2 per barrel.

Mocoh had probably bid at least $1.80 higher than anybody else because we hadn't fully anticipated how hard it might be to sell the cargo, particularly given that we weren't a big player with a refining system or a large global trader who might have access to more potential buyers.

We were pretty relieved when we managed to sell the Shaikan cargo to a bitumen business in Philadelphia in the U.S. But then the U.S. government publicly announced that it was unacceptable for the Kurdish authorities to sell their oil independently from Iraq's national oil company, SOMO. Suddenly our trade got a whole lot more complicated.

The U.S. position was that Iraq was a single country and that Kurdistan should not aspire towards independence, either politically or economically. Kurdish oil should therefore be sold through SOMO rather than via Kurdish tenders like the one we had won, and any revenues from Kurdish oil should be remitted to the Iraqi Central Bank in Baghdad.

The U.S. guidance wasn't as severe as full sanctions, but it had the same chilling effect. The U.S. authorities stopped short of an outright ban on U.S. companies buying Kurdish oil, but they did warn firms of potential legal risks, which obviously made our buyer and our financing banks extremely nervous.

We and our buyer had a problem. Our vessel was already heading across to the U.S. when the buyer told us that he wouldn't be able to discharge Kurdish oil onto U.S. soil because of the government guidance. Of course, then the banks started to call us asking what our alternative plans were for the cargo.

We had ended up overpaying to get the wrong cargo in the wrong place at the wrong time. Of course, everyone in the market knew we were holding Shaikan, so every conversation we had with anybody would start with them asking, 'how are you doing with your Shaikan?' When you are in that position, it's like having a wart on your nose that everybody is staring at.

Resolving the Shaikan

The positive element of the trade was that we were holding a letter of credit from a first-class U.S. bank, entitling us to receive full payment under the terms and conditions of our contract.

That provided motivation for our buyer to work with us and to look for a solution. If we had agreed different terms in our contract, it might have been a different story. If we had agreed payment after discharge, for example, and the buyer had refused to discharge, then our only alternative would have been to look for another buyer somewhere else in the world, which would have been a very costly business.

The professional terms negotiated in this sale ensured that our buyer had to cooperate with us rather than refuse to discuss the issue. In a situation like that, your counterparty can become your best friend or your worst enemy. You can either threaten to sue each other, or you can try to make the best out of a difficult situation.

We both agreed to store the oil outside the U.S. for several months and to share the profit when eventually the cargo was sold.

We were fortunate enough to sell the crude from storage at a level that made a return for us, our initial buyer and our financing banks. The buyer was so pleased that we had decided to work with them, rather than just cashing in our letter of credit, that the experience ended up deepening our relationship and we continued to sell oil to them for some time.

We had managed to work through the situation with the buyer, and we had kept our banks fully informed throughout. The way we managed this problem with transparency and professionalism solidified our relationship with our banks and stakeholders.

Sliding doors

We had come from similar starting points with both our Albanian and our Kurdish trades – we believed we could unlock value from a niche grade – but we ended up having very different experiences along the way.

As a trader, there is simply no way that you can get every decision right. You do what you do, and you will make mistakes at times. Blaming yourself or running through 'could haves, should haves' doesn't solve anything.

I founded Mocoh in 1998, and there are not many private independent trading companies that have lasted that long. To survive, there has to be some luck involved. There are choices we made along the way that were either fantastic or disastrous, but sometimes it's hard to tell afterwards exactly what led us to make a particular decision. Perhaps, intuition and years of experience lead to the right decision.

Store of value

I launched Mocoh using my own savings as our initial capital. We picked up some business in Madagascar that got us started, but we really established our name in the marketplace by taking over the contract to manage the Saldanha Bay storage from South Africa's Engen.

Saldanha has six underground caverns, and each cavern can hold 7 million barrels of crude oil. It's a huge facility that was built during the apartheid era to make sure that South Africa always had a few months of oil in storage. They are concrete underground caverns where storage levels can't be assessed from the sky.

The Saldanha facility wasn't that well known when we took on the obligation. I decided to sell the risk and our lease to another trading firm, Arcadia. Little did I know at the time of the sale of this lease that this transaction would lead to one of the most famous, or perhaps infamous, trading plays in the North Sea market.

Between 21 August and 5 September 2000, Arcadia bought such a large number of Brent cargoes that they ended up acquiring more Brent than was actually available, sending the value of the Dated Brent benchmark surging by more than $3 per barrel.

Everybody was wondering at the time what Arcadia was going to do with all their Brent cargoes if they were delivered. The buyers were expecting that Arcadia might have to sell the oil back at a loss. But, of course, Arcadia just shipped all the cargoes down to South Africa and stored them in Saldanha.

Arcadia's Brent play attracted a huge amount of adverse comment as well as regulatory scrutiny, but it certainly put South African storage on the map. Saldanha was very high profile after that, and we had a lot of interest in the facility from other trading houses.

In retrospect, taking on such a large amount of storage was a large position for a start up like Mocoh, but we cautiously and professionally shifted the risk to Arcadia. The line between success and failure is sometimes very narrow. Think about cycling and how many times you might have a near miss and almost get knocked off. If you love cycling, you accept that occasional risk and it doesn't put you off.

Reputation first

In a large oil company, it can be hard to reach a final decision. Any idea passes through so many management layers that by the time it gets to the final sign off by a senior decision maker, it is hardly worth talking about.

In a smaller organization like ours, we can make decisions quicker, and once we make the trade, we accept all the risks and follow through whatever happens. We are 'committed' to the trade: as a smaller firm, we have to see our deals through and make them work, whether that is in Saldanha, Albania or with Kurdish oil.

Our commitment to the trade is so important because trading is not always about money: maintaining our reputation is much more critical. One thing that I constantly try to instil in the traders is that we have to do what we say we are going to do, even if it costs the company money.

It's not great to make a losing trade, but you can always come back from a bad trade. If you lose your reputation, and you do not fulfil your contractual obligations, then you will not be accepted in the market. There are plenty of examples of traders who have misbehaved or let people down. Those traders can never come back again.

If you get a reputation that you are untrustworthy or that you are too aggressive, then I don't think it can work out in the long term.

People in the oil markets still value honesty and integrity, and if you have that, then hopefully people will approach you with projects or stand by you when deals get complicated. It would be extremely difficult to build a successful long-term trading business without respect for your partners and stakeholders.

23 Smoothing logistics

Chris Del Vecchio began his career in energy in 1983 working as an inventory controller within the New Haven Terminal and eventually rose to a position as a crude and products forwarder with Northeast Petroleum. In 1990, Chris moved to BP, where he spent 16 years working as senior lead operator. Stints at Goldman Sachs, Musket Corp and Saracen Energy followed, before he joined PetroChina International Americas in Houston in 2010 and BioUrja Trading in 2013. Chris co-founded the Matrix Global group of companies in 2015, which operates the widely used Matrix Auction Platform, and where he serves as chief commercial officer.

If there's a constant theme throughout my career, it's that I have always looked for better ways to make things work.

I would look at the way we were trading and say to myself, 'well, if I manage to upgrade this one aspect, it's going to increase our profitability. So how can I best optimize it? Let me talk to the facility, let me talk to the pipeline or to the shipping people'.

My goal was always constant optimization. I'd want to understand how the trade was performing on a daily basis and whether it was making money or losing money. Then my next step was to ask myself what I could do to impact our performance.

I guess that attitude must have been hardwired into my character. In part, I don't like just accepting how other people have set things up. Maybe I'm also naturally lazy in some way: I was always asking, 'why are we doing this in 10 steps, when we could do it in five?'

That's how I got where I did: I grew up in a farming community in Connecticut and I never went to college. People loved to tell me that I wouldn't get anywhere without a college degree. But it never held me back in my career because I was always able to come up with better ways of doing things, and my bosses appreciated that skill.

Whenever new projects started up, they would always throw them at me and say, 'go figure out the best way to make this work'. I'd come up with what to my mind was the best way of doing something and then I would let people see if they could shoot holes in my thinking.

DOI: 10.4324/9781003144335-28

Logistic strength

To my mind, logistics is the key to successful trading. A lot of oil traders don't do their time in logistics at the start of their career, or they don't spend enough hours learning about operations and scheduling. They just jump right into trading and that means they don't always understand how the physical market really works.

One of my jobs was always to make sure that our traders weren't committing the firm to something that couldn't possibly happen. When you understand logistics, sometimes you have to step in and bring the guys on the desk back to earth.

Other times you can step in and help fix a problem. I remember back in the mid-1990s, I was working as part of BP's trading and refining group in Cleveland, Ohio, and we were not totally satisfied with the way we were managing our crude oil flows from Colombia.

Our group was handling the trading side on behalf of our exploration and production (E&P) division, which owned equity crude oil production in Colombia in partnership with Ecopetrol, Colombia's state-owned oil company, and French major Total.

The grade we were producing was called Cusiana, and it was a light sweet crude oil, which was produced in the Andes and exported from the Coveñas terminal on the Caribbean coast.

The oil was typically exported in 500,000-barrel cargoes, which were allocated each month in line with the percentage of ownership of the current production. Ecopetrol held the largest share of equity, followed by BP and Total.

It seemed to us like Ecopetrol always received the best loading slots each month. That timing advantage meant that Ecopetrol was able to sell their cargoes at the best prices, and we could never match them.

Our initial focus was to see if there was any way we could get the port facility to give us better loading windows. We came up with the concept that if we started lifting larger parcels – 1 million barrels rather than the normal 500,000 barrels – from the facility, then we should get preferential treatment when they came to assign the loading windows.

There are only so many loading windows that a terminal can allocate in a month, and so we argued that by taking larger cargoes, we would be allowing more cargoes to load throughout the month.

One cargo that loads twice as much volume would free up an additional loading window, which allows another ship to go out each month. My sales pitch was that Coveñas only had 15 loading windows per month, but that Colombian production was only going to continue to rise.

If the terminal would allow up to three of these double cargoes to load out each month, then the terminal would have more loading windows available. That would mean that the Colombians would not need to worry about containment at the facility and about potentially shutting in oil production, which was the last thing that anyone wanted to see happen.

Selling the concept

Once we were clear on the benefits of double-loading, we had to get to sell the concept to our partners and to the Colombian government. That meant lots of visits to Bogotá, and a bunch of calls and emails to show them how it was going to work.

We met with all of the group together, as well as side meetings with each party. We had done the analysis, but we needed to make our case in a way that was understandable not only to the traders around the table but also to the government officials.

We also needed to make sure that everyone understood that double-loading would benefit the entire group, which it would, and that we deserved to get priority on loading dates in exchange for freeing up more slots for everyone.

After all, we were the only ones at that time that were willing to load 1 million barrel parcels of Cusiana, even though in theory any of the other partners could have offered to do the same. Our firm's willingness to double-load was going to help everyone avoid running into issues with containment, so it wasn't unreasonable for us to ask for first pick of the loading slots in return.

After some back and forth, our partners accepted and approved our concept: they would allow 1 million barrel cargos to load, and we would be able to choose their loading windows before the rest of the cargoes in the month were assigned.

Second phase

The first piece of our strategy was in place. We had started out to look at how we could optimize our lifting slots at Coveñas, and we had achieved that.

Now we had to figure out how we could optimize the marketing side. We were going to be bringing bigger vessels to the U.S., but we were going to have a hard time selling those larger cargoes to customers in a single trade.

For a start, there weren't that many ports in the U.S. at that time that could take a fully laden 1-million barrel vessel, and we certainly didn't want to be unloading at multiple ports of discharge as that would hurt our economics.

We clearly needed a better marketing plan for our Cusiana barrels.

We came up with the concept of bringing our double-sized cargoes onshore and storing them in a cavern that we leased at the Louisiana Offshore Oil Port (LOOP). That would allow our customers to decide if they wanted to buy the full cargo or if they wanted to buy smaller parcels.

It also meant that the customers could decide if they wanted to buy Cusiana on an import basis or if they preferred to think of it as a domestic tradeable grade that they could buy rateably.

Our 'Cusiana Cavern' at LOOP gave us total flexibility and upended the marketing model for Cusiana, which had always previously been sold in full cargoes.

We decided to use a BP-owned vessel to basically do a 'milk run' between the terminal at Coveñas and LOOP. That meant that we were using the safest ships, and, if we timed it right, we would even be able to squeeze in two trips per month.

Internally, it was an easy sell. We were optimizing the use of a BP vessel as well as optimizing BP's Colombian equity. It also worked really well on a trading and marketing basis because we could determine when we wanted to lift, and we could offer great flexibility to our customers in the U.S.

Logistic knowledge

The new arrangements turned out great and we marketed our Cusiana production on that basis for quite a few years, significantly enhancing the profitability of our Colombian output.

The strategy only really stopped working quite as well when Ecopetrol decided that they also wanted to lift and market their crude entitlement in larger vessels. That was totally understandable, but it obviously took away some of our unique marketing advantage.

I enjoyed coming up with the strategy – we took the original desire to improve our loading windows and morphed that into a broader concept, where we used a storage play to totally change the marketing side of Cusiana, which we made into a domestic 'foreign' crude.

Of course, to make the concept work, I had to know and understand all of the U.S. customs rules and regulations that would allow us to 'domesticize' Cusiana as well as understand the inner workings of the Coveñas facility.

It's all very well coming up with a strategy that looks like a winner on paper. Often the real skill and the real challenge is in the implementation, which is when a deep understanding of logistics is critical.

The strategy would also never have gotten off the ground if we hadn't been able to build trust with our partners and persuade them that our proposal would help everyone maximize the loading slots available at the terminal.

Now, obviously, I had a secondary agenda, which was that I wanted to be able to lift in certain windows when the market was in our favour, but we never proposed anything that wasn't of benefit to the wider group.

It was a long process, but it ended up being totally worthwhile. Effecting change in this industry is always tough. The oil market is essentially pretty conservative, and you can go crazy trying to persuade people to change the way that they have always done things, even if you are suggesting an improvement.

Everyone says they want to see improvements, particularly in trading and logistics, but often people are reluctant to take any concrete action themselves or to even show interest until the change looks like it will definitely happen.

It's a funky market – I've been involved in it long enough to understand that. You need a lot of patience and a lot of persistence if you want to effect change.

That's always a challenge, but it's a challenge I find hard to resist because I love to try out new concepts and think of ways to optimize.

I still clearly remember the day that we completed all of the paperwork to support our new Colombian strategy. We had gotten exactly what we wanted, and we were about to load our first double-cargo. Instead of celebrating, all I could think about was, now what can I fix next?

24 Trading floating storage

Daphne Teo joined Korean refiner GS Caltex after school in their accounts department in Singapore, before later moving to the operations team. After five years with GS Caltex, she joined Koch Refining as a trading assistant. Daphne moved the Singapore branch of Norwegian oil firm Statoil (now Equinor) in 2000 as an operator for crude oil and refined products. In 2006, she was appointed to the crude oil trading desk. Then in 2011, Daphne moved to Azeri state-owned producer SOCAR Trading as head of crude oil for Asia. Since her retirement in 2016, she has been running a sleep wellness business in Singapore.

I was a very reluctant crude oil trader.

I guess a lot of people that work in commodities might dream of becoming a crude oil trader, but that was never the case for me. I was quite happy working in operations. To be honest, to this day, I still prefer operations to trading.

I guess that's kind of ironic, given how much time I spent trading, but I really enjoyed my time as an operator handling cargoes. It was a real struggle for me when I was asked to move to the trading desk because that wasn't what I wanted at all. I was quite happy where I was.

In the end, they offered me quite good money and so I said 'OK' to the move. I was still young and I thought I could try trading for a while and if I didn't like it, I could always move back to operations.

Although I missed my previous role a lot, my background as an operator gave me a comparative advantage over a lot of young traders or even over some seasoned traders. If you don't know operations properly, then in my opinion you will lack some key expertise when you are trading cargoes.

My time in operations and before that in finance meant that I was very comfortable working through all the potential costs and revenues for my trades. My more technical background meant that I could develop very accurate projections of our risks and of our likely profits.

Floating storage

My background helped me to make a lot of good decisions over the years. I developed a trading style where I focussed on the physical movement of crude

DOI: 10.4324/9781003144335-29

oil, like storage plays or arbitrage trades, which are where you move oil between different regions.

My strategy wasn't necessarily to trade huge volumes of crude, it was more about making decent profits on a particular cargo whenever an opportunity presented itself.

In 2015, the market experienced a very steep contango, which is a period when the price of oil is much cheaper now than it is expected to be in the future.

Whenever a contango structure develops, it makes sense to buy as much oil as you possibly can at the cheap current price level. You store the physical oil and you use the futures market to lock in a higher future price for the oil.

The profit in the trade comes from this time structure – the difference between cheap prices now and higher prices in the future – which has to be higher than the cost of storage and financing to make the trade work.

When you see a contango develop, the first thing that happens is that traders rush out to buy cheap oil and to fill up all of the oil tanks onshore all around the world.

Once all of those tanks on land are full up with oil, the next thing that happens is that some traders will take a long-term charter on an oil tanker and then just anchor the vessel somewhere – basically turning the vessel into another type of tank.

Oil traders call this strategy of using vessels to hold oil, 'floating storage', and when a contango emerged in 2015, everyone started putting cargoes on the water to try to make money out of the strategy.

Early start

At that time, I was running Asian trading for SOCAR Trading, which is part of the national oil company of Azerbaijan. One of my main responsibilities was bringing our benchmark crude oil, Azeri Light, to Asia and selling it. It typically went to Singapore or Thailand, but also sometimes to China.

Before the contango properly developed, we made the call to load a cargo of Azeri Light onto a very large crude carrier (VLCC) tanker that we put on a very long-term charter. Our plan was to bring the VLCC to Asia and to anchor it offshore Singapore as floating storage.

We took that position before the contango even began. It's the skill of a trader to spot a contango developing right at the beginning, before anyone can be sure that it will be a deep contango. You can't wait for the contango to be obvious before you lock in a storage trade.

That's because it takes time to look for a vessel that you can charter at a reasonable price, to organize the loading of a cargo and to figure out where to dock the ship for a long period. You have to take the decision very early on, based on your reading of the market cycle.

By the time that the contango is already obvious, every other trader will be trying to take the same position. When every trader is chasing tankers to use as floating storage, then the cost of chartering a vessel will obviously get expensive and then the trade won't work anymore.

The key to making money on a floating storage play is to get your timing right. That usually means that you have enough experience of the market that you have seen similar situations develop in the past and can recognize the patterns.

Anyway, I was sure we were entering a deep contango and my management was supportive, so we decided to act. We found an available VLCC, loaded it with 2 million barrels of Azeri Light, shipped it across and then let the oil sit for almost a year off the coast of Singapore, while the price of crude slowly rose once more, increasing the value of the cargo.

The crude oil onboard does not spoil, of course, even over such a long period of storage because the vessel has heated tanks, and the oil is kept gently moving.

One's plenty

My boss was sitting in our corporate headquarters in Azerbaijan and when I only booked one VLCC, he was not happy at all. After all, some of the trading houses were putting four or five VLCCs of crude on the water to try to take advantage of the contango.

I was under some pressure to match that. Every day colleagues were calling me to ask, 'why only do one? why aren't you floating more?'

I was getting questioned every day during endless calls from my HQ. It almost got to the point where they were questioning my integrity. They were always asking, 'why are other people doing this, but you can't?'

I faced the pressure head on. It wasn't easy for me to challenge my bosses, but I literally refused and I just put on one VLCC. My experience told me that one was enough.

I had spent years trading for Statoil where we were very focused on inter-regional arbitrages, and I knew that ultimately demand and supply would have to rebalance.

When you enter a floating storage play, you also have to think about how you will exit it. I was convinced that I would not maximize my profits if I stored more than one cargo.

Finding a way out

I knew very well that when a contango comes to an end, there is a sudden rush for the exits.

At that point, everyone wants to end their storage plays and sell the crude that they are holding. That means that a market that is only just recovering from a demand perspective gets suddenly flooded with lots of cargoes, which cannot all sell at the same time. Traders then have to offer heavy discounts just to find a buyer for their oil.

After the contango finishes, the price of oil isn't rising any more, but you still have to pay the costs of chartering the vessel where you are storing the oil. It all comes back to doing a proper cost analysis. Sometimes traders fail to take into account how quickly the costs will add up if they don't get the timing right and sell their oil from storage before it becomes distressed. Otherwise, at that point, the size of the discounts you have to offer is so deep, it can wipe out your profits from the floating storage.

The hard part of a floating storage play isn't just spotting the start of the contango, it's also spotting when it will stop.

You need to predict the trend and to be ahead of it. You must get to work when there's just a slight contango developing and then you must look to exit when you first see signs of the contango disappearing.

Timing is extremely important in this scenario. One day late on a decision can make a huge amount of difference. That's real trading skill: you store the oil for a year, but then you have to pick exactly the right day to sell it.

I timed the market right that time. I managed to sell my 2 million barrels of Azeri Light before the contango disappeared. Because I hadn't been greedy and hadn't stored too much crude, it wasn't too hard for me to find a buyer for my cargo at a very respectable price.

The fact I made over $10 million of profit on that one single cargo justified my decision not to store too much crude.

Other people's decision making was not quite so fortunate. I remember towards the end of the contango, there were traders stuck with distressed cargoes that couldn't find a home. I'm not sure if some of the others managed to recover their losses on those storage trades that year.

Lingering doubts

I was very happy with how my strategy had played out. I got a lot of credit for the performance of that cargo from HQ, but then after the congratulations, sometimes I would hear the comment, 'maybe you would have made three times as much if you had put on three VLCCs like we suggested'.

Of course, I couldn't listen to that. I was pretty direct. I told them, 'I guarantee that if we had put on three, we wouldn't have made anything'.

It's not easy for a Singaporean woman to stand up to Azeri men. The cultures are very different and we both have our own different values. It was not easy to develop trust, and I had to be very strong and very gutsy. But over the years, I proved myself to my bosses, and ultimately they gave me a lot of authority to put on the positions that I wanted.

Even after I announced my retirement, I ended up staying on at SOCAR Trading for another seven months to help my boss find a successor to run the desk. I was enjoying myself and I wanted to help the firm carry on making money.

Time pressure

I always enjoyed the physical aspect of trading. Even making decisions around major plays like the floating storage trade wasn't really stressful for me. For me, the stressful thing was watching the oil futures markets.

I traded a lot of Brent and WTI futures, and those markets are trading around the clock, so it was really time-consuming. The futures can move so much that you don't really want to take your eye off them.

Trading definitely impacted my family life because I didn't spend much time at home. I would usually get to the office at around 11 am and spend the working day there. After that, I would go out for entertainment in the evening with our customers or counterparties, after which I would work on the Brent market and then later the WTI market. I would get to bed around 4 am every day.

It was only Saturday and Sunday that I was at home. So my son didn't really see me that much. Of course, he was already in his teens when I was working those hours, but it was still very tough. That's the part of my career that I did not enjoy.

There were many years when I didn't really sleep properly. My health definitely suffered from my work, and in 2016, I suffered a slipped disc that meant I was not able to walk or sit properly for a while. That was when I started to think seriously about retirement. More money is always useful, but it's important to have a life. When your health suffers, your perspective switches.

Drinking culture

Although operations was and remains my first love, I don't regret moving to the trading side of the business.

The move did change me, though, as a person. The atmosphere was very different, and I found I had to be more manly. When I started out, the men were pretty rough. I was quite a sweet girl, but I realized I had to get tougher, especially when I stepped into the trading environment.

When I was first promoted in the mid-2000s, there weren't many senior female traders around. In fact, there can't have been more than four or five of us in the industry. We had to look out for each other because it was challenging, you still had to be aware of how some of the guys might start behaving whenever we had parties or client functions or even after a few drinks.

I had to toughen up fast, especially when I was negotiating deals. Some male traders tend to be harder on female traders, so I had to be equally hard as well to get anything through.

The drinking was also another thing I had to get used to. Whenever we had a problem with a trade, the men would say, 'let's have a beer and talk it over'. We always had to have a few beers to get anything sorted.

I am actually allergic to alcohol, so in the beginning, it was pretty bad. After a while, my immune system kind of gave up the struggle, and I stopped being so sensitive to alcohol. Part of my training as a trader was training my body to tolerate alcohol.

I still remember in my younger days when I was in Korea. We had a dinner, and there was one crate of the Korean spirit soju for every two people. I just had to swallow it down. As a female, you couldn't afford not to be seen to be tough.

Oil trading was a male-dominated environment, but most of the time I enjoyed the work, and although I used to dread some of those drinking sessions, I ended up making a lot of very good friends in the industry.

I miss the excitement of the market, and those moments where you spot something happening, like a contango developing, and you back yourself to profit from your experience. Those are the best times, when you are sure you are right and your results prove it.

What I don't miss are the working hours. Trading is not an easy job for someone like me who has workaholic tendencies because there's always something happening 24 hours a day. I was never one of those traders that was able to distance myself from the market; I was always too deeply involved.

25 Trading around strategic storage assets

Justus van der Spuy majored in law and economics at the University of Stellenbosch before obtaining an MBA from the University of the Witwatersrand. After graduating, he worked in the international trade division of Credit Suisse in Zurich as an exchange student. Justus joined Standard Bank Group (SBSA) upon his return to South Africa, where, as a member of the international division, he worked in foreign exchange and bond trading. He worked on the rescheduling of South Africa's foreign currency debts following its 1987 default and was a member of SBSA's foreign trade team. In 1990, he joined the Strategic Fuel Fund, which was responsible for South Africa's crude imports and its strategic petroleum reserves. Justus later joined independent energy trader Masefield in London, eventually becoming chief executive. After leaving Masefield in 2010, Justus was appointed managing director of Ambrian Energy. In 2012, he left to co-found Capital Energy Resources with Enrico Ganter, which provides energy advisory, transaction structuring and management services.

I had been working for the Standard Bank Group as a foreign exchange and bond trader when I was seconded across to work within the Strategic Fuel Fund (SFF) of South Africa.

It was 1990, and at that time, the SFF was responsible for procuring around 400,000 barrels per day of crude oil for four major refineries as well as maintaining an enormous strategic petroleum reserve (SPR) of around 125 million barrels of crude oil, which was equivalent to 300+ days of net crude oil imports for the country.

This huge SPR was a consequence of the international sanctions against apartheid-era South Africa, which had left the government extremely concerned about sanctions-driven disruption of the country's liquid fuels supply.

By the time I joined the SFF, South Africa was heading towards free and fair elections for all its citizens, and while the sanctions environment had relaxed somewhat, the energy environment was still very challenging. Saddam Hussein's August 1990 invasion of Kuwait took the oil price from the low teens to the high 30s, as well as dramatically changing relative prices along the forward curve.

DOI: 10.4324/9781003144335-30

The effect of the events in Kuwait across 125 million barrels of SPR oil and 400,000 barrels per day of imports was, to say the least, thought-provoking for a small, young SFF team keen to implement some new ideas.

Despite the disruption, the SFF's policy priority changed from guaranteeing supply to reducing the cost of oil being procured, identifying and managing extreme price risk and implementing a more conscious management of our SPR assets.

In the apartheid era, international traders like John Deuss and Marc Rich had combined both the physical supply and the pricing mechanism, which obviously was not ideal for South Africa, albeit at the time the government's priority was simply to maintain supply.

Our team decided to disintermediate pricing and supply, which led to us independently hedging the price of the oil that we were buying. We had just experienced the impact of significant market changes on the assets we owned, so we enthusiastically grasped the opportunity to make sense of these structures and reduce the cost of the SPR programme.

SPR policy

I can confidently say that the whole concept of proactively managing SPR stocks originated in the work of the SFF in South Africa in the early 1990s.

At that point in time, no other agency paid attention to the real cost of maintaining a SPR or the impact of relative prices over time on storage assets/inventory, let alone to proactively harnessing market structure or any other mechanisms to lower the cost of holding SPR stocks.

This was surprising to us, to say the least, given how many countries had by that time invested billions in building up their SPR programmes. It seemed to us that, much as had been the case with South Africa under apartheid, economic rationality was an early casualty once the word 'strategic' was invoked.

After the oil shocks of the 1970s and 1980s, more and more governments had adopted the policy of acquiring and holding static stocks of liquid fuels to protect their economies from any future supply disruption.

This approach was later formalized and standardized, so that member countries of the International Energy Agency (IEA) are today obliged to hold 90 days of net oil imports as an SPR.

While many government SPR agencies were highly indifferent to the cost of these energy supply security policies, the SFF had proactively managed South Africa's SPR with enormously beneficial financial consequences.

When I went in 1992 to work for Jim Daley's newly created trading house, Masefield, we immediately began to work with national SPR agencies to encourage them to manage their strategic stockpiles more efficiently.

Masefield partnered with at least a dozen SPR agencies over the years, but it was rarely a straightforward process. Strategic stocks are typically treated as an insurance policy, and one that is not later subjected to critical or actuarial review.

The simplest course of action, particularly if prescribed by law, is to do nothing: buy the oil, store it and sit on it, perhaps with occasional quality exchanges or 'refreshments'.

Doing anything more innovative typically requires a change of regulation, which is difficult and time-consuming. Ministers are understandably reluctant to see their energy agencies entering into hedge transactions or buying, selling and swapping oil.

The risks are all skewed to the downside. Officials who make costly mistakes can get fired, but, even if they save their country tens of millions of dollars annually, they will not receive a bonus or stock, as they might in a privately owned business. All of this makes it difficult for agencies to change the way they have historically run their SPR programmes.

Our approach was to run educational seminars for officials in which we explained that it was entirely possible to run an SPR more efficiently and to do so safely and within the existing SPR policies. If they showed interest, we invariably offered to enter a small trade that illustrated all facets of the transaction: operational risks, management of price risk/exposure, margins, risks, and costs.

These smaller transactions provide lessons that can be applied across the SPR, thereby hopefully increasing the willingness of the Men from the Energy Ministry to do more of the same.

The value of time

We used different techniques to create value around SPR assets, depending on the shape of the forward oil price curve.

In a backwardated market, where future prices decline progressively from prompt values, an agency can upgrade its stockpile and make gains by executing a hedged time swap. This presumes a willingness or ability to reduce the volume of oil held in the SPR for a defined period while one grade is removed first and it, or an alternative grade, is resupplied in the future.

In the late 1990s, one European SPR agency wished to dispose of a heavy sour crude oil melange that had been in storage since the mid-1980s and upgrade it to lighter, sweeter crude grades that their local refineries were more likely to process in an emergency.

The question for the agency was how it could avoid or reduce the upgrading cost as implied by the quality differential between the crude it was disposing of and the market price of the higher-quality oil which it would later purchase, once the storage had been vacated?

Our solution was to ship the blend of medium gravity, sour crudes that had been held in the Wilhelmshaven caverns to an Asian refinery on a formula discounted by $3 per barrel to Dated Brent, while we simultaneously hedged the later purchase price of the replacement North Sea Forties crude using the appropriate forward Brent month and paying a small quality premium of around 20 cents per barrel.

The Brent price for the future delivery month was $6.50 below Dated Brent, which gave us a $6.50 margin to subsidise the $3.20 quality difference between the two grades. We used the remaining $3.30 to recover a net shortfall in freight costs received from the Asian buyer, pay freight on the Forties being resupplied to the SPR and still bank in excess of $1 per barrel after all transaction costs were covered.

The SPR agency's willingness to allow a six-month delay between the time of disposing of the 'old oil' and receiving the 'new oil' made it possible for us to harness the $6.50 backwardation, thereby securing the financial objectives required to deliver a zero-cost SPR quality upgrade for our client.

We also carried out a similar transaction for South Korea's KNOC in which we harnessed backwardation to swap two Middle East sours, creating a significant increase in the volume of the return oil at no cost to the client. These transactions represented massive leaps into the relative unknown for these agencies.

Excess holdings

In the years after the 2008–2009 financial crisis, global petroleum demand was weaker, and we met several governments to point out that, while following the IEA guidelines and holding strategic reserves equivalent to 90 days of pre-crisis net imports, they were now in effect holding, say, 120 days of net imports in the SPR. This is also what happened following the COVID-19 pandemic.

With demand not predicted to return to normal pre-crisis levels for another 12–18 months, it made sense for the SPR agency to release some of the surplus 30 days of coverage to the market. By taking prompt delivery and on-selling this oil at current prices, Masefield used the opportunity to immediately hedge the future replacement of the oil at a discount to the prompt value. In exchange, we paid a share of that gain to the SPR agency in lieu of a fee for the interim use of the oil.

The alternative of the SPR agency 'sitting on' the oil would have meant forgoing a share of this gain, while the underlying oil had no defined SPR 'insurance' purpose in the meantime. Releasing the oil meant that the policy objective of holding 90 days of net imports was still being observed. By having the right to redeliver the oil and repay the oil 'loan' early, Masefield obtained a valuable option to take advantage of the contango and buy oil at a discount to the future contracted redelivery month, if this change in market structure were to occur in the meantime.

These were highly rewarding, low-risk transactions, and by sharing the hedged profit with the SPR agencies concerned, whether through a cash payment, better quality oil being returned or more oil being returned than the volume released to us originally – or a combination of all of these – Masefield created significant non-speculative value.

There are other techniques that can be employed in a backwardated market to secure value from storage assets, which ordinarily tend to be less than full in those market conditions. For example, government storage owners can earn option income by granting producers or traders the right (but not the obligation) to access their spare storage in the future, in return for a few cents per barrel per month being paid now.

Other reasons for acquiring such an option include a producer or trader securing a bolthole to be used if the value of their particular grade were to come under pressure, or they need to take some oil off the market due to unforeseen events. In this situation, access to land storage may be cheaper than floating storage, particularly if freight rates are high.

In all these instances, a few cents per barrel buys an insurance policy or an option on harnessing a future contango, while the storage holder – the government – earns some additional income.

Harnessing contango

There are different techniques that SPR programmes can use when the market exhibits a contango structure, which is when prices for future delivery are progressively higher than prices today.

The market was in a deep contango in the early 1990s, and we realized in South Africa that our enormous storage caverns in Saldanha Bay provided us with some attractive trading opportunities.

We started to pre-purchase bulk supplies of crude oil for Caltex's Cape Town refinery, put it into storage and then pump smaller batch volumes to them over the rest of the year. The cost of buying the oil, putting it in storage, hedging and financing the future sales was still much lower than the value received from selling hedged oil for pipeline delivery in the future.

Later as Masefield, we brought larger quantities of prompt oil into Saldanha Bay and then, during the months that followed, delivered pre-hedged oil in smaller (300–400,000 barrel) parcels to satisfy our term supply agreements into Madagascar and Tanzania.

No one could understand how we could compete with the majors to supply East African refiners in these quantities, but our ability to buy and ship in bulk and to lock in the contango on later sales paid for the additional logistic costs.

From the government SPR storage facility owner's point of view, securing rights of first refusal to buy the oil being stored by third parties in your storage facilities before this oil is one day re-exported or sold can effectively count towards holding SPR reserves – all at no financing cost to the host government.

Using options

Beyond the physical trades we were able to pull off, I would like to see SPR agencies making more use of derivatives and options in particular.

After all, the real risk for most governments is not that the country will not be able to secure oil from somewhere. (No disruption event since the 1970s has ever seriously or sustainably compromised the physical availability of oil.) It is more that at some point during a rise in market prices, there is a pain threshold for an economy, which becomes unbearable. Why not buy some out-of-the-money call options to mitigate against that price risk?

For every additional physical barrel of oil in the SPR, there is a declining probability of its 'deployment in anger'; of its being used for the purpose intended. Yet the cost of buying, storing, financing and managing that oil is more or less constant.

Why not then hold lower physical inventories and augment SPR policy by holding a constant portfolio of call options, which can be more flexibly deployed or traded if oil prices rise, regardless of whether driven by a supply disruption or not?

Even if such an options portfolio continually degrades to zero, the option premium paid may be lower than the real cost of holding physical oil in storage.

This approach would also allow governments to think more deeply about their country's unique trade-off between supply risk and cost and to define what level of price rise is tolerable for their economy.

If, for example, a government is willing to take the first $15 of price risk or define an absolute 'pain threshold', such as $100 per barrel, then it could buy out-of-the-money call options at a relatively low cost.

Market neutral

We continue to run seminars for government agencies to heighten their awareness of the inherent value that they are holding and understand the consequence of outright and relative oil prices on these assets over time. Whether or not the officials then act is a different matter.

Paradoxically, it was often the smaller countries that ought to have felt themselves very vulnerable to disruption – South Africa, Taiwan, Israel, South Korea, Ireland and Hungary – that were more willing to experiment and look for efficiency gains.

In contrast, the biggest SPR asset owners of all – Japan, India, China and the U.S. – face the biggest bureaucratic hurdles, whether arising from legislation and public procurement policies or from a desire to maintain secrecy around SPR assets and objectives. The systems in those countries do not incentivize innovation.

It is obviously each different government's prerogative to do whatever they feel necessary to ensure security of energy supply. If they want to put oil in storage because it helps them to sleep at night, then that is fine, but they ought to at least be able to quantify the cost of their approach.

In my opinion, the IEA should be at the forefront of questioning the validity of current SPR policy guidelines. They do a lot of good work, but the policy approach to strategic storage of liquid fuels has not visibly altered since the 1980s, unlike the energy landscape, which has changed and continues to change dramatically. Submitting the 90 days rule to actuarial scrutiny would be a good place to start.

Whatever its origins, it is a crude (pardon the pun) and unsubstantiated one-size-fits-all policy that ignores modern energy interdependence as well as the unique disruption exposures faced by each IEA member country in terms of geographic location, gross domestic product (GDP) impact of liquid fuels prices and so on

Shifting energy mix

These policies are outdated and expensive in the face of an energy sector which is changing incredibly fast, and to see governments still making 30-year investment decisions by committing capital to buy oil and build storage tanks seems to be a non-optimal or even irrational allocation of capital. Calling something 'strategic' ought not to provide immunity to commercial and actuarial 'interrogation'.

I have said that every further barrel added to an SPR programme has a declining probability of deployment, so it is worth each country determining at what point on the range between holding 0 and 90 days SPR inventory, or more in the case of Japan and others, the probability-adjusted cost of holding each additional barrel in storage exceeds its usefulness as a physical insurance policy and could be replaced or augmented by option strategies.

Arguably, the drive towards 'net zero' may bring about an early and sustained ceiling to oil demand and supply. Oil demand destruction poses a graver risk to producer countries, whose economies are also often more one-dimensional and exposed to oil demand and prices than to consumer countries.

In any case, as the energy transition gathers pace, governments that are truly concerned about securing uninterrupted supplies of energy to drive their economies need to move way beyond traditional liquid fuels policies.

A modern government could be looking to ensure continued access to, or inventories of, rare minerals, battery metals, microchips or the materials required to harness solar and wind energy and so on as part of a comprehensive energy supply security plan.

In a world where renewable energy is ever more important, genuine energy security should be about more than storing crude oil in the ground.

Trading new crude oil grades

Crude oil is a finite physical commodity. New fields are discovered, their oil is produced, and then, they are eventually depleted and decommissioned. This means that the market is constantly dealing with the launch of new varieties of crude oil, known as 'grades', as well as with the decline or changing nature of older well-known grades.

Typically, grades start out as the output of a single large field development, such as the famous Brent field in the U.K. North Sea, but as those fields mature and production falls, often the output of similar nearby crude fields is blended into the existing grade, eventually becoming the main source of supply, even though the original brand name is retained.

Any change in the make-up of a grade affects its quality, which is most commonly expressed in terms of API and sulphur content. The API – American Petroleum Institute – gravity measures the density of the petroleum – how free-flowing it is – while the sulphur content affects how complex it will be to process the crude oil into low-sulphur products like gasoline and diesel.

The following chapters illustrate how, as with all changes in the established market structure, the launch of new grades represents both a challenge and an opportunity for traders.

Sellers have the opportunity to market a new grade in a new way, to find new buyers or to develop new logistics. Buyers that are more advanced, such as India's Reliance, can try to find bargains before a grade becomes popular. Meanwhile, others can take a view on the impact of the new grade on regional and global supply–demand balances.

The emergence of new grades or blends can also be an important time for the producing country, which may be expecting both an uplift in revenues and to make a statement to the market and to the world.

DOI: 10.4324/9781003144335-31

26 Marketing the first Brent

Richard Johnstone joined BP's supply department in 1966, after graduating in chemistry from Oxford University. In 1969, he was posted to BP's Italian subsidiary in Milan, and on return to London in 1971, he was appointed assistant crude oil sales manager. Richard worked in international marketing for Kuwait National Petroleum Company from 1972 to 1974 and was product manager for Marlin Oil Trading between 1974 and 1978. He was one of the first oil traders to join the British National Oil Corporation (BNOC) in 1978, and in 1981 was appointed manager, crude oil trading, before being promoted to general manager, supply in 1982. In 1985, he joined BNOC's successor, the Oil and Pipelines Agency, as general manager, supply, trading and participation. Richard joined BG Group in 1990 as manager of oil sales and transportation, a role he held until 1997, when he left to set up his own energy consultancy, where he specializes in advice on trading, contractual issues and training.

When I joined BP as a graduate in 1966, the profession of oil trader didn't exist and neither did the oil markets as we know them today.

Most of the companies I worked for in those days simply sold the commodities that they had produced themselves, whether it was crude oil or refined products. What we were doing was really marketing more than genuine trading.

The department at BP that I joined as a graduate was called the supply department, for example, and I think Shell used the same name. Nowadays, that function might be called 'supply and trading' or even just 'trading', but the focus on trading came along a lot later.

It wasn't that we never traded oil, though. We regularly swapped cargoes in one location for another more convenient one, or we swapped different types of refined products, and so on. We just didn't think of what we were doing as trading.

That kind of business at BP and Shell was called 'exchanges'. The section responsible for those transactions would find a counterparty to, say, take a cargo in Italy and give another back in northwest Europe, or to take a grade from the Middle East and provide a different one from Venezuela.

Once we produced a huge surplus of gasoil, for example, which lasted for some months, and we did an exchange for some heavy fuel oil with Amerada

DOI: 10.4324/9781003144335-32

Hess. Those exchange deals were relatively rare, and they attracted a lot of attention internally. Deals were done at a very senior level indeed: the product exchange was handled by one of our general managers directly with Leon Hess himself.

Growth of trading

Of course, this was oil trading in all but name, although the term wouldn't have meant much to us at that time. We did become more aware of trading as a concept over the next few years, during the 1970s. In particular, we started to hear more about those companies that had started getting into the business as trading intermediaries.

These were firms that had no real physical assets to speak of, but who were increasingly finding a role stepping in to take positions in between the larger traditional oil majors and the national oil companies (NOCs).

Much of what those early traders – people like Bulk Oil and Mabanaft – were doing was what we would now call 'breaking bulk'. Firms would bring larger vessels filled with refined products into northwest Europe and then redistribute the cargo in smaller barges.

People like Marc Rich of Philipp Brothers, who later founded Marc Rich + Co, the forerunner of Glencore, were also beginning to find a niche as an intermediary between countries and companies that perhaps didn't want to openly trade with one another.

Marc Rich became one of the most prominent of the early oil traders and probably came to define the popular image of an oil trader. He certainly rose a long way from when in 1972 he acted as a broker to help me sell a cargo of Iranian crude oil to a Spanish refiner. The oil was valued at just $1.27 per barrel, and I paid Marc one cent per barrel in commission for his assistance. Hard to imagine those prices now...

Trader as a profession

The first time that my business card actually said 'oil trader' on it would have been in 1978 when I joined the British National Oil Corporation (BNOC), which had been established in 1976 as the U.K.'s state-owned oil company.

After leaving BP in 1972, I had stints at what was then called the Kuwait National Petroleum Company, and then at Marlin Oil Trading, which was the marketing arm of a large private Italian refiner.

I had just returned from holiday, and when I got back to the United Kingdom, I opened up that week's *Petroleum Argus* and to my astonishment – and I don't think Argus has done this before or since – they were reporting a job advertisement looking for people to go and work for BNOC.

I joined BNOC as one of its first oil traders. U.K. North Sea oil production had only just started, and BNOC's access to oil was in its very early stages, but they were assembling a team because they knew that output would build up quickly.

BNOC's total sales volume eventually got up to around 800,000 barrels per day, which made us one of the biggest crude sellers outside the large national oil companies (NOCs). BNOC became a very influential company with a leading position in the international oil business.

When I arrived there in 1978, we truly were trading rather than simply marketing. We both bought and sold crude oil. A lot of that buying was still on a term basis, but not all of it, and we started to buy and sell crude on a spot, one–off basis.

The bedrock of BNOC's activity was clearly marketing the oil that was coming in from other North Sea producers as well as our own equity oil, but we also made third-party purchases to balance our system and to optimize the portfolio.

U.K. North Sea develops

I arrived at BNOC at a very exciting time for the British oil industry: production from the giant Forties field in the U.K. sector of the North Sea had begun in November 1975, and the first oil from the world-famous Brent field had been produced in November 1976 and initially loaded into tankers offshore.

Incidentally, Shell-Esso named all of their U.K. North Sea fields after seabirds, with Brent named for the Brent Goose. But the rumour in the industry was that Shell-Esso had in fact named their first discovery, A-UK, because it was their first commercial field in the U.K. They planned to name the next fields B-UK, C-UK and so on. But they swiftly realized they were going to have an issue with the F field…

In this version of the story, the partners decided instead that A-UK would be better read as Auk, a seabird, which then led onto Brent, Cormorant, Dunlin, Eider, and the rest of the seabird fields.

Whatever the truth about the origins of its name, Brent crude oil and oil from the nearby Ninian field, together with crude production from other producing oilfields in the area – the two streams were later combined into Brent Blend – were pumped through pipelines to a new terminal facility built at Sullom Voe in the Shetlands, which first became operational in November 1978.

I was part of the team that sold that first cargo loaded from Sullom Voe. That cargo went to a German refiner: at the time, we mainly sold to European refiners, but we quickly decided to diversify our sales and we started to promote North Sea oil to buyers in the U.S.

I remember plenty of marketing trips to visit refiners in New York and Houston during my first few months at BNOC. We were very fortunate in our timing: just as the U.K. North Sea was starting to develop, the oil market was thrown into an uproar by events in Iran.

In the same month that we sold that first Brent cargo from Sullom Voe, the Iranian oil workers' strike reduced production from around 6 million barrels per day to around 1.5 million barrels. The situation escalated in February 1979 when the Shah left Iran to go into exile and Ayatollah Khomeini was invited back to Iran. In November, Iranian revolutionaries seized the American Embassy, and the U.S. government responded by imposing an embargo on Iranian oil.

Not surprisingly, there was a shortage of oil globally throughout 1979–80, and the oil price more than doubled within 12 months.

Stand and deliver

The U.S. was really pleased to see the U.K. North Sea take off because events in Iran had disrupted everything. The U.S. was the world's biggest importer, and obviously, the U.S. refiners were very concerned about their oil supply.

We received numerous visits from various U.S. buyers to BNOC's headquarters in London. Some of the delegations came from the absolute middle of the U.S., where they were right at the end of the pipelines that brought oil up from the Gulf coast.

They might not have understood much about the global oil markets or about what was happening in the U.K. North Sea, but they certainly understood that we had crude oil, which they needed desperately, and so we were suddenly their best friends.

From the start of production in the mid-1970s, the U.K. got up to 1.5 million barrels per day by 1980 and to 2.5 million barrels by 1985, so we were a significant help in filling the gap left by Iran.

The events of 1979 ensured that this was clearly a seller's market, and so we started to consider whether we could sell our crude oil in a different way in order to maximize its value.

Until then, we had exported all of our crude oil to the U.S. and elsewhere on a free-on-board (FOB) basis, which means that the buyers brought their own vessels to load our oil, which gave the buyers a lot of flexibility.

We decided that we might be better shipping the oil ourselves to the U.S. and selling it on a delivered basis.

Selling on a delivered basis would allow us potentially to make some extra money on the shipping side. (Remember that, in that period, the cost of shipping was really quite a large percentage of the final price.) Selling our oil on a delivered basis would also give us more control over where our crude was ultimately going.

We decided to approach a number of our existing U.S. customers to see if they would be prepared to buy on a different basis.

I went on a road trip to see our U.S. customers along with three colleagues: a shipping guy, a lawyer and a planning/technical colleague. We first went to Houston and had meetings there, and then, we flew up to Oklahoma City for a meeting there. Then, we hired a car to drive to Tulsa, before flying to Chicago and New York.

Driving along the turnpike between Oklahoma City and Tulsa, we passed farms and houses that each had an oil well in their back garden. Those little nodding donkeys that perhaps produced five or ten barrels per day brought it home to me just how different the U.S. oil industry was from the rest of the world and particularly from the North Sea, where we were working on giant developments far offshore.

Our discussions were not straightforward but they were ultimately successful. The U.S. refiners were keen to retain access to U.K. oil, and so they accepted our proposition. Partly because of the jetlag and partly because I was nervous about ensuring the trip was a success, I hadn't slept much throughout the trip, but I still managed a very nice dinner in New York with some very good wine to celebrate a successful mission.

Stand and deliver

The strategic move to delivered sales worked well for BNOC, although it wasn't always simple from an operational perspective. The vessels were often delivering to multiple companies, and so we would have to mathematically allocate what was discharged and then invoice the buyers accordingly.

Although successful for a time, the switch to delivered didn't end up lasting too long though. The oil markets are always cyclical, and the oil supply crisis that was brought on by the Iranian Revolution eventually corrected itself.

As the tightness in the market eased, it became clear to us that selling on a delivered basis would no longer be so profitable or easy and that there would be more resistance from our customers.

We were fortunate that we didn't have long-term shipping contracts in place, and so we were able to extract ourselves from the delivered strategy and revert to selling on an FOB basis.

This was the first time that North Sea crude oil had been exported on a delivered basis, and it was another couple of decades before that happened again regularly. Of course, nowadays, it is not unusual to see North Sea grades sold on a delivered basis, although now the destination is typically Asia.

This period also marked the start of the era of transatlantic sales of Brent and other North Sea grades, which regularly moved to the U.S. and Canada for the next few decades. That trade route became crucial for the global oil markets because it established the relative price of the European Brent benchmark and the U.S. WTI benchmark.

From that point onwards, the WTI price in the U.S. would always need to be high enough to attract North Sea crude imports, which meant that WTI had to be at least equivalent to the Brent price plus the cost of transatlantic freight.

That price relationship proved to be very enduring and lasted until around 2010, when a surplus of Canadian crude oil and U.S. shale oil, added to a lack of infrastructure between the U.S. Midwest and the Gulf Coast, led to the reversal of the Brent-WTI spread. Since then, with U.S. production surging and North Sea output in decline, the trade route that we pioneered has reversed and U.S. crude oil now flows towards Europe.

Trading grows

Even though I had held similar roles ever since beginning my career in 1966, the emphasis on trading definitely increased in the late 1970s and early 1980s.

The 15-day forward Brent market began operating in the early 1980s, and that obviously led to a sharp increase in firms buying and selling North Sea cargoes on a spot basis.

Firms like BNOC saw that trading enhanced profits, while the independent trading houses went from strength to strength, in many cases driven by traders who had started their careers in the academies otherwise known as BP and Shell.

My good fortune was to land in BP's supply department, just as the industry began to gravitate towards active trading and to join BNOC just as U.K. North Sea production was coming to prominence.

The trading team at BNOC was a disparate group. We all came from different companies with different corporate cultures. I believe we managed to retain the best aspects of everyone's backgrounds, which was a credit to the team and to its management.

Maybe it helped that we were all conscious that we were working on behalf of the U.K. by trying to maximize the value of the recent discoveries in the North Sea. We were acting in the national interest, but in practical and commercial ways.

The move towards active trading definitely suited my personality. As a BP university apprentice, I had spent a vacation stint at the BP research centre in Sunbury, which had taught me that I absolutely did not want to spend my career inside a laboratory.

Trading was, and remains, a people-centric business. Throughout my career, I most enjoyed the personal contact with colleagues, counterparties and trainees, many of whom I am still in contact with decades later. The social focus, and the opportunity to work with so many different cultures, have suited me; maybe that's why I had some success in the trading business: ultimately, I like people and I enjoy relating to them.

27 Flexibility plays

A mechanical engineering graduate, Rajaraman Jayaraman joined the state-owned Indian Oil Corporation (IOC) in 1982 after completing his studies. He held several roles of increasing seniority within IOC, rising to be deputy manager in charge of domestic refined products logistics. Following the deregulation of the Indian oil industry, Raja joined Reliance Industries Ltd in 1994, as the private-sector company prepared for the commissioning of its first refinery in 1998. Initially, in a senior logistics role, Raja joined Reliance's trading group in 2000 and was subsequently appointed senior vice president and head of crude oil trading in 2003. In 2016, he took over the role of heading physical trading, which spans crude imports and product exports along with associated commercial chartering and trading operations.

Reliance's Jamnagar refinery in western India is the largest single-site refinery in the world. It has the capacity to process close to 1.4 million barrels of crude oil per day.

Crude is obviously the largest raw material for the complex, and we import nearly 100% of our crude oil needs. When you are not a well-head refinery, you are always thinking of your crude diet, so keeping the refinery supplied with its optimal diet at the lowest landed cost is the priority for my team.

Where we are incredibly fortunate, though, is that the planners of the Jamnagar refinery thought very deeply about the configuration. They had a great vision, and they enshrined the maximum flexibility possible during the design process.

When we are in the market buying and trading oil, we know that we are starting from the advantage of having one of the most flexible processing kits in the world. Whatever grades my traders are considering, we know that the one thing we will never hear from our colleagues on the refinery side is: 'no, I cannot process this particular crude'.

When it was commissioned in 1999, the kind of configuration we have at Jamnagar was very unusual for Asia. This set-up was common in the U.S. Gulf Coast, but not in Asia. When we began operations, it was like we were starting up a large complex U.S. Gulf Coast refinery, except that market conditions in East of Suez are very different. Our regional market is dominated

DOI: 10.4324/9781003144335-33

by Middle East national oil companies (NOCs) that establish their own prices for their oil and predominantly sell on term contracts.

Different terms

Asia has traditionally looked to the Middle East for supply because of its proximity, and Asian refiners have also preferred to buy their oil on a long-term basis because of their concerns about ensuring the security of supply.

Asian refiners traditionally worked on the basis of something like 80% long-term supplies and 20% spot purchases, but we took the conscious call to be lighter on term to the extent we could because we were aware that one of the most important tools for the refinery is to alter its feedstock in response to crude oil market dynamics and refined product market dynamics.

We wanted to be nimble enough to respond to the product market because ultimately Reliance, like every oil refinery, is in the business of adding value to a raw material.

Refiners need to respond to how the refined product markets are performing, and obviously, they also need to respond to how the various price differentials for different crude grades are performing, how tight is the freight market and how is the differential between light and heavy crude oil.

What gives us such great flexibility is our ability to look at globally traded grades of crude oil and identify what works well. We realized early on that operating a huge refining system in one location has its own challenges.

A huge single-site refinery is a different proposition to running a huge global refining system where you have the option to optimize around the globe by switching your term supplies between different regions.

Hardcore techno

That background explains why our approach to crude oil trading is based on what I call a 'techno-commercial strategy'.

At Reliance, we try not to isolate the technical problem or the commercial problem but to address them both together. For example, there might be some technical challenges to processing a tough grade of crude, but we will consider the trade-off against the commercial improvement in our economics and decide if there is sufficient upside.

Our 'one team' techno-commercial approach forces the traders to work extremely closely with the refinery operators. That degree of closeness is perhaps something that's unique to Reliance and that explains why we are so happy to experiment with different crude grades.

I don't think any other refinery in the world has run as many types of crude oil as we have run at Jamnagar. We crossed the milestone of 200 different grades during the early part of the 2020 pandemic, and a year on, we must have reached somewhere around 225 grades.

I can confidently say that we have refined all of the major traded grades of crude. Early on, the largest cluster of our buying tended to be in the heavier crudes, but later on, we kept adjusting our optimal diet, where we blend an extra heavy crude oil with an extra light cargo or a cargo of condensate.

There might be a few grades that we haven't run at Jamnagar, but in those cases, I would guess that they are very small streams or they load in small vessels. Frankly, there must be something very tough about the economics of that grade if we haven't already tried it!

Our techno-commercial trading strategy also enables us to quickly review and to clear new grades of crude oil when they launch. We have developed a good process to clear a grade quickly, and sometimes, we can even clear the grade without seeing a sample because we are prepared to take some calculated risks.

Reliance was the first refinery to process Iraq's Basrah Heavy grade, for example, and more recently, we were the first refinery in Asia to take Canadian Heavy grades on a term basis from the U.S. Gulf Coast.

Our voracious appetite for new and different grades clearly requires a lot of support from the people that run the refinery, as our approach inevitably brings lots of blending issues and lots of compatibility issues. This approach would not succeed if we didn't run the whole business as an integrated whole.

Private move

When I started my career, I wanted to join the private sector because I thought that there was more scope to be entrepreneurial. I like to understand how my role is affecting business performance from a bottom-line point of view.

But when I first graduated, an opportunity at state-owned Indian Oil Corporation (IOC) came along, and, well, that was one of the best jobs an engineer could hope for at that time. It was a very fashionable option for a young graduate.

I joined the marketing division of IOC, where I focused on supply and distribution, particularly domestic logistics. I enjoyed my time at IOC enormously, but with the deregulation of the Indian petroleum sector, a role came up at Reliance.

It's always a bit of a tough one to leave a secure public-sector job, but by that time, Reliance was a well-respected private-sector company so it wasn't such a difficult decision. They were already a major player in petrochemicals, and they had further ambitions to develop the downstream by building refineries that would tie in petrochemical feedstocks.

I thought I should give the private sector a try because it would give me the chance to work for a business that was going to look at its activities in a more commercial way.

When I started at Reliance, I first worked on visualizing the logistics of the refined product distribution from our new refinery. I spent 1994 to 1998 thinking about logistics and helping to finalize our plans. We commissioned the refinery in 1998, and then, I spent a further year and a half finishing up all of the product distribution and placement in the domestic market.

I moved across to the trading side of the business in 2000. This was a significant career change for someone who had previously specialized in logistics, and it was nice of Reliance at that stage of my career to give me an opportunity in what was considered quite a specialist area.

Trading was a very different world of course. My background in operations was very helpful, and I learnt a lot during my one-year stint in London as a Reliance deputee to Shell's trading company STASCO, but there's a huge amount to learn and absorb, particularly when you are dealing – as we are – with so many grades and so many different sellers.

Different cultures

If you are trading with the same kind of counterparties every day, it must be fairly straightforward. But because our approach is to deal with everybody and to try everything, we have to learn to adapt to work with different cultures and different negotiating styles.

Each of our counterparties has a different personality. On one side, there are a set of sellers who would like to sell only term and to sell on official selling prices (OSPs). On the other side of the spectrum, you have trading houses who are extremely commercial. Then, you also have smaller independent producers who don't have a refining system but have over time set up smart trading outfits to monetize their production.

That variety is what makes trading for Reliance fun. How we approach a problem depends on with whom we are dealing. Our negotiation tactics clearly need to be based on the best way of approaching a particular counterpart.

The continuous learning and recalibration has its own charm, particularly as you become more experienced and you start mentoring your team. You can help the team navigate some of the pitfalls and help them be mindful of their approaches to different issues.

There are certain outfits for whom the relationship is the most important factor. For other outfits, the only thing that is important is price. You need to handle these elements tactfully while at the same time remembering your endgame.

There's sometimes a balancing act that requires us to look beyond an individual transaction and to apply some form of bigger-picture approach to a specific issue.

As the saying goes, there's never a dull moment in trading. It feels like there's always something to resolve.

Reliance University

The area where you start your career stays with you. To this day, I still find I have an immediate connection to the logistics issues around trading. Something that Reliance practiced from day one was that the trading team was built with engineers, such as myself.

We brought in people with an engineering background and then we groomed them in the commercial nature of the business. The guys are generally quick to pick that side up. After all, they all come with a well-rounded field operations background, and many of them are naturals with numbers and logistics.

Reliance maintains an internal programme to build up the trading bench rather than bringing external candidates in. Of course, the quality of our training programme means that a lot of Reliance-trained traders then move on to take roles in other companies.

There are traders that have been trained by Reliance all over the world now in different countries. The discipline and knowledge required by our techno-commercial trading strategy has made Reliance training very valuable, and we have become one of the most important 'universities', developing talent for the oil trading industry.

Next evolution

Going forward, the landscape for the oil industry will inevitably change. In the medium-to-long term, the emphasis on carbon neutrality will change how corporates and countries do business.

A roadmap towards carbon neutrality is going to bring in some new aspects to the energy business, which could make a material difference to our operations.

Over the next decade, we will all be asking ourselves how fossil fuel consumption will be impacted and how might the refining sector adapt.

In January 2021, Reliance's Jamnagar refinery received the world's first major shipment of carbon-neutral crude oil. It was 2 million barrels of U.S. WTI Midland crude that we acquired from U.S. oil major Occidental's Oxy Low Carbon Ventures (OLCV). OLCV announced after delivering the shipment that the greenhouse gas emissions associated with the entire crude lifecycle of the cargo had been offset.

The shape of the deal was that of a structured product. Obviously, nobody today has the ability to do net-carbon zero oil production at this scale. The credits and the carbon impact of the oil were squared off by OLCV with Australian bank Macquarie arranging a bundled offset supply and retirement. This led to the supply of a carbon-neutral shipment to Reliance.

Reliance had several discussions with Occidental on this subject, and we were pleased that OLCV elected to supply its first major shipment to us. We intend continuing to engage in this area.

It is obviously early days for the sector, but this is probably something that is going to change the landscape going forward.

The search for carbon reductions brings a new dynamic to refineries and will make a material difference to how we approach our business over the medium to long term.

As I said before, there's never a dull moment in trading. One of the most enjoyable elements of my role is that there is always something new to learn and to explore, whether it is new grades of crude oil, new counterparties, or new and developing areas like carbon-neutral crude procurement.

28 Refining the first Norwegian oil

After graduating from Trinity College, Dublin, with a natural science degree, Bridie Tobin joined Shell International in 1963 as one of the company's early female graduate recruits. Bridie first worked in supply operations, and then in trading and supply roles in London, before transferring with Shell to The Hague in 1968. In 1971, she left Shell to join a new independent oil trading company Magna Oil and within six months was transferred to Houston, Texas. Bridie returned to London after a year, still with Magna. In 1984, she was recruited by U.K. oil producer Britoil as head of supply and trading. After Britoil was taken over by BP, she was transferred to BP Oil U.S., first in Cleveland, Ohio and then in Houston, Texas. She returned to London in 1992 and retired from the oil industry in 1996. Since then, she has worked with non-profit organizations.

Throughout my lengthy career in the oil industry, I always had the good fortune to be in the right place at the right time. I was even fortunate with my timing in terms of being able to join the industry in the first place.

I had studied geology and geography at Trinity College, Dublin. I loved my subjects but didn't want a career in a laboratory. In 1963, I applied to Shell International in London as part of the graduate intake.

The company had only recently agreed to a request by the U.K. Department of Employment to consider recruiting women graduates alongside the male intake. Previously, women had only been recruited as secretaries.

There were, I think, five women taken on by Shell that year, amongst several hundred males. We were placed in backroom functions, like personnel, planning or supply, which were not departments where graduate trainees were normally found.

A colleague and I were put in Supply Operations. My first awareness of the difference in treatment was when Personnel had to insist to my manager that I be released for the normal graduate training courses. He resisted, questioning their value... It took nine months until I attended the first course.

Similarly, I was not at first given a salary increase comparable with other graduate intakes until Personnel intervened.

The manager was unused to viewing staff from the point of potential. Even a couple of years later, at a salary review, when I queried that the space to show potential had been left open on my report, my division head said,

DOI: 10.4324/9781003144335-34

'oh, my dear, I bet you £5 that this time next year you will be married'. He meant it.

In Supply Operations, my first job involved the movement of refined products in and out of the Pernis refinery in the Netherlands.

Pernis was Shell's largest refinery in Europe. It was what we called a 'balancing refinery', in that it maintained the balance between supply and demand by processing much of the crude oil that couldn't find a home elsewhere. In the 1960s, Pernis acted as the balancing refinery not just for the Shell group of companies but, in effect, for the whole of northern Europe.

Chilly welcome

The job initially involved my attending the important monthly planning meeting that was held alternately between London and the refinery.

I had never been to a refinery, so my first visit was to include a tour. It was mid-winter and very cold. I wore my very warmest bright red coat and thought no more about it. But the whistling began at every site of the facility, and it was a huge place. By the end of the tour, my face was the colour of my coat.

I was exhausted with embarrassment. It didn't get any easier when I was taken to lunch in the senior dining room at the refinery. Everyone fell absolutely silent. They had never had a woman sitting in that dining room at the refinery before.

My Dutch colleagues were polite, but after that first meeting, my department head had a call from his opposite number at the refinery, emphasizing just how important these meetings were and that they expected London to be represented by an appropriate person.

My boss in London ignored their veiled comments and sent me to Pernis again two months later for the next meeting. After that one, the head of the refinery sent a note to the division head in London – my boss's boss – explaining that they were going to upgrade the meetings from now on and would only be inviting senior people.

At that point, my division head told me there was not much more he could do and so London went along with their decision and I stopped visiting Pernis. That was one of my first experiences in the industry.

Birth of spot trading

I transferred from supply operations to a department responsible for processing, exchanging, and trading worldwide on behalf of the group. In the 1960s, most of this activity was between the 'seven sisters' group of major oil companies and governments.

Spot trading was virtually non-existent, and the majors dealt primarily with one another. Change was brought about initially by wars, disasters or embargoes leading to emergency changes at short notice. The need for flexibility led to the breakdown of old attitudes as supply shortages had to be covered.

So began the development of spot trading.

I had been with the group for about five years when I was transferred to The Hague, but I found a different situation in the Netherlands in terms of gender equality.

When I first arrived, the human resources department gave me a list of names and addresses. When I asked what they were, I was told that it was a list of respectable Dutch families that I could stay with. At that point, I was an independent woman who hadn't lived with her family for over ten years.

I went back to my manager and required him to explain who I was and my role in the company. I also asked him to ensure that I received the same expenses and so on as my male colleagues. Previously, female staff had only ever been on short temporary secretarial assignments.

Things did start to change a bit, but I had to prove constantly that I was a serious representative of the company, even with other parts of Shell – I remember, for instance, that the general manager in Finland was impossible to deal with and wouldn't even agree that I should visit the State Oil Company in Helsinki as they held meetings in a sauna!

My role in The Hague was to manage various supply deals and exchanges that Shell had with companies operating in Greece, Portugal and the Scandinavian countries.

Norwegians would

I noted before that I have always been fortunate in my timing, and this role meant that I was lucky enough to be in the right place for the start of the development of the Norwegian section of the North Sea.

In late 1969, I was at a meeting in Oslo with Shell Norway and some representatives from Mobil, when it was abruptly interrupted, and my general manager stepped out. This was to tell him that Phillips had hit oil at its Ekofisk development on the Norwegian Continental Shelf.

That discovery is a famous tale in the industry. It was the last well that Phillips was planning to drill in Norway, after it had spent two years exploring for oil without finding anything. They only drilled it because they decided that it was cheaper to drill another hole than to pay a fine to the Norwegians for not completing their drilling programme.

Their discovery of the giant Ekofisk field obviously changed everything. For my Shell colleagues on the upstream side, they were obviously disappointed that Phillips had succeeded where so far Shell had failed.

From my side, our first thoughts were about the commercial implications. Not surprisingly, the Norwegian government wanted the first cargo of Norwegian oil to be processed in Norway itself. We knew that Phillips would not be able to refine the crude itself because they didn't have a refinery in Norway, whereas Shell had a refinery nearby on the west coast of Norway at Sola. We stepped in quickly and offered to process the first Ekofisk cargo and subsequent crude on behalf of Phillips, satisfying the Norwegian government's desire.

Shell Norway was at this stage purely a marketing company. I went back to The Hague and at their request and with the assistance of a senior Dutch lawyer, we drafted an elegant and straightforward processing contract and forwarded it to my Norwegian colleagues.

This was the first processing deal for Norwegian oil. The only recollection and regret that I have is that our simple text returned to me in The Hague with some added amendments and was no longer so elegant.

The initial consignment of Ekofisk arrived at Sola on 4 August 1971. This was a huge deal at the time. It's easy to forget that back then Norway was not the wealthy country it has become. It was still considered to be a small and relatively undeveloped country. The Norwegians were incredibly proud to have found oil and to have processed it in Norway itself.

After all, the first Norwegian refinery had only been constructed 11 years before in 1960 by Esso, while Shell had completed the Sola refinery in late 1967, just a few years before that first cargo of Ekofisk arrived.

It was incredibly impressive to see how Norway dealt with that first oil discovery. The first element that stands out was the creation of Norway's state-owned oil company Statoil, now known as Equinor, which had a right to a certain proportion of oil discovered in Norway, and quickly developed into a major global player. The other key development was the establishment of what has become an incredibly wealthy state investment fund, built on the profits generated by Norwegian oil.

Shell received a lot of credit in Norway for participating in that first oil deal, and given how important that discovery was to the country and how significant Ekofisk has become as a crude oil grade, being associated with the initial deal remains a significant event in my career.

Trading up

I was lucky to join Shell when I did, and I was very lucky to be on the spot for the birth of the North Sea crude oil industry, but perhaps my greatest fortune was to land in the part of the oil industry – supply and trading – just when it was about to change forever.

I was assigned as a graduate to a department responsible for processing, exchanging, and trading oil in Shell, just at the time that major problems started to emerge with global oil supply. If I had joined the firm a few years earlier, I might have already moved on to some other part of the industry. Instead, I stayed on the trading side, which meant I was there for the explosion of opportunity and flexibility that Shell quickly developed in response to the various oil crises of the time.

When I transferred to The Hague, Shell International was decentralizing. Previously, all downstream activities were headquartered at Shell in

London, while Shell in The Hague was upstream: exploration, production and engineering.

Shell created a small organization of maybe 200 or so staff, separate from headquarters, to coordinate all Shell's supply and marketing activities in Europe. This group was staffed with a cross-section of the brightest and best from Shell's European companies.

It was a very stimulating time. This small group helped Shell to stay at the forefront of the trading scene, which was based in Rotterdam.

The origin of modern oil trading is, after all, the barges of heating oil that were traded and then sent up the Rhine from the refineries in Rotterdam, like Pernis, following the model of the earlier coal market.

That was just the beginning. I returned to London at the end of 1971, left Shell and within six months I was involved in introducing international spot trading in Houston, Texas.

29 Marketing a new stream

Originally from Georgia, David Jorbenaze holds academic qualifications from Gubkin Russian State University of Oil and Gas, Cambridge University and the London School of Economics. He began his career in 1995 as an oil trader with French major Total, based in Geneva, before moving to London in 1998 to join Chevron, where he worked as an oil trader and as director of business development. In 2007, David joined the U.K. trading arm of Chinese major Unipec, where he held the role of trading manager. In 2017, David co-founded BG Energy Ltd U.K., where he serves as senior trader and business development manager.

Not many traders get the opportunity to bring a new grade of crude oil to the market.

We launched CPC Blend from Kazakhstan in 2001 and I quickly learnt that successfully developing a market for a new grade takes a bit of imagination and a lot of extra work.

It always takes some time for the oil market to get used to something new. Refiners are generally pretty reluctant to buy a new grade of crude oil unless it is heavily discounted or they are otherwise encouraged.

There is usually a psychological barrier towards new grades that you have to overcome. The first step is to send all of the potential buyers a comprehensive presentation about the new grade as well as a sample of the oil itself.

Refiners understandably need a lot of reassurance. First of all, they want to be sure that the volumes will be consistent, otherwise why waste their time experimenting with something new?

Second, they want to be sure that the quality will be consistent. Then, third, they want to see how their individual refinery is going to react to the new grade. That's not a quick process: it can take months to process a cargo of crude oil in a refinery and then to sell all of the refined products.

Only once that whole multi-month cycle is complete, will the buyer be confident that the new grade works for the refinery. At that point, hopefully, the buyer will add the new grade to the list of crude oils that they can run regularly in their refinery.

DOI: 10.4324/9781003144335-35

Overcoming doubts

It is always going to take time to overcome that initial reluctance and to get the market comfortable with a new grade of crude oil.

The easiest way to market a new grade is obviously to just sell it very cheaply. If a trader goes to a refinery with a cargo that should be worth 50 cents more than the benchmark and offers it for minus ten cents, then he or she will easily move the cargo because everyone's going to jump on a bargain.

But at the same time, when you are marketing a new grade, your job is to make sure that you are moving cargoes at as high a price as possible and to as many people as possible. Trading is all about relative value. If you are convinced of the actual fundamental value of your crude, then you need to achieve as close as possible to that price.

That requires you to be creative.

We launched CPC Blend crude oil at the end of 2001, after the commissioning of a 1,580km pipeline by the Caspian Pipeline Consortium (CPC) that linked the oil fields in western Kazakhstan to the Black Sea export terminal at Novorossiysk in Russia.

The CPC pipeline collected crude oil from different assets that were owned by two U.S. producers, Chevron and Texaco, which had recently merged. Texaco's specialty was heavy oil and their production had an API of 20–21°, but the bulk of CPC Blend came from the much lighter Tenghiz fields, which had been developed by Chevron and had an API of 37–38°.

I was in charge of the marketing and distribution side of CPC Blend, and our first job was to design a blend of the two types of oil that would be attractive to European refiners. We created a special group that focused on CPC quality – what the final blend should look like and how to regulate quality. In the end, we fixed the quality of CPC Blend at 45° API and 0.56% sulphur.

Fixing the quality and ensuring that it would be consistent removed one of the obvious objections that a potential buyer might have. That meant that any difficulties we would encounter in selling the grade would not be related to CPC itself, but to people's reluctance to embrace something new.

A huge amount of work was done in the background to make the quality of CPC Blend palatable to European refiners, but the issues we faced were more psychological. It was going to be hard work to move the first cargoes at respectable prices.

Sales diversity

If we were going to make CPC Blend a success, we were clearly going to need to diversify our potential pool of buyers. We decided on a three-pronged trading strategy: we would sell within Europe where possible, but look at sales out of the region as needed, and meanwhile, we would develop Chevron's capacity to run CPC within our own refining system.

When CPC was launched, the market wasn't ready to digest as much CPC as started hitting the market. Out of five cargoes that we had for sale each month, it was easy to sell two or three in the Black Sea and Mediterranean or even into the northwest European market.

After those deals, though, we would struggle to sell the remaining one or two cargoes. At that point, we had to look at other markets further afield, like the U.S. or Asia. Early on, we moved CPC Blend to South Korea – it must have been the first Suezmax tanker to ever leave the Black Sea.

Getting that trade done wasn't straightforward, and I had to push and pull on both sides of the deal.

I had to convince our Korean buyers that this new grade was going to be important and that it was worth them taking their time to investigate it. I also had to work with my upstream partners to persuade them why we would want to ship oil all the way to South Korea rather than keeping it in Europe.

Our view as a trading team was that, if we were going to have excess cargoes of CPC Blend, it would be better to compromise a bit more on one or two cargoes by providing buyers outside of Europe with a deeper discount. By pushing cargoes away from Europe, we would support the remaining cargoes in our home region by reducing the alternative supply.

The initial Korean sale appeared kind of revolutionary to some of our colleagues because on paper it didn't look too attractive to move that cargo out of the region. Obviously, we didn't discount the oil too heavily but it was still a difficult deal to push through.

We were getting plenty of questions from senior staff or from the upstream side, along the lines of 'why, when you just sold CPC at flat to the benchmark in Europe, why would you want to discount it to take it somewhere else?'

They all assumed the next sale in Europe would also be flat or maybe slightly lower, but I knew that we had hit the limit of European demand and that the next local sale might be minus 50 cents or even minus $1. It was clearly better for us to acknowledge that reality, to sell our cargo at minus 50, but to then take that oil out of the region, shortening the supply side.

Shipping to Asia

The logistics we needed to work through to make any sales to Asia were not straightforward.

When we wanted to sell CPC into China, for example, we started by shipping two parcels of 1 million barrels to a location off the Egyptian coast where we used ship-to-ship transfer to load them onto a very large crude carrier (VLCC).

We then shipped that VLCC to China, but instead of a single discharge there, we moored the VLCC in a lightering zone, where it discharged into a number of smaller Aframax vessels that could travel up rivers to feed some inland Chinese refiners.

It's a hell of a journey. That oil was originally loaded in the Black Sea. It passed through the Bosporus then through the Suez Canal to reach the Red Sea, where it was uploaded into a larger vessel and then was shipped through the Indian Ocean and the South China Sea before being transhipped again to move inland through the Chinese river network.

The whole journey from Kazakhstan to the Far East used to take around three months, but all of that time and effort was well worth it when the arbitrage was open because the trading margin was quite attractive.

The cost of all that shipping and handling was high, but if you were looking at prices of more than a dollar below fair value in Europe, then the difference between those levels and the price we could achieve relative to the Dubai benchmark in the Far East would cover all of our costs and leave us with a profit.

You have to be prepared well in advance for those arbitrage sales, though, because those windows of opportunity tend to close very quickly. We had to anticipate the situation well ahead of the actual physical loading by taking derivative positions early and getting a VLCC in place.

The beauty of equity flow is that you know the flow of oil will be consistent, which allows you, as a trader, to be a lot more prepared. By the time you get to the physical loading of your vessel, you should have a very clear idea of what you are going to do with it.

Of course, even apart from the profits from individual sales into Asia, arbitrage deals also had the additional benefit of removing some of the excess oil from Europe, which supported the value of CPC in our 'home' market.

Sweet talking

The frequent to-ing and fro-ing before a deal gets done is one of the sides of oil trading that a lot of people don't see. It takes a huge amount of convincing to get some physical deals done and you often need to be both persuasive and creative.

As a trader, you are a salesperson. That's particularly true if you are trying to market a new grade or if you find yourself in an environment where the market is long and everyone is trying to sell cargoes to the same buyers. That's when you have to paint a very clear picture to the buyer of why they should buy from you rather than from a rival supplier.

In order to sell at the best possible price, you need to have a very clear understanding of the market, how many other sellers are out there, what are they offering and at what price. Physical oil trading is all about timing, offering the right grade at the right time to the right person.

We had started to build up our customer base for CPC Blend and our occasional strategic sales outside the region were working well for us. Obviously, as the output of the grade grew, that early development work of building the customer base became even more valuable.

The next big thing we did for CPC Blend was to connect it to our Pembroke refinery in Wales. We looked at the cost of shipping the crude to the U.K. by taking a long-term charter on a tanker. We presented the economics of processing the grade to our management, and the technical people then came up with an idea about how to slightly upgrade the refinery to run CPC optimally.

That work went ahead. Chevron later sold the Pembroke refinery to Valero, but the deal we put in place worked so well that even after all those years that contract remains in place and Pembroke still takes CPC.

Pre-CPC routes

Throughout all my time with various oil majors, I was always excited about finding new solutions and new ways of doing things: expanding the markets and growing the customer base.

I loved discovering new ways of managing logistics and coming up with new options: elements that gave us an edge and put us in a better place versus our competition.

Our ability to innovate paid off for CPC Blend, which has become a well-accepted grade globally, but the need for innovation was perhaps even more critical before the CPC pipeline came online.

Before the CPC pipeline was constructed, we were trying to find a way to the market for the growing volumes of Kazakh oil in any way we could. We were trying to get the oil out via any of the pipelines that were available at the time, which were mostly Russian pipelines, and we used a lot of rail transport – trains would bring the oil through Russia via Ukraine to the Black Sea ports.

Another route, which I put together, was by barge across the Caspian, by rail through Azerbaijan and Georgia, and then by ship from the Georgian port of Batumi.

There were a lot of pioneering developments at that time because the volumes that were being produced were unprecedented and the transport side had not caught up. There were bottlenecks everywhere. We were trying to find anything we could to carry the oil: pipeline, barge, rail, taxi, donkey, you name it…

We were pushing the oil in any direction, even if it might look unprofitable on paper. After all, the key was to keep the oil moving. Shutting in production and stopping the wells is a much more expensive proposition for a company than spending a little more on transportation.

To make things even more complex, at that time, the Russian pipeline operator Transneft did not take into account the quality of the crude you introduced into their system. Everything was treated as if it were Urals Blend, which was a medium-sour grade with 32–34° API.

That was great for Texaco, whose production was heavy oil with an API of 20–21°. Transneft's policy meant that every barrel we moved through the Russian pipeline system would get an automatic upgrade because it was treated as if it was more valuable Urals. That added a few dollars to the value of our crude.

Transneft's policy was great for Texaco's heavy oil but it was a disaster for Chevron's Tenghiz fields, which produced oil of 37–38° API. Tenghiz was much better quality than Urals but it was treated as Urals, and we were losing a lot of value. That's why we were so focused on alternative routes: even if our transportation cost was higher, the difference was made up by avoiding the quality loss.

Once Chevron and Texaco merged, it was clear that we needed to develop an alternative pipeline route to market to the Transneft system. Tenghiz production was so much higher than the heavy Texaco output that using the Russian pipelines was a very costly proposition for us.

The costs we were incurring from that Transneft policy were the driver behind the construction of the CPC system, and therefore the development of CPC Blend.

Major driver

The physical market for crude oil is essentially an enormous jigsaw puzzle. As a seller, you have to put an enormous number of pieces together in order to know whether to sell now, to hold tight, or to store your crude.

As a trader at a major oil company, multiple teams are feeding you with information, and you need to constantly review whether you are positioned in the best way. It's a continual ongoing review process, particularly when you deal with multiple grades of crude.

Everybody in the market sees the same fundamental indicators, more or less. All the information is out there, but at a major, you do have some proprietary knowledge relating to your own system.

I spent virtually all of my trading career in majors, although I had offers from trading houses. Although the majors typically pay less and offer lower bonuses, they give you more chips to play with, they are more consistent and they work to longer time horizons.

After all, only by working at a major oil company would you would get an opportunity to get involved in the development and marketing of a brand-new grade like CPC Blend, which has gone on to establish itself as a core part of the European market.

Helping launch a new blend of crude oil, and establishing its proper value, well, that is something truly interesting that not many people can say they have done. The physical crude oil market is always a very testing environment, and so I got a particularly big kick out of seeing our hard work on CPC Blend pay off.

30 Splitting Basrah

Thomas Løvind Andersen began his career in the oil markets with Shell Scandinavia, where he started as an assistant trading manager in 1996. In 1998, he moved to Shell's London office to work on the North Sea crude oil trading desk. Thomas joined Caltex Trading in Singapore in 2000, where he worked as a senior crude oil trader, before moving to Goldman Sachs and then to Trafigura, where he served as crude oil derivatives manager. In 2007, Thomas joined Bank of America Merrill Lynch (BAML) as trading manager for the Far East, later moving to London in 2011 to become BAML's global head of crude and product trading. He joined Litasco in Geneva as head of crude oil in 2014, retiring from there in 2017 to return to his native Denmark. Thomas currently serves as chief executive of People in Sport, which provides agency and commercial management services to professional athletes.

Crude oil, and specifically the Basrah stream, is the heart and soul of the Iraqi economy. Oil dominates the Iraqi budget and accounts for the overwhelming majority of Iraq's foreign currency earnings.

Basrah crude oil is such a key part of the overall picture for Iraq that any development that touches on the grade is obviously going to be incredibly sensitive.

In the mid-2010s, I was working for Russia's Lukoil, which was one of the biggest producers in Iraq because of our involvement in the West Qurna-2 crude oil development.

The oil from West Qurna-2 was heavy, at around 21° API, and it was also high in sulphur. As production from West Qurna-2 ramped up from 2014 onwards and was blended into the Basrah Light stream, the characteristics of Basrah Light began to change dramatically.

At that time, Iraq lacked the infrastructure to blend the new production into the Basrah stream reliably and consistently, and nor could they successfully segregate it. Inevitably, different cargoes ended up containing different proportions of the new crude from West Qurna-2.

Getting heavy

Sizeable differences emerged from loading to loading. A customer would turn up with their vessel, and one time they would get a traditional Basrah

DOI: 10.4324/9781003144335-36

Light, but then the next time they would get a heavy sour cargo, and then somebody else might get something in between.

You can imagine the difficulties that caused. Bear in mind as well that, because all these cargoes were theoretically supposed to be the same quality, each of these customers would have to pay based on the same benchmark price for their oil. There were sulphur and API escalators in place but these did not provide sufficient compensation.

Even before the specifications started fluctuating, Basrah Light was already a complicated grade to manage. Basrah had a sulphur escalator and a freight de-escalator; some cargoes had destination restrictions while others were free; there were often delays at the load port and different demurrage arrangements; as well as different pricing benchmarks and pricing periods for sales to different regions.

The quality fluctuations made a complicated grade even more complex and risky, and the buyers were soon up in arms. Some of the lifters started reneging on deals and outright refusing to load Basrah Light. Others lobbied heavily for cargoes of a certain quality.

It became clear that something would have to be done and quickly. West Qurna-2 looked set to be Iraq's fastest-growing field for a few years from 2014, so the problem was not going away.

Time to split

Eventually, in June 2015, the Iraqi authorities decided to split the Basrah stream into two grades: Basrah Light and Basrah Heavy.

It was absolutely the right decision, even though that brought with it a period of greater complication. The Iraqis acknowledged that the overall quality of their output was changing and that they would be better served by marketing two separate distinct grades that would each have more reliable quality specifications.

The risk otherwise was that buyers were bidding for every cargo as if they were going to get a delivery of the lowest common denominator, which was effectively West Qurna-2.

The overall theory of splitting into two grades was excellent, but the implementation of the split was a challenge.

No one among our potential buyers had any idea what Basrah Heavy looked like and how it might behave in their refinery.

When you launch a new grade, you often ramp up output slowly and provide a few small test parcels for refiners to trial. There was nothing like that in this case. Instead, suddenly Lukoil and other producers had millions of barrels of Basrah Heavy to sell every month.

You could almost call Basrah Heavy unsellable at first. The grade worked very well for highly sophisticated refineries, but of course other crudes were competing for that access as well.

Heavy marketing

As if marketing a new grade with complex characteristics was not enough of a challenge, we were also facing the issue that Iraq's state-owned oil producer SOMO didn't fully appreciate how difficult it would be for the market to consume their new grade.

In a normal scenario, I estimate that it takes 9–12 months for any new grade to be fully accepted by refiners. During that first period, a producer usually needs to accept a discounted price for their crude in order to encourage refineries to try it out.

SOMO found it difficult to accept that discounts were needed, and so each month we found ourselves faced with an official selling price (OSP) set by SOMO for Basrah Heavy that was simply too high.

We went through a period of around half a year when we were buying the grade at the OSP but selling it at a market price that was inevitably lower. We were looking at huge potential losses as a trading desk. If you buy at the OSP but consistently sell at $1–2 per barrel below OSP, then that will rack up the red ink very quickly.

The situation was clearly unsustainable, and so we had to decide which buttons we would start to push.

Our first thought was to talk to our own upstream division, who were producing the oil, and to see if they could renegotiate a new deal.

The upstream division was earning around $1 per barrel for every barrel that they produced. That payment was irrespective of the quality of the crude, so in theory our colleagues didn't mind whether the oil was heavy, light or in between, or whether the OSP was too high or too low.

For them, as for all upstream companies, it was all about volume: producing as much as you can, as quickly as you can, in order to recoup their massive upfront investment in developing the field.

The upstream division had established other very specific success criteria for the giant West Qurna-2 project, so as a trading desk, we had to look at other ways of solving the issue.

SOMO FOMO

The second button for us was to go to SOMO and to try to explain to them what was going on in the market and what the feedback was regarding Basrah Heavy and its OSP.

I ended up travelling numerous times to Baghdad to visit SOMO for a combination of begging, arguing and convincing. I was always trying to persuade them to lower the OSP, particularly in the first six months after the launch of Basrah Heavy.

Simultaneously, we worked with a couple of professional consultancy services whom we hired to produce independent reviews of the Basrah Heavy crude price. We wanted SOMO to hear from external experts what was going on in the market and why the OSP should be lower.

I felt that one of my roles as a representative of one of the biggest producers in Iraq was to feed SOMO market intelligence, price data and analysis around market behaviour and what might be a fair price for Iraqi oil.

After all, as the global head of crude oil trading, marketing and supply for Litasco, I was the person responsible for marketing and selling our equity crude from Iraq and supplying oil to all the Lukoil refineries around the world.

Interacting with SOMO was a key part of my job. Going down to see them was a hairy experience because at that time Baghdad was not the safest place in the world to visit. It was very binary, either nothing happened, and it was like any other work trip, or something happened, and you were in real trouble.

Every time I went there, I had six armed guards picking me up at the airport, usually Russian or American ex-military in three armoured vehicles, and I was provided with body armour and a helmet. They would drive me into the Green Zone, where I would spend the night in a guarded guesthouse.

The first time I spent the night there, there was an explosion just outside the Green Zone and across the river. We could hear and smell the explosion. Everything was shaking. Of course, we were all thinking was it really worth being here?

But, on the other hand, we took all the proper precautions and then you had to think of all the people who were living there without any protection at all. What was frightening for us was normal life for millions of Iraqis.

Other companies decided early on to do all their meetings with SOMO as videoconferences. We took the decision to go there regularly, and my boss Tim Bullock led by example, visiting several times for meetings himself.

Contrary agendas

SOMO highly appreciated us coming to Baghdad in person even though we were always at odds. The agenda of every meeting was that we would ask for lower prices, while they pushed for higher ones.

Our counterparts at SOMO were and are highly intelligent and well-educated people, and I honestly think they were interested in our views on the market, even if they could not accept our commercial logic.

Our meetings reminded me a lot of when I worked for Shell in Europe in the mid-1990s, and I used to represent the firm at the Norwegian Petroleum Price Council – better known as the Norm Board – which sets tax reference prices for Norwegian crude.

I used to go to Oslo every three months to present Shell's case on what the official selling price of Norwegian oil should be. The experience of spending 15 minutes trying to win over 20 Norwegian bureaucrats was good preparation for our debates with SOMO.

In both cases, I was going in to represent my firm's interests, but with an agenda that was almost diametrically opposed to the people that I was meeting. Saying that, at least no one from SOMO ever fell asleep during our meetings, which happened to me twice in Oslo.

Stimulating demand

As well as trying to improve our Iraqi economics by talking to our own upstream division and to SOMO, we also had to make sure we were marketing the new grade to the best of our abilities.

The benefit of being part of an integrated firm like Lukoil was that we had access to a lot of detailed analysis from our own refineries.

We learnt very quickly about the ideal way of refining Basrah Heavy, the best way to blend it at the refinery, what precautions you had to take, how you had to treat it in storage, and so on.

Of course, we immediately shared any discoveries with our customers. That ability to do much of the testing in the Lukoil refineries was key to getting Basrah Heavy adopted widely as quickly as possible. We saved our customers a lot of time by doing the experimentation ourselves in-house.

Obviously, a lot of the work that we did benefited the other equity owners of Basrah Heavy as well as ourselves, but at the end of the day what goes around, comes around. After all, we all had the joint aim of trying to build up the market for the new grade.

We could also – because we were such a big lifter of Basrah Heavy – offer our customers significant flexibility around loading dates. We would allow them to move dates and so on because we had so many cargoes on offer.

Our refining know-how and our operational flexibility enabled us to offer benefits to our customers that none of the other lifters could match at that point in time.

We also had a very professional set-up in terms of crude trading and marketing, with offices in Singapore, Houston and Geneva. I had a team of very experienced and capable traders who all had contacts at the right level to quickly market and trade those barrels.

We were able to move a lot of Basrah Heavy to Asia, mainly to India and China, and some to the U.S. Marketing the grade got easier with time. The global refining system was increasing in complexity with every year, and by 2018, the more 'difficult' grades like Basrah Heavy were actually in demand.

Light sweet crude like Nigerian or North Sea grades were less popular and the light–heavy price differential narrowed because there was more than enough refinery capacity to run heavy crudes. Refiners were willing to pay almost parity to light crude.

Profit and loss

We incurred huge losses on some of the early cargoes of Basrah Heavy, but we were successful in limiting those losses relatively quickly by developing a market for the grade at top speed, along with our fellow producers.

We were also successful at explaining to SOMO that they should be more flexible about the pricing of their newly introduced grade. By 2016, our Basrah trading was no longer about mitigating losses, it was back to contributing to the firm's overall profits.

Of course, making money in a trading company is the number one thing that makes everybody happy, but the launch of Basrah Heavy was so much more important than trading profits. Making a success of the split of Basrah Light justified the decisions made by the Iraqi authorities and by the very top of our company.

As a trading and marketing desk, we had to get it right, there was no way around it. Of course, no head of a trading company will ever tell you, 'don't worry about day-today profits, focus on this strategic project instead'. But making Basrah Heavy a success was absolutely one of the key success criteria in that period for Litasco and most definitely for our parent company Lukoil.

Diplomatic license

I believe our success in turning a difficult situation around came largely from our ability to manage appropriately our complex relationships with our refiner customers, our upstream division, and with SOMO.

I am Danish and I come from a good Danish social-democratic background, where you are encouraged to seek compromises, to look for alternative solutions and to try to get people together. That was exactly the skillset required at this time.

Some of the best traders that I have met have few or no diplomatic skills, and there may have been times in my career when my attitude has been a hindrance, but I think overall it has been a strength and certainly it paid dividends in our Iraq business.

I have worked for Goldman Sachs, Merrill Lynch, Trafigura and Lukoil, amongst others, which means that I have been exposed to some of the most fierce and competitive environments that you can possibly imagine, but if you are able to keep your head above water and swim, then those experiences will make you stronger.

My time trading has changed me for sure. I am not the same person that I was 20 years ago when I started my career in oil in Denmark and not just because I am older and wiser nowadays.

Trading changed my mindset, and it improved my ability to cope with pressure and setbacks. I hope I have still stayed faithful and honest to my core values, but that has absolutely been challenging at times.

We live in an environment where traders get measured every day. Every single day at the end of the day, you can see exactly how much you have lost and gained. If you run a team, you can watch the results at a global level for all your traders, and in the most sophisticated environments, you can update your positions with live prices every minute. The stress that potentially puts you and your people under is incredible; it is enormous.

If you talk to people who have worked with me over the years, very few of them will say that I am absolutely the best trader they have ever met. They will hopefully, though, tell you that I was a good people manager and that I was good at reading people in different situations, which made me a good judge of strategic opportunities and gave me an ability to manage complex relationships in difficult circumstances.

31 Asia's shift to sour

A mathematician by training, Andrew Dodson, started his career in the oil markets in 2003 as an analyst with Trafigura, before joining Arcadia Petroleum as an oil trader in 2007. Andy rose to become book leader for Arcadia's ex-U.S. oil trading. He held this role until 2013 when he joined Brazilian financial group BTG Pactual as global head of non-U.S. oil. In 2015, Andy moved to investment manager Millennium as a partner and as a portfolio manager. In 2017, he founded the boutique energy investment firm Philipp Advisors, which operates the Philipp Oil Fund, and where he serves as managing partner.

To make real money from crude oil trading nowadays, you have to be alert to the structural and thematic shifts in the way that the oil world turns.

There are a lot of traders who can make a few million dollars per year for their firms in a relatively straightforward way: they know how the prompt market works and how the flat price functions, and that's about all they need to run a successful desk.

But if your ambitions are broader and you want to make a multiple of those profits, then you have to make bigger structural trades. Those opportunities to deliver outsized returns only tend to come when you correctly identify a shift in trade flows or a disruption to trade flows that will change the way that the market works.

Chances to make serious money only come along once in a while. They are infrequent because you usually need a confluence of events to occur. One such confluence played out in 2010–11 when there was a fundamental rebalancing of the pricing relationship in Asia between light sweet crude oil and the medium or heavy sour grades.

Heavy demand

This rebalancing was the culmination of a number of multi-year events.

The first change was in the configuration of Asian refineries. Traditionally, most refineries in the region had been tooled to run light sweet crude oil, but then Reliance developed a major refinery in Jamnagar (see Chapter 27) that was designed to take medium and heavy sour grades. The Chinese

DOI: 10.4324/9781003144335-37

also built a lot of new refineries specifically tooled to run a slate predominantly composed of medium and heavy sour crudes.

Throughout the 2000s, more and more Asian refineries followed this path and started to add desulphurization plants and more sophisticated units to their configurations, enabling them to process what were historically the less attractive medium and heavy sour barrels.

Refinery demand for these less popular grades increased, but at the same time, the local supply of these barrels was quite limited because the OPEC countries, particularly the Gulf States, had cut their output quite dramatically.

OPEC was keen to lift the oil price once more. Prices had stayed stubbornly low ever since the financial crisis of 2008–09, which had obviously had a major impact on demand for oil, and OPEC responded by reducing its output to match the lower demand.

OPEC had artificially reduced the volumes of medium and heavy sour crude coming to the Asian market at exactly the time when a large number of regional refineries had come online that preferred those medium and heavy sours.

Sweet and sour

The combination of these two factors materially changed the supply–demand dynamic for sour barrels in the East of Suez market.

The market was a lot tighter than it had been historically, lifting the price of sour crude, as represented by the Dubai benchmark, relative to light sweet crude, as represented by the Brent benchmark.

The Brent-Dubai spread had been narrowing for some time anyway because globally refiners were getting better at managing sulphur and heavier average molecular density crudes, so the discount for medium and heavy sours was lessening.

That sweet–sour spread became even narrower still in 2010, and we reached the point where the spread occasionally inverted, meaning that the medium and heavy sour Dubai-linked grades were actually sometimes worth more than the traditionally more valuable light sweet Brent-linked grades.

It was clear that Asia was desperate for additional volumes of sour crude, and so we started to scour the world for alternative suppliers.

My firm managed to secure deals with several suppliers of medium and heavy crudes in Colombia, including Ecopetrol, to market their Castilla and Vasconia grades on a destination-restricted basis to Asian customers, and we started to move a large amount of Colombian crude oil into Asia.

The Colombian sales proved to be a very profitable business for us, but at the same time, we were fully aware that if you could move Colombian crude oil to Asia, reliably and regularly, then that meant that the price of medium and heavy sours had become pretty heady.

The success of our Colombian business and the high prices we achieved acted as something of a red flag for us, warning us that it was time to start thinking about what might happen next. We felt it was unlikely that these frothy prices for sour crude could persist for too long, and so we started to consider what might cause sour differentials to ease once more.

ESPO emerges

The other multi-year development that was taking place in the background was the construction of the giant Eastern Siberia-Pacific Ocean (ESPO) pipeline, which Russia was building to transport crude oil from its fields in the Russian Far East.

The new ESPO grade would load onto tankers at the port terminal of Kozmino on the Russian Pacific as well as move directly to Daqing in China via a spur pipeline.

We realized that when the first supplies of ESPO pipeline were made available in early 2011, there would suddenly be a lot of new medium sour crude oil available locally in Asia at an economic price. That meant that the supply–demand balance was going to change once more.

We knew ESPO would meet a large part of the booming Asian demand for medium and heavy sours and might end up replacing some of the supplies, like our Colombian barrels, that had been drawn to Asia from halfway around the world.

We took that view not only because of the imminent arrival of ESPO in the Asian market but also because we expected that as the oil price recovered and demand picked up after the economic crisis, the compliance of the OPEC countries with their self-imposed production restrictions would start to weaken.

We felt there was about to be a big shift in how the world of oil was looking, and we needed to position ourselves to take advantage of our insights. The tea leaves were predicting that the spread between Brent and Dubai, which had been so narrow, would start to widen out again.

Accumulating EFS

Throughout early 2010, we watched the progress of the ESPO pipeline project. We wanted to be sure that there weren't going to be any really substantial delays in its completion before we placed our trade.

By the middle of the year, it was clear that the project was going to complete broadly on schedule and launch as planned in early 2011. But clearly, that additional supply was going to take a bit of time to bed in: obviously, it wouldn't be the case that the moment ESPO came online, there would be a complete collapse in the price of medium and heavy sours.

We were looking to choose a point in time where there would be the maximum chance that the Brent-Dubai spread would behave as we were expecting, but which would also allow for delays and other contingencies.

We finally settled on the second quarter of 2011 as the most likely period when the sweet–sour spread would rebalance. We felt that by then ESPO would be a significant presence in the Asian market and that OPEC discipline might also be starting to slip.

From the middle of 2010 onwards, we started building up a position in Brent-Dubai derivatives, which are known as the exchange of futures for swaps (EFS). By buying the EFS, we were effectively shorting Dubai and going long Brent. We bought EFS that would settle in the second quarter of 2011.

Obviously, you don't just pile in and buy derivatives aggressively; otherwise, you would drive up your purchase cost and alert others to your strategy. We built the position up over time via different brokers and by buying directly from different counterparts. We were able to amass reasonably sized positions very discreetly.

Thinking inside the box

Apart from acquiring significant volumes of the second quarter EFS, we also saw an opportunity to capture the last moments when Brent-Dubai was still very narrow, before the OPEC barrels came back online and before the exports of ESPO picked up.

There was a brief moment in time, where there was a really good opportunity to be short of the prompt EFS – to bet on the short-term continuation of the trend whereby light sweet was pricing at similar levels to medium and sour barrels – and also to get long of the EFS for that later period when we were confident the situation would change.

When you trade a nearby spread against a spread further out in time, the trade is called a box because the two spreads together create four points.

We decided to go short of Brent-Dubai for the fourth quarter of 2010, while concurrently buying the second quarter of 2011.

That box structure of fourth-quarter 2010 versus second-quarter 2011 also allowed us to increase the volumes we were trading substantially because a box trade typically benefits from substantial exchange margin offsets, reducing the capital we required to finance the trade.

Waiting game

Once we had built up our positions, we had to wait for the changes in the market to actually happen. That was a stressful period. However sure we were about our overall analysis, certain things could have taken place that would have derailed the success of the trade.

One of our biggest risks was that OPEC could have decided to increase its output once more, so we were keeping a close eye on their messaging. We were fortunate that they maintained production discipline throughout the fourth quarter of 2010.

OPEC had been so hurt by the collapse in prices that they were very keen to see an aggressive recovery, particularly as a lot of member states had got used to factoring prices close to $100 per barrel into their budgets.

We also had more micro concerns that maybe a large number of refiners would go into maintenance in the fourth quarter of 2010, reducing demand for medium and heavy sours, impacting the first part of our box trade.

In the end, we were fortunate that our trade wasn't derailed. Brent-Dubai traded at around the $2 mark at the end of 2010, making the first part of our box trade profitable, and then by April 2011, as ESPO volumes ramped up, the Brent-Dubai spread blew out to $5–6, which was a change in our favour of a significant magnitude.

Recalibration events

Our expectations for the Brent-Dubai sweet–sour relationship had proved correct, and our trades had worked out to be very profitable for the firm.

As a crude oil trader, I firmly believe that serious money comes from identifying these thematic shifts. But there are only a handful of trading houses that choose to position themselves for these thematic and multi-year events in the paper markets: many will try and capture them through the real optionality of their physical merchant business.

Most traders are still very focused on their traditional day-to-day merchant business, and on what I would call micro oil concerns, such as participating in refinery supply tenders or bidding for spot cargoes.

Dealing with the daily routine is obviously still the core role of an oil trader, but we also made sure that we spent a lot of time thinking about the macro picture and making sure that we were very plugged into geopolitical trends.

A couple of decades ago, there were opportunities to make $1 or $2 per barrel just by being the trader on the spot in a particular country at the right time, but there are too many traders now chasing those types of deals, while producers and buyers are increasingly sophisticated and are less dependent on using traders as intermediaries.

The overall pie has shrunk and so trading margins from traditional merchant business have shrunk dramatically as well. The only way to make outsized profits is to take advantage of longer term themes that are emerging and that will come to dominate the market.

To be a successful trader of macro themes, you need to understand the future state of supply and demand, not just of crude oil generally, but also of specific grades, which means taking a view, as we did, on how the relative value of the different grades will play out.

You need to know what new fields are coming on, what type of crude they will produce, and how new refineries are configured. With that knowledge, you have a good chance of predicting how supply–demand for particular types of crude oil should develop over time.

In 2010–11, we experienced a multi-year recalibration event that occurred when a new stream of crude oil was introduced just as there was a thematic shift in the Asian refinery slate and a change in OPEC behaviour.

It was an interesting point in time. We analysed the implications, and we made our trading decisions accordingly. These kinds of opportunities don't come along too often, but when they do, you have to back yourself and your analysis to the maximum extent.

Trading crude oil derivatives

Although there were earlier attempts, which you will read about shortly, the first successful launch of crude oil futures was that of WTI by NYMEX (now CME Group) in New York in 1983. Brent futures were also tried a couple of times without success in London before their 1988 relaunch finally caught on.

As we will hear, to trade WTI and Brent originally required the trader to stand in a circular pit on an open-outcry trading floor, although all of the activity has since migrated to electronic screen trading and matching.

Since their launch and particularly since the electronic revolution, futures volumes have exploded, providing traders with a tremendous tool to either hedge their risk or take a view on the future direction of the market.

Although WTI and Brent dominate, there are dozens of other crude oil derivatives that are available. Some represent different grades, such as DME Oman or Dubai, others might be versions of WTI and Brent in different currencies, while others provide more granular ways for physical players to hedge, such as the array of instruments that make up the Dated Brent complex.

The derivative markets attract a much more varied range of participants than the physical oil markets. Oil companies trade futures with hedge funds, pension funds and individual traders, as well as with sophisticated algorithmic traders, some of whom are official exchange market makers.

The huge variety of participant types, each following their own strategy to meet their own needs, combined with the global significance of crude oil as a commodity, is what makes the crude oil futures markets the most active commodity markets on the planet.

DOI: 10.4324/9781003144335-38

32 WTI proves itself

Thomas McMahon began his career broking and trading soft commodities, before moving to trade oil futures at NYMEX (now CME Group) in 1981. Thom worked on the NYMEX trading floors until 2003. He served as chairman of both the natural gas advisory committee and the petroleum advisory committee and became a member of the board of directors. Between 2003 and 2007, Thom established NYMEX's representative offices in Tokyo and Singapore. In 2007, he was appointed president of the newly established Hong Kong Mercantile Exchange and in 2009 became the first chief executive of the Singapore Mercantile Exchange (now ICE Futures Singapore). Thom has subsequently founded a number of businesses focusing on commodity trading and financial technology, such as the Pan-Asia Clearing Enterprise, Abaxx Exchange and AirCarbon Exchange, where he currently serves as chief executive.

I first went to work on the New York trading floors when I was 13 years old as a summer page on the NY Cotton Exchange. Every summer throughout high school, I took a job as a page – a glorified errand boy in an exchange jacket – running pieces of paper to and from the different traders in the different trading pits.

Each year you learned a bit more. Then at 16, you could get bonded, and I graduated to running warehouse receipts and settlement documents around Wall and Broad Street. I would take receipts for delivery on cotton and depositary receipts for metals up and down the Street, between the exchanges and the depositary banks.

I was lucky to get such great experience. When you're a kid, sure, you're excited to work on Wall Street, but maybe you don't think too much about it. Now, I look back and think what a fantastic opportunity it was to start so young and to learn the trading business from the physical delivery and trade finance documentation side.

I finished college and I went straight back to the trading floors. I started on the New York Cotton Exchange (now part of ICE) in February 1977, originally as a phone clerk.

DOI: 10.4324/9781003144335-39

Fully juiced

My big break came the next year. I had been handling the hedges for a group of Florida orange juice producers who ran a big commercial hedging book. They would go long or short orange juice futures depending on where they were in the growing and production season.

The group had to be very long, just when a freeze in January 1978 sent orange juice prices from 22 cents per pound up to over $1.00, which in juice terms was a massive move. The guys from Florida did hugely well from that futures position as well as from a significant boost to their spot sales.

As we sorted out the contracts ahead of March delivery, my clients realized that they had somehow ended up long two extra contracts.

I had done a pretty good job for them, and when no one claimed the contracts, they opened a trading account for me and put the two lots into the account as a kind of bonus.

I was later able to sell those two contracts for $24,000. A seat on the New York Cotton Exchange at that time cost $26,000 so I bought a seat with the money in September 1978 and that established me in the business. It got me off the phones and into the pits.

Birth of oil futures

My workplace, the New York Cotton Exchange, had listed the first oil futures contracts in 1975 in response to the Second Arab Oil Embargo of 1973–74. The contract was based on delivery in Rotterdam, and each lot was 100,000 barrels in size.

The exchange stuck the oil contract in an old pit over in the corner of the trading floor, which was the old wool futures pit. A few guys hung around down there, but oil futures never really took off. The main problem was that the contract was just too big. At 100,000 barrels, it was 100 times the size of the futures contracts that we trade today. No trader wanted to take that amount of risk apart from major oil companies. The other issue was that delivery was based on delivery in Rotterdam so there was no U.S. angle.

The Cotton Exchange's new propane contract was more successful than crude oil. Propane was used for drying cotton and for freezing orange juice for concentrate so our agricultural traders were interested in hedging propane alongside their crop hedges.

Trading propane was my first exposure to the energy markets, which were growing in importance. In 1978, the New York Mercantile Exchange (NYMEX, now CME Group) had launched its first energy contract, a heating oil contract based on the barge market in New York Harbor.

Heating oil proved to be quite active so now you had two energy contracts trading in the pits of the Commodity Exchange Center at 4 World Trade Center: propane on the Cotton Exchange and heating oil on NYMEX.

NYMEX was going through a significant transition at the time: they had had a big default in their potato futures market, and so they were looking for something new. The Merc's young chairman Michael Marks had the vision to take a shot at energy.

The agricultural markets in NY went quiet in 1981, and I was offered the chance to move across to the fast-growing NYMEX energy markets, after a spot opened up in the new leaded gasoline pit (unleaded and RBOB came later). I made the move from the Cotton to the Merc by literally walking 150 feet across the floor of the Commodity Exchange Center.

WTI emerges

NYMEX started to look at crude oil in 1980. The Rotterdam contract had been too big and too cumbersome, but the concept of crude oil futures was good.

A window of opportunity was opening up. Oilmen like T. Boone Pickens were supportive and convinced that there could be a single price for crude domestically in the U.S.

We obviously needed a delivery location with a lot of storage and a lot of connectivity. There were plenty of debates about where delivery should take place. Cushing, Oklahoma was not the original choice but was ultimately chosen because there was excess storage there.

Cushing was a relatively underutilized interchange at that time, but it had tanks that were available as well as a robust architecture. Cushing was also handy for Texas and the production areas in the central U.S.

Domestic Light Sweet Crude Oil Futures, better known as WTI, were launched in March 1983, and hopes were high on the floor. By that time, the refined product futures were doing well: they were attracting a lot of commercial participants, and European suppliers were using NYMEX to hedge the cargoes they were sending to the U.S.

We expected a similarly strong start for WTI, but there were challenges ahead. On the first day of trading in WTI, there was a lot of noise; there was a bit less noise on the second day; then on the third day, there must have only been five people in the pit.

One guy stood there on the top step and made a market continuously. He had a 1,200 lot buy order to fill, which was a big ticket in those days and a massive ticket for a new market. It took him two weeks to fill that order, which tells you a lot about how slow trading was in the beginning.

WTI definitely struggled with adoption. The market in 1983 was dominated by the major oil companies, and they were largely unconvinced about the need for crude oil futures. WTI did make progress, but it was slow going.

Much of the support for WTI in the early days came from speculators and the oil independents. Before the launch of WTI, the only way you could take a direct exposure to oil was by holding oil company stock, which doesn't give you a very pure exposure.

The concept of commodity futures funds was beginning to emerge. Paul Tudor Jones had already done some early work on what ultimately became his Tudor group of funds, and he was starting to expand from the cotton and juice markets into energy. Commodities were developing as an asset class, and oil became an intrinsic part of that.

Despite some promising signs, from 1983 until 1986, the WTI market was very humble. It had credibility and open interest, but it was only in April 1986 that it came into its own.

Catching a falling knife

There was a global surplus of oil in the mid-1980s, in part because many OPEC members were producing way in excess of the quotas designed to keep prices stable. In September 1985, Saudi Arabia, which had previously reduced its own output to compensate for overproduction elsewhere, decided to change direction and produce at full capacity.

To guarantee demand for the extra Saudi oil, the Saudi oil minister Sheikh Ahmed Yamani introduced netback pricing for Saudi crude. Netback pricing meant that refiners paid for Saudi crude on the basis of refined product prices, and it effectively removed the price risk from buying Saudi oil. Netback pricing was obviously popular with refiners who bought plenty of Saudi oil. But once other producers copied the Saudi move, a severe glut of crude oil developed.

The overhang of crude grew and grew until, finally, in April 1986, the market just tanked. The netback deals had already put pressure on the refined markets. I remember one day we opened at $24 per barrel, we traded down to $20, and then closed at between $16 and $18. Then, the next day we opened at $11 and traded down to $9 on the opening. We've seen these moves since in electronic markets but never in the pits.

Those days were manic. I'd never seen more people in the WTI pit. If you had gone home long the previous day, you lost everything in seconds. If you had gone home short, you just couldn't believe what was happening. Your only worry was picking a time to step in and take profits.

I was flat crude the day of the big collapse. I began the day in the gasoline pit, but when crude opened, I stepped across into the WTI pit and watched as crude traded down from $16, to $11, to $10 per barrel.

Late in the opening another large sell order came in for around 600 lots. The first 500 went through as low as $9 per barrel; 100 offered at $9 I bought 50 and held my breath. Then, the market went into an enforced two-minute pause. All the back months were limit down and offered. Prices had fallen so fast that the exchange rules enforced a brief pause in trading.

Those were the scariest two minutes of my entire trading career.

We were standing there in the WTI pit, waiting for the reopen. We were all looking at each other and wondering where the hell will prices go when we restart?

The market reopened at $10 bid, and I sold half of my position. The market then went $11 bid, and I offered $12 and got lifted. I walked out of the pit. The market went on to recover later that day, but the volume and volatility of April 1986 provided learning lessons for market corrections to come.

Reputation builder

I had bought WTI at the bottom of the market, a profitable trade for me, but it's sometimes better to be lucky than to be good, at least in retrospect.

But, more importantly, it was the trading on that day that made the reputation of WTI crude oil futures. The crude oil market outside NYMEX was in freefall: there were no buyers, there was nobody willing to put a bottom in the market on that morning.

The day after and in the days beyond, people realized that those bunch of whack-jobs on Wall Street, those Merc-jerks, had succeeded in providing a credible discoverable price for crude oil at a time when none of the over-the-counter markets were functioning.

As a result, WTI gained an immense amount of credibility in the financial markets. The pit had bought crude oil when nobody else in the world wanted it.

Crucially, the exchange also stood behind every trade. Elsewhere, counterparties were walking away from each other and counterparties were defaulting. On NYMEX, everybody got settled. In the futures market, we took performing on a trade for granted, but others were impressed.

That day in April 1986 is what really solidified the validity of NYMEX as an exchange and WTI as a contract. Then, in June 1988, the International Petroleum Exchange (IPE, now ICE) successfully launched Brent crude oil futures and the WTI-Brent spread developed, further boosting activity levels, and inevitably linking the two global benchmarks.

Setting a floor

In retrospect, being part of the formative years of the global benchmark was just another day in the pits. Nowadays, most market makers are professional electronic trading firms, but then the individual guys on the floor were the liquidity providers. We stood there and ground it out.

These were good traders and tough people. There wasn't a lot of blue blood in the commodity pits. Those guys all gravitated to trading equities on the New York Stock Exchange, or they went to the bond markets.

The vast majority of the commodity guys came from the streets, and the markets often split on an ethnic basis. Irish, Jewish and Italians and others were a big part of the cotton market, and the coffee, sugar and cocoa markets.

The Merc traders were often drawn from the soft produce community in lower Manhattan, a legacy of the old Produce Exchange, while the gold and silver markets attracted a lot of guys from Brooklyn and Staten Island who had been phone clerks on other floors before being recruited to COMEX in 1974, becoming members when gold reopened for trading in 1974.

Paul Jones and I were admitted as members of the Cotton Exchange on the same day, and we got razzed in the board room that we were college boys. Most of the guys had been to night school or maybe had studied later in life through the G.I. Bill.

None of those guys got paid to provide liquidity for new contracts, like WTI. Instead, they put their own money up to trade and to build up new markets.

In the modern electronic markets, there is a contractual obligation for an orderly market. But when we worked in the pit, there was no question. Yes, we were opportunistic, and no one wanted to lose money but, fundamentally, we all knew we had to keep the market going in every situation.

There were days like that session in April 1986 when you had to step in, trade the gaps, try to calm the market and to get it moving again. Maybe not everyone thought like that, but there were enough of us that did, that the market performed as intended. People stepped up and they built the benchmarks on which the world still depends today.

Last resort

NYMEX succeeded as an exchange on the back of WTI crude oil futures, and WTI succeeded on the back of an oil market that was under enormous stress.

The traders on NYMEX acted as the buyer of last resort for oil in April 1986. When the oil price was collapsing and refinery stocks were full, the New York market stepped in and found liquidity on the downside.

Each time since that oil prices have surged or collapsed, the exchange puts a bottom or a ceiling in the market. When prices soared in July 2008, NYMEX traders were the seller of last resort, and they were the buyer of last resort when prices subsequently collapsed during the financial crisis.

When I hear people – sometimes OPEC members – blaming speculators for falls in the oil price, it makes me smile. Back in 1986, and plenty of times since, if our markets hadn't existed, then the oil price would have fallen even lower.

When the oil price collapses, it's not the big oil producers that step in to buy oil and provide support for prices. Instead, they rely on the traders in our markets, who make sure there is always a tradeable price for their commodity. It may not be the price you want, but it's a price all the same. Exchange traders provide the transparency and the liquidity that everyone needs but no one else is able to provide, either as a buyer or as a seller of last resort.

33 From floor to screen

Steve Roberts began his career in the early 1980s, holding a number of trading roles in agricultural commodities. He began trading oil on the floor of the International Petroleum Exchange (IPE, later ICE) in 1994 and worked in the trading pits until 2005. Steve later joined ICE as director of oil marketing in 2008, before co-founding independent trading firm Oak Futures in 2010 and creating its parent company Oak Capital in 2012. After seven years at Oak, first as chief executive and then as chairman, he was appointed non-executive chair of TTG Energy in 2018. Steve co-founded BlueChip Holdings in 2020, where he acts as chief executive.

I must have made thousands upon thousands of crude oil trades during my two decades buying and selling oil futures on the floor of the IPE.

I would consider myself an astute trader with good reactions to constantly changing dynamics, but the best move I ever made was to understand that the oil markets had dramatically and permanently changed once the exchanges introduced electronic trading, ushering in a new world that required new skills, new trading strategies and new ways of working.

The IPE had tried to launch futures on Brent crude oil – the North Sea benchmark – a couple of times already before the product finally took off in 1988. From that point on, the Brent contract never looked back and trading volumes kept on increasing.

The Brent crude oil market quickly started to dwarf other European commodity futures markets in terms of its daily activity levels, and this helped to attract traders like myself, who had previously traded other commodities such as sugar, cocoa and coffee.

It's hard for anyone who was not around at that time to picture the IPE's Brent crude oil trading floor during its heyday in the 1990s and early 2000s.

All of the trading in those years was conducted in the open-outcry trading floor, where traders representing different companies or trading on their own behalf used hand signals or shouts to transfer information and to conclude deals within a defined part of the floor, known as a pit.

DOI: 10.4324/9781003144335-40

Volume of trade

As a visitor to the trading floor, probably the first thing that would strike you would be the noise from hundreds of traders all operating in a restricted space.

If you were an experienced oil futures trader, the intensity of that noise would give you information about the state of the market before you ever saw any price information. Those sounds would tell me within the first few seconds whether the market was moving quickly or slowly that day, and even whether the oil price was rising or falling.

If it was a busy trading session, then you would hear the noise grow on the floor. You would see the anxiety on people's faces as they looked to get out of a position. When you were trading there all day, every day, you got a real physical understanding of the market.

Standing in a pit, you feel the noise, the hubbub, and you appreciate whether certain individuals are adding their weight to the sell side or the buy side of the market. On a screen, you don't know whom you're trading with, which is right and fair. But that makes it a very different trading experience to standing next to guys on the floor and understanding them and their motivations.

At times, as an independent trader – what we called a 'local' – you would need to rely on your neighbour to have your back. When you stand next to someone for several hours a day, you talk about life, kids, whatever else, and then you hope that they will watch out for you because good traders knew exactly who was short and who was long in the pit.

Good traders would look around and know very quickly where the axis of the market was and where to take positions. They also understood the daily cycle of the floor.

The London open was always a very busy time. Other intense periods were pre-lunchtime when the U.S. woke up, the official NYMEX open at 2–2.30pm, and the London markers at 4–4.30pm. The floor would then quieten down until the final close at 7–7.30pm.

In between, there were times that we would call a 'no-trade zone' when you would try not to put on a significant new position because the next active period might take the market in a totally different direction.

Trading places

The nature of Brent trading started to change when the exchange introduced electronic trading screens that competed with the floor as a venue to transact. As the popularity of electronic trading grew, ICE took the decision to close down the trading floor in April 2005.

When the floor closed, I traded on the screen from home for a while. I was not too concerned about making the transition to electronic trading because my trading strategies had a bit more built-in diversification than those of my peer group.

My results were good but I certainly wasn't enjoying myself. I like working with people, I like being around people. Although it could be challenging and stressful, the trading floor was fun. Looking at a screen at home was not.

A couple of us started to consider whether we could recreate some of the environment we had known and enjoyed on the open outcry floor, but with a set-up that was tailored for the new world of electronic trading.

We created what became Oak Futures, which brought independent energy traders together in a single office space. At first, each trader was trading on their own account – later we offered salaried positions – but crucially they were sharing an experience that was not a million miles away from what they had experienced on the trading floor.

We created a space that was conducive to the sharing of ideas and being able to work with like-minded individuals sharing similar values. We tried to replicate elements of the floor like the humour, while also trying to create some structure.

We cherry-picked people to join us that we knew would get on with others. We also made sure that people who needed a bit of a hand with their trading style could sit alongside traders that were happy to share their experience and strategies.

Arcade fire

The concept of 'trading arcades' quickly took off. The arcades weren't offering traders anything that they couldn't get at home in terms of market access, but they provided a supportive environment that helped people achieve their best performance, while working in an atmosphere that made people enjoy their working day.

One of the first things we recognized was that many of the former floor traders relied on just a few strategies. People were very dependent on trading Brent versus WTI or on the Brent time structure: the first three monthly calendar spreads, the six-monthlies or the yearlies. That was all a lot of people knew.

We started to introduce our traders to the correlation between Brent futures and some of the other over-the-counter energy markets. That was an eye-opener for many of the guys. Oak introduced learning sessions: we wanted our traders to understand all parts of the barrel and geopolitics, essentially anything that would help them trade better.

The first step for a proprietary trader is to understand why oil prices or refined product cracks are moving; the nuances, the reasons. But the most important piece of the puzzle is the second step: how to take that knowledge and turn it into a successful trading strategy.

Some of the guys from the floor immediately took to electronic trading and this new way of working, but others struggled. The success rate of traders that left the floor wasn't great. I would say comfortably below 50% successfully made the transition.

Some traders couldn't move past their old strategies. They might have periods of a few months when those worked, but overall the traders would be making at best slightly more than the average U.K. salary. Even so, many would still be spending the same, subsidizing their lifestyles with their savings from the floor.

You can't help some people. I remember one guy who joined us, who had no experience but was keen to become a trader. He started with a significant amount of money in his account, and at first, everything worked amazingly: in his first few months, he was making between several thousand dollars and $20,000 per week. But then he did what most amateurs do, which is to stick with the same strategy over and over again. Despite one-to-one sessions with our trading manager, risk department and even the management of Oak Futures, he wouldn't change his ways, just because it had worked the first time.

That initial success is often luck rather than a winning strategy. We'd show him some different techniques, but his attitude was 'it's my money, I'll trade how I want'. Obviously, he ended up losing what he'd made as well as some of the money he'd started out with.

At that point, as management, we would step in with him and with others to say, 'this isn't for you, you're sticking with trading June–December or June–December–June because you've had some initial success, but once the market comes out of that cycle, what are you left with?'

Speed kills

The main challenge for independent traders was speed. The growing sophistication and prevalence of high-frequency traders, who use sophisticated algorithms and the fastest means of connection to exchanges, puts enormous pressure on the 'point and click' guys, who trade onscreen manually.

High-frequency trading changed the whole pace of the market. Let's say the market was 93 bid at 94 or 95, then suddenly you'd see 91 trade and then 72. Huge gaps would emerge as stop-losses were triggered, which then triggered other stops, and so on.

Oak Capital had pretty sophisticated systems ourselves, but we could never compete with the high-frequency guys, so there were plenty of times when they jumped in front of us in the queue, which generated a lot of irritation and frustration.

In that more cut-throat environment, the only way to compete was to take on larger positions, which was not the way most independents had typically traded.

On the floor and even in the early days of electronic trading, people would trade the flat price without any safety net. They would go long or short and try to ride the market up or down. But once the sophisticated high-frequency guys came in, the market could move 30 or 40 cents, and that could happen in two seconds.

Moves on the screen would happen in seconds, which would have taken an hour on the floor. People had to learn to trade with a bit more cover, and so they began to trade spreads rather than flat price, even though they could make more money by pure flat-price trading. Instead of ten lots of flat price, they might do 250 lots of spreads to achieve the same potential profit, which was obviously good for exchange volumes.

Different world

Over 50% of Brent trading volume done on the floor came from the independent 'locals'. I'm not sure that the value that the locals created was ever fully appreciated.

The suggestion that it was just a bunch of oiks on the floor is a stereotype that gets used quite often, but it's wrong, because there were a lot of talented people there.

People must have had talent because they were very successful. Trading open outcry wasn't necessarily an easier way to trade, although it might have been simpler in some senses. It certainly wasn't as fast paced or as sophisticated as screen trading is now, and certainly, the talent on the floor was often not what was required in the electronic trading space.

People used to come to our office and say, 'well, I used to be a good trader on the floor'. That doesn't matter. It's like being great at football and also expecting to be good at rugby. They might both be both ball games, but they require very different skills.

People think that trading is trading, but it isn't the same. The floor was very unique: you needed to be likeable, you needed to have common sense, good banter and a quick mind. But you didn't have to process the amount of information that you do now.

On the floor, we knew that Brent was going up or down for just a few reasons: a news headline, someone significant was long or short, or we were coming up to a particular time of day.

Today the markets move so quickly and all the financial and commodity markets are interlinked. There are so many more factors to process.

A trader with a degree in economics, for example, will do much better in the new electronic world because he or she can break down and understand the elements of the market much better than a guy that used to work on the floor.

That doesn't mean that the guy from the floor was a bad trader. He was just playing a completely different game. If you took one of the guys with a First from Cambridge who is trading onscreen superbly now and put him on the floor, I guarantee he wouldn't have the same success.

The crude oil futures market has evolved and it's changed. The underlying oil market might be the same but the way that we access that market and execute trades is completely different, and I have no doubt that the market will continue to evolve further.

As a trader and a manager of traders, the key to long-term success is to understand that different trading environments require different skillsets and different mindsets.

34 Bringing Brent onscreen

After completing his master's degree in mathematical analysis in his native country, Slovakia, Milan Kratka undertook a doctorate in mathematics from the University of Chicago, where he became a junior faculty member and was instrumental in establishing a master's program in financial mathematics. His first commercial role was as a quantitative analyst at investment giant Citadel in Chicago, after which he moved to become deputy head of research at proprietary trading firm TradeLink. Milan went on to work in commodity pricing and trading roles for Morgan Stanley, Wolverine Trading, and Sirius Investment Management. In 2006, Milan was appointed head of energy trading by Sun Trading LLC, and he then founded his own electronic trading firm ArbHouse in 2009. In 2018, Milan joined broker-dealer AOS, Inc. as their chief technology officer.

One of my key aims is to make sure that my trading each day is boring and drama-free.

I have worked as a professional market maker in the energy markets for almost two decades. Exchanges pay us stipends and provide other incentives to make sure that there are always bids and offer visible on their screens and that there is always someone prepared to take the other side when one of their customers wants to trade.

Like everyone active in the oil markets, market makers need to make money. But unlike speculative oil traders, the aim of every market maker is to make money in a very plain steady way.

Market makers are pure service providers for the exchanges, so we avoid speculation and limit our risks as much as possible. Market makers don't take a view on the oil price, they aren't gamblers, and they always try to control their exposure by hedging all of their positions as completely and quickly as possible.

Because we don't speculate on oil prices, the direction of the market is irrelevant to us. After all, if you don't take directional risk, then up or down feels the same.

Many people can spend their lives trading oil without even being aware of the existence of market makers. After all, we don't move prices and we are market neutral. But it is the market makers that provide the liquidity and

DOI: 10.4324/9781003144335-41

competitive pricing that serves the customers of the exchanges. We add value to the oil market by showing prices that are as fair as possible while minimizing our risk.

The big screen

Without market makers, the oil markets would never have transitioned from the trading floors of the IPE and NYMEX (now ICE and CME Group) to the electronic model that has improved trading liquidity enormously and has enabled customers all over the world to access Brent and WTI.

I was the first person to quote Brent futures electronically on ICE back in 2003, and although it proved to be too early to work, over time the market never looked back.

I started my career as a market maker in weather futures and options. The firm I was working for liked the weather markets because we felt that it was a market with a relatively level playing field. To take a view on the weather, you just need to have access to quality weather forecasts. Unlike the oil markets, for example, it is hard for firms to have proprietary information on how the weather will play out, or at least that was our thinking at the time.

After that experience, I started my own firm and I met David Goone who asked if I could help ICE by electronically quoting crude oil and natural gas. Back in 2003, ICE was essentially a natural gas exchange, but they wanted to expand into crude oil because they thought that the electronic marketplaces that they were building would eventually catch on right across the energy markets.

Getting started as an electronic market maker for Brent crude oil was hard.

Our first difficulty was to raise the money I needed to start trading. Investors generally want to see a three-year record of profitability before they will back a trader. That was obviously impossible for us because at that time electronic trading hadn't even been in existence for three years.

We approached around 80 potential investors, and only one was interested. He gave us an initial $1 million, which was a start but wasn't really enough to build out a significant trading operation.

The technology we were using to quote electronically was also in its infancy. ICE had given us access to their application programming interface (API), but we were still using Excel spreadsheets to write to that interface and show our prices.

Adverse reaction

Once we were live-streaming Brent prices, a couple of things happened that we hadn't expected.

ICE started marketing this new ability to trade Brent electronically to its customers and people started seeing our prices. It was at that point that I started to get harassing messages. A censored version of them would read something like, 'hey, what do you think you are doing?'

People were furious with us showing prices on screens for everyone with access to see. The traders on the floor of the IPE clearly did not want an electronic marketplace to succeed and to replace them and so they put up a fight.

Their resistance also meant that we couldn't get people to trade with us on screen. I was quoting five lots (5,000 barrels) with about 5–10 cents spread between the bid and the offer for the first six months that ICE listed. Almost nothing was traded.

No one wanted to trade with us, especially the floor traders, even if the floor prices traded through our electronic prices. Let's say that the bid was 8 and the offer was 9, but even if I was bidding 11 people would not sell me the 11 because the floor did not want electronic trading to take off. This kind of open arbitrage happened hundreds of times.

That certainly didn't help our business. If you don't trade, you don't make money. As a market maker, you have to trade in and out, in and out. At that time, there was just no 'out'. When you provide liquidity at competitive prices, you expect to trade but we barely traded. I was one guy with a technology partner, and we had expected a minimum of five times more volume than the volume we were seeing on the screen.

In the end, the lack of liquidity killed us, and we ended up returning the money to our original investor. I realized that I couldn't make it on my own, in part because I didn't have enough capital. My partner's mom died, and my father died within few weeks of each other, so we decided to exit the business. Although not for long, as I joined an up-and-coming high-frequency trading (HFT) firm that was interested in commodities.

Success criteria

The experience of making markets in Brent was obviously difficult, but it ended up benefiting me enormously because I went on to join another firm, and as electronic trading developed, we became one of the biggest participants in the back months of Brent and WTI.

We had also developed a deep understanding of the ICE API, helped to debug their interfaces and built up a good relationship that has lasted to the current day.

For a market maker to succeed, a lot of things have to go right. The primary ingredients of success here are speed, cost and experience.

Speed is crucial to a market maker. You have to be fast, and you have to process information as fast as anyone else. If you parse information slower than your competition, then you are exposed to risk or you could start being unprofitable.

Having information is a key valuable asset, and if you process that information quickly, then you have more value than the competitor who takes longer to do so.

Speed is necessary but not a sufficient condition for success on its own. You can respond to market conditions within five nanoseconds if you have your technology configured correctly, but if you respond the wrong way, then you will lose money.

Another condition for success is that your cost has to be lower than your expenses. Typically, when you provide liquidity you show a bid and when somebody hits your bid, you go and hedge it. That leaves you with a spread position, which you will need to eventually close off. That means every round trip trade that a market maker makes generates four transactions.

Your fixed cost is therefore the cost of the fees of four transactions. Essentially, the spread that a market maker shows between the bid and the offer has to be wide enough that your edge can pay for the cost of four transactions, while leaving something as profit.

If you have to pay, say, $1 in transaction fees, then you can create a formula to calculate how tight you can make the market. An exchange therefore has to ensure that fees for market makers are less than a quarter of their desired bid-ask spread. Otherwise, it will not be a sustainable business for market makers to make markets over a longer time period.

Information flow

Information is the most important commodity of all. You need to have at least as much information as your competition. That's why I have always preferred to stay away from trading in the front month. There is more liquidity, but I have no edge because I have less knowledge than anybody else might.

As a market maker, we did not have any access to information about the physical oil markets, which meant we had no advantage in the prompt market.

We always avoided quoting the front-month Oman contract for the Dubai Mercantile Exchange (DME), for example, because we lacked the necessary physical knowledge and did not want to run into trouble when quoting for and trading against companies who had big teams of people counting tankers, storage levels, and so on.

Our advantage was that I knew how to price the back months of oil contracts, whether it was Oman, Brent or WTI. You can analyse the forward curve and how it moves, especially as the further months tend not to move that radically. With modelling of the curve and limited risks, we could provide liquidity and then hedge.

We maximized what we could do with the knowledge we had. When ICE listed the back-month Brent contracts electronically, we could grow our volumes because we had the technology and the speed. We had to take some risks but not excessive risks.

I have seen people try to make money quickly, but I have stuck with providing liquidity as safely as possible. If you want to be a speculator, you can play the lottery. But if you want to stay trading sustainably for a long time, then you need to base your trades on knowledge and managing risks.

A market maker has to be the smartest person in the room. In order to process information quickly, you need to have the right technology, but you also need to have basic fundamental knowledge. You have to have the experience that will enable you to add value. After all, speed is only one component of information.

When I was first market making Brent on the screen, there were times when I wished I were back in a big bank with all of their resources. Still, we tried to do our best with limited capital and with all of the constraints we faced at that time.

Looking back at what Brent has become, we were definitely on the right track. We were ahead of our time, and the market caught up with us eventually. It was a challenging period, but we tried something new, and the knowledge and information we developed did pay off in the end.

35 Trading opaque markets

Greg Newman is the chief executive of Onyx Commodities, a proprietary trading firm that he co-founded in 2018 and which focuses on making markets in oil derivatives. Before Onyx, Greg was head of crude oil and distillate trading for another proprietary firm, Mandara Capital, which he joined as a crude oil derivative trader. After studying biochemical engineering, Greg started his career in the oil markets as a trading analyst at Gazprom Marketing & Trading in London.

I was pretty young when I started on the oil derivatives desk at Mandara Capital in 2013, and one of the first pieces of advice I remember hearing from the more experienced guys was 'whatever you do, don't get into the Dated Brent market'.

They made it sound like that market was basically the Wild West. Dated Brent was considered to be incredibly opaque. It was dominated by large commercial players, like the oil majors and the big independent trading houses, and it required huge technical knowledge, even to understand the various instruments and how they interrelated.

To a certain extent, the guys were right. The North Sea is by far the most complicated oil market in the world.

As well as the core Brent futures product that everyone knows about, there are a number of derivative contracts that help manage price risk related to the Platts Dated Brent assessment that is the benchmark for physical North Sea crude oil. These include contracts for difference (CFDs) that hedge the average of weekly Dated assessments, Dated-to-Frontlines (DFLs) that cover the spread between Dated and Brent futures, as well as Exchanges of Futures for Physical (EFPs) that can be used to convert positions from futures into physical North Sea cargoes and vice versa.

In short, there are a lot of instruments to watch in the North Sea, and it was definitely not a market for the faint-hearted, particularly for a trader like myself that wasn't receiving a constant flow of information from activity in physical oil production or refining.

But I was fascinated by Brent and I wouldn't be deterred. It took me about a year and a half to really get into the market, and at first, I started small. I was just trying to make a few cents here and there by trading the Dated curve.

DOI: 10.4324/9781003144335-42

When I first started trading Brent in 2013, it was a niche market with so few major participants that it felt a bit like a club. The existing players tended quickly to get frustrated with new participants if they weren't perceived to be adding any value to the market. There I was, just taking value out of the curve and people didn't like that particularly.

Then the stars aligned, and everything changed.

Changing circumstances

The market was just coming out of the big oil crash of 2014 and was beginning to reset its dynamics. There was a big oil glut throughout 2015 that depressed the time spreads, which represent the difference between prompt oil prices and oil prices further out in time.

The prices we were seeing in the Brent futures were incentivizing a trade that is known in the oil markets as 'cash and carry' whereby traders buy cheap prompt oil and store it in order to resell it at higher prices later on.

When the difference between the front-month Brent futures and second-month futures reaches minus 50–70 cents per barrel, you would expect all crude oil storage on land to be full up. And when it gets to minus $1 per barrel, then traders will also fill up all the oil tankers that they can charter, just to use the tankers as floating storage facilities for crude oil.

This massive utilization of storage by oil companies meant that all the firms wanted to hedge their positions. They were primarily looking to hedge in the Dated Brent market because that was their actual physical price exposure, so most of the hedging was originated in the over-the-counter Dated market and then transferred into the listed futures market by trading in the Dated-to-Frontline market.

At the same time, as we were deep into this 'cash and carry' storage market, there was a significant technical change planned to the way the Brent market operated. In mid-October 2015, exchange operator ICE had announced that from March 2016 onwards its Brent futures expiry calendar would move to a month-ahead basis rather than being based on 15 days of activity.

These changes by the exchange were very sensible because it meant that the Brent futures expiry would encompass twice the previous volume of crude oil. That made the exchange process more robust and harder to push around.

A change of this magnitude was bound to have a big impact on trading behaviour, and in particular in the price of the exchange of futures for physical (EFP) market, which is the price at which market participants are willing to take a futures position into the expiry process. Dated Brent market participants are really interested in the level of the EFP because the price of their actual physical crude is linked to Dated Brent rather than to the futures.

Seeking protection

All of this meant that the North Sea market was facing two challenges: first, managing the risk of the big oil glut we were experiencing, and at the same time, managing the change in expiry that ICE had announced and which was expected to have a significant impact on the value of Dated Brent in February 2016.

The market knew that the relationship between Dated and the futures would change next February and so lots of market participants wanted to get very long in the February DFL relative to the March and April time spread.

After ICE's announcement in mid-October, every trader wanted to manage the same risk, so there was a huge volume of business to be done. You could talk about almost an unlimited volume of buying interest in that February DFL. Meanwhile, the current trading month, November 2015, was still incredibly weak because of all the oversupply and storage. There was a huge amount of selling interest and the market was moving lower and lower.

This was a long way from being a normal market, and I began to see an opportunity to get involved. There was interest in trading so much volume on both sides that it really needed a market maker to step in. It became clear that if I could strip out the Dated component from all the instruments that were trading and then trade them against each other, then I would have a pretty good relative value trade right there.

Everyone wanted to buy as much February DFL as they could get their hands on. Once people knew I was there to sell, I even had people coming to me directly. There was a clear liquidity pool right there that I could rely on. Then, there was also a lot of spread buying in the December-Dated versus February-Dated time spreads.

I knew that if I sold February DFLs, I would also be able to sell December–February Dated to get all of the Dated risks into December. I would just be matching up my December selling with my February selling.

Then, there was also significant buying in the November contract-for-difference (CFD) market to cover floating storage positions, so I was selling those contracts to bring my December position forward into November, which was still extremely weak because of the glut.

I knew I would have to wait until the pricing window when everyone was selling the November CFDs because their pricing was so weak. At that point, in theory, I would have a great short position: everyone wanted to sell November and so I would hopefully be able to buy it back at a lower level and cover my short position.

There was essentially a brief time period where all of these different Brent-related markets seemed to be lining up and moving in my favour. You could buy an unlimited number of November CFDs, you could sell an unlimited number of February DFLs, and then, you could sell an unlimited amount of spreads to link it all together.

Execution time

I was confident that I was thinking along the right lines and that the markets were going the way I needed them to go, so I decided to take the plunge and do as much trading as I possibly could, bearing in mind my risk limits.

This was a crazy time. To put it into context, a normal trade that a proprietary trader like myself would do would be for 100,000 barrels, while a medium-sized trader might do 200–400,000 barrels and the largest players might look at trades of 600,000 barrels. During that period, I was regularly trading 1.5 to 2.0 million barrels on every single deal. The market was going nuts.

The whole life cycle of the strategy was around six weeks. Two weeks in October to execute and then the trades would price out over the month of November. It was six weeks of total madness. I thought I knew what I was doing, but I still had to back myself by writing some huge tickets. I was filling orders all day every day for two weeks.

The North Sea market was never as active as that before, and I doubt it ever will be again. I was trading with huge numbers of different participants – we were even getting calls from Singapore and the United States. Because of the unique situation in the market, everyone was getting involved.

It was a nerve-wracking time. Most proprietary traders would not have been comfortable with the amount of separate legs involved in setting up such a complex strategy. It takes some nuance and some execution skill to extract value out of the Brent structure, particularly when you don't have the information flow or muscle of the large oil companies.

It also requires a huge outflow in fees. I probably paid out 50% of my gross profits in fees because I had to bear all of the costs of buying, selling and expiries, as well as financing margin payments to the exchanges.

Making this strategy work also required a great trading system that could cope with complex strategies and that was able to track costs and total value at risk (VAR). Of course, even the best systems can only take the trades into account that have been posted, so the firm would see some huge swings in VAR when I had placed one leg of the strategy without yet placing the others. That sometimes led to emails where the risk managers would point out that I was 50 times beyond my VAR limit. My management was remarkably understanding, or at least until the volumes started to go crazy…

Ultimately, I was fortunate that everything came in. Every leg of the strategy worked and for that short time span there was liquidity in every part of the North Sea market. The volume was there on the February DFL and on the December–February Dated; I was making my edge on the relative value of Dated Brent, and my position in the EFP came off.

That settlement period was a different level of stress because instead of the normal 1 or 2 million barrels of exposure that I had to roll off, I was sitting on 24 million barrels of exposure.

I would get to every pricing window and would be waiting to see where my EFP futures were pricing versus Dated Brent. It was pricing in my favour every day, but I was close to a heart attack on a few occasions because the day-to-day price swings were wild. Ultimately, I had been marking my book with the EFP at −25 cents, but it ended up pricing at −40 cents because the market was just so weak.

Transparency calling

I was 25 years old at that point, and it's no exaggeration to say that that month and that year made my career. That was the month that I announced myself to the market. I was trading with everyone and every broker knew me because I was probably the biggest payer of brokerage fees that month. Then, internally, Mandara was delighted with the performance of the strategy.

That fourth quarter of 2015 was a good time for many people. The brokers had record years, the oil companies were doing well out of their 'cash and carry' strategy, and my own strategy was working. It was a genuinely enjoyable time in the market.

That experience later gave me the confidence to go ahead and set up my own trading company. We are still applying the principles behind the trading strategy I have described to the way we trade today.

When I first started out, North Sea crude oil was a niche market dominated by a group of big players who weren't particularly convinced of the value that a proprietary trader could bring. But as soon as I started trading bigger size, people started to think I was actually useful. The difference was that majors or big trading houses were used to financial players running away from big positions rather than taking all the size that they could provide.

I think we showed in those weeks that there could be a role for proprietary trading in the most complex oil market of them all. Proprietary traders could make money, and they could also provide a service. I ultimately left Mandara to start Onyx, but Mandara still has a very active North Sea crude desk and there are other market makers that have started up.

In the North Sea, we've gone from a situation where a few people had most of the market knowledge and there was limited liquidity to a more active market, which is unbelievably efficient. On the screen, the bid-offer spread for prompt contracts is now just one cent wide, whereas it used to be 15 or 20 cents. Those tight spreads mean hedgers pay less to manage their risk.

The volumes we were trading in November 2015 were unprecedented, but overall volumes in 2019–20 weren't far off. That's largely because people feel they can trade with greater confidence.

The veil has been lifted from North Sea crude oil. Greater transparency means that price discovery is much better, which also makes it easier for Platts to produce their assessments. A good indicator is the EFP market. In 2015, the EFP traded in a range of nearly 50 cents. Nowadays, the range is no more than ten cents. Of course, the EFP can still move around, but it's more stable and it's better aligned with the real physical market.

The whole North Sea ecosystem is very well priced and very transparent. The only people who might complain about that are those that might have preferred to dominate an illiquid and opaque market.

From my perspective, the entry of proprietary traders like ourselves can create a virtuous cycle. We enter a new market, we increase liquidity and transparency, and everyone benefits. Markets always adapt and traders have to adapt with them. If I have learnt one thing, it's that markets usually only go one way: towards greater transparency.

36 Trading as a calling card

Gary King obtained bachelor's and master's degrees in petroleum geology from the University of London. He worked as a geologist before transitioning into oil trading, where he held increasingly senior roles at Neste, Morgan Stanley, TransCanada and ENOC and Dragon Oil Plc. Gary went on to create one of the first private equity funds in the Middle East focused on oil and gas for Standard Bank and then to become the inaugural chief executive of the Dubai Mercantile Exchange (DME). After launching the DME, Gary took up various chief executive roles in the natural resource and security sectors, including sovereign wealth fund Dubai Natural Resources World and Dutco Natural Resources Investments in Houston, U.S. He also served as an independent board member for listed companies Parker Drilling in Houston and Serinus Energy in Calgary. Gary continues to advise the global oil and gas industry through his Matrix Organisation consultancy, while also serving as chief executive of security technology firm, Radio Physics Solutions.

One thing I've learnt in my career is that you can never be sure about someone's motivation or drivers for putting on a trade. You often don't know if a firm is hedging or speculating; you don't know if a physical trade is offset by a derivative position or if an individual deal is part of a wider market play or a long-term agreement.

In my case, some of the best trades I ever made were in a market that ultimately disappeared. Neither did they make a major contribution to the global profits of my employer at that time. My motivation for making those trades was not about the money itself but about leveraging those trades and providing a service to clients that could potentially lead to deeper business relationships in a part of the market that other people ignored, avoided or were reluctant to participate in.

I had been working for the Finnish oil firm Neste Oy for over a decade in London and Dubai before they decided to move me down to Singapore as a manager in their crude oil trading business unit, with the idea that my upstream knowledge and the relationships and knowledge that I had built up of the Middle East crude markets would be very useful, particularly given how much Gulf oil was flowing into Asia.

DOI: 10.4324/9781003144335-43

I had previously been involved in the physical trading of Oman and Dubai crude oil for Neste and that's how I came to the attention of Morgan Stanley in Singapore. They were looking to develop their oil business further in Asia, and I believe they liked the fact that I had been a geologist with oil and gas 'DNA' and had many years work experience with a refiner and integrated oil company trading in the physical markets.

I felt a strong rapport and clicked with my colleagues and folks at Morgan Stanley, and I was fortunate to join them back in 1994. Joining an investment bank with a strong focus on derivatives was a real eye-opener and steep learning curve for me. I had mostly dealt with aspects associated with trading and hedging physical crude oil at Neste and for me derivatives were something of a dark art. But it was a tremendous experience – it 'rounded me off' in the sense that I was developing a grasp of the paper side, which complemented all the previous experience that I had in physical crude oil and the upstream sector of the industry.

A need unmet

I spent a great deal of my time with Morgan in Singapore looking at and studying the APPI crude oil market. The APPI has disappeared now, but back then – and in fact through till the early 2000s – the Asian Petroleum Price Index (APPI) was a key benchmark price for crude oil in the Far East.

APPI assessments were used to price crude oil blends from countries such as Australia, China, Indonesia and Malaysia. Their assessments were published each week on Tuesdays and Thursdays by Seapac Services in Hong Kong.

I'd hesitate to use the word 'primitive' about the APPI system, but quite honestly it wasn't far off. Instead of being set by a price reporting agency, the APPI benchmarks were set by a panel of market participants who sent in submissions on the price of the prices of the various crude oils that APPI covered, with the highest and lowest panel submissions discarded from the published average. At that time, the submissions were sent in by fax!

Despite its obvious drawbacks, APPI Tapis developed as a major benchmark for Malaysian crudes, while official selling prices from Indonesia (the ICPs) were originally based entirely off APPI assessments, particularly of Minas crude oil. This usage by the national oil companies (NOCs) of Malaysia and Indonesia made APPI assessments extremely important for the Asian crude oil market at that time.

Clearly, though, the nature of the APPI methodology – only published twice a week, assessments based on a panel system – made life incredibly difficult for traders and buyers of Malaysian and Indonesian crude oil, who were exposed to a potentially volatile benchmark that was thinly traded in the Asia time zone and considered to be unhedgeable.

By 1995, I had been at the bank long enough to feel comfortable with derivatives. At the same time, we were constantly hearing and listening to comments and observations from our customers and from the broader market around aspects like, 'there's no way of hedging APPI' or 'I'd love to manage my APPI risk'.

That looked like an opportunity to the firm and so we started to offer Tapis and Minas swaps actively to the Asian market.

Managing risk

As you can imagine, offering to buy or sell Tapis and Minas derivatives and/or offer a two-way price was far from a straightforward process, particularly in the Asian time zone when the U.S. or London markets were closed. At that time, the risk management function of Morgan Stanley was one of the most advanced on the street. Without that and without the great trading systems we had in place, I doubt we would have been able to get the initiative off the ground.

The desk would show bids and offers for Minas and Tapis forward markets, sometimes two-way prices, and then the moment someone transacted with us, we would need to manage that risk. We often hedged our exposure with Brent or WTI, and we spent a lot of time analyzing the historical correlations and standard deviations between Minas, Tapis, and the major western benchmarks.

We would also look to shift Minas exposure into Tapis where possible. Compared to Minas, Tapis was fairly liquid as there were a few regular market participants, like Glencore, Vitol, BP, Shell, Conoco and Malaysia's Petronas and occasionally Texaco, as well as other investment banks like the J Aron division of Goldman Sachs.

Even so, it was often difficult if not impossible to get the perfect hedge in place, given the nature of the instrument, so there were plenty of moments where we were crossing our fingers waiting for the APPI numbers to be published or else just waiting nervously for London to open so that we could put a hedge on in a more liquid market than the pretty thin Asian trading window.

Calling card

Despite our best efforts at Morgan Stanley, Tapis and Minas swaps never really took off as a significant derivative market.

Liquidity was always pretty thin, and we had to show fairly wide bid-offer spreads in order to protect ourselves against unexpected moves in the APPI assessments. We did quite a few trades, but ultimately the market didn't catch on. Traders didn't want to pay wider spreads than in other crude oil derivative markets, and there were only a limited number of counterparts in the Minas and Tapis markets anyway.

Ultimately, firms went back to hedging directly in the Brent futures or Dubai swap markets and just living with the basis risk. Money looks for liquidity: most traders will always prefer an imperfect hedge in a liquid market, rather than a perfect hedge in a market that is too illiquid to enter and exit easily.

As a consequence, the APPI swaps market just faded away slowly towards the end of the mid-1990s. Nonetheless, APPI Minas and Tapis remained important benchmarks for physical crude oil trading as late as the late 2000s when they started to disconnect from other crude oil markers. The declining physical volumes underpinning exports of Tapis and Minas made the benchmarks prone to supply constraints, while the panel methodology employed by APPI led to some unusual outcomes.

Australia and Papua New Guinea shifted away from using APPI in favour of Platts Dated Brent assessment in 2009. Malaysia and Vietnam then followed suit in 2011. Indonesia kept faith with APPI a little longer, continuing to use it in its LNG formula until finally dropping it in February 2012.

APPI is now a footnote in oil history, and our swaps offering was not exactly the most profitable part of Morgan Stanley's commodity business, so why did the bank want to get involved and why did we consider the project so successful? After all, major Wall Street investment banks don't typically want to take large risks on illiquid products that only trade sporadically.

In my personal opinion, one of the reasons we persevered and continued to participate was that APPI Minas and Tapis swaps were in effect one of the best calling cards that we could have had in the Asian market.

Back then a lot of firms didn't have the capacity to hedge for themselves, so they were very appreciative that we were offering new and innovative markets for them to manage risk, particularly with regard to hedging refining margins.

Talking to customers about Minas and Tapis swaps allowed us to create, develop and build on relationships with important corporate clients with whom we could do other business with down the line.

We could help customers hedge their Brent and Dubai exposure; we could help refiners lock in their refining margins; assist airlines with managing their jet fuel price exposure; or help producers lock in the long-term profitability of their oilfield production. We could also provide strategic advisory services for firms' trading or risk management activities, or we could introduce them to other parts of the bank that could help with their financing and other corporate investment banking needs.

One of the strengths of Morgan Stanley was that we looked at business with a long-term lens and we never lost sight of the big picture and that the customer comes first.

Offering Tapis and Minas swaps provided a way to engage with the Asian oil community and the physical crude oil market and showed that we were prepared to innovate and to take risk; we could demonstrate that we were a participant across the entire spectrum of crude oil and product trading. As a bank entering a commodity market, there's always some suspicion from commercial oil firms who want to know if you will bring anything new to the market and if you are bringing added value to the table.

Participating in the Tapis and Minas swaps market showed that Morgan Stanley in Singapore was serious about adding value and also that we were comfortable having a conversation about physical crude oil and about dealing in complex benchmarks and working with clients in these areas.

Banker on tour

I travelled extensively with colleagues promoting our oil trading business capabilities, including our Minas and Tapis offering – to China, Japan, Korea, Vietnam, India, everywhere in Asia really. We focused on visiting the pure commercial players, like Showa Shell, that were importing crude oil from Malaysia and Indonesia.

These were mainly business development and educational trips but a lot of the customers that I met during that period ended up transacting with Morgan Stanley in one form or another.

The Minas and Tapis swaps provided one way for us to get in front of clients and to talk to them, listen to their requirements and then promote our capabilities and experience to them, particularly in Brent-Dubai, where we were a very large player, and in refinery crack hedging and aviation jet fuel hedging.

This was all a great experience (and fun) for me. As a former physical oil trader, I could engage when they brought the engineers in to talk about the refinery, and as a former geologist, I could relate when they wanted to talk about long-term oilfield production profiles and producer hedging strategies.

As a Wall Street refiner, I could engage as a 'real oil guy' and that helped me develop great long-term personal relationships with some of the big physical players. It was clear that building good long-term relationships with the national oil companies (NOCs) and corporates in Asia was an important part of the firm's success.

My oil industry background combined with the bank's participation in Minas and Tapis swaps hopefully added to our credibility that opened doors and helped build these important commercial and personal relationships.

By using Minas and Tapis swaps as a calling card, we weren't acting the way the industry expected a Wall Street investment bank to act, and at the same time, I was very far away from your typical bank paper trader. In fact, with my background in the upstream and physical oil space, I always felt more like a poacher turned gamekeeper and felt very comfortable sitting on the customers' side of the table.

My contribution to our global trading profits from trading Tapis and Minas was very limited, and very often, the stress of managing some of the positions was way higher than the potential upside on each trade! But we believed in leveraging our trading offering as a broader business platform to build on our very strong brand and reputation and increase our business interaction with the industry by developing long-term strategic relationships.

The relationships that we made through those very early initiatives and relationships endured and, with my colleagues on the trading desks, supported the bank's ability to build on its business activities in Asia, but also the Middle East. Ultimately, the experience that I gained during these early days played an important role in my subsequent career, particularly in Dubai and the Middle East when I later moved into the exchange space with the DME, and subsequently into asset management and other associated areas.

I was lucky to meet and get to know so many talented people during my time as a trader that I was able to build an extensive personal commercial and political network across the markets in Asia and the Middle East. As a plus, many of the people with whom I traded Minas or Tapis swaps went on to become very senior and highly respected legendary players in the industry, and I count myself fortunate in having had the opportunity to meet and to get to know them during those early days.

37 A chart for success

Kevin McCormack has spent his career on Wall Street in various roles in the commodities space. After graduating with a degree in business and commerce, he entered the NYMEX trading floors in the late 1980s, where he worked as a broker and trader of crude oil, natural gas and refined products. In the mid-2000s, Kevin joined environmental commodity firm, the Flett Exchange, as well as working at a number of proprietary trading firms and over-the-counter brokers. Since 2010, he has held various positions as an importer and trader of physical crude oil, jet fuel and diesel, while also trading crude oil futures on a personal and proprietary basis.

I trade crude oil nowadays without worrying about what is happening in the physical oil markets. Honestly, I don't even look at the news that much. Instead, I base all of my trading decisions on the technical analysis of statistical trends – what people in the market refer to as 'charting'.

Information about fundamentals is out of the window for me – I don't watch what OPEC is doing or try to figure out where supply and demand are going. My method is to use various charting tools to generate short-term trading signals from previous price movements.

Let's say I focus on the three-month chart; I'll watch the oil price over the past three months – how it has behaved and what its typical trading range has been during that period. Then, when I perceive that the oil market is breaking out of that price range, because it is moving either to the upside or to the downside, I will take that as a signal to establish a trading position.

In early February 2021, the market experienced what I understood to be a significant break-out to the upside and so I bought oil quite heavily and, as it turned out, very profitably.

For the previous three months, oil prices had been fairly rangebound, trading between around $50 and $54 per barrel for front-month WTI futures. There was maybe the occasional dip under $50 here and there, but then it would head back up to $54. The market was effectively stuck in that range for quite a while.

I had identified resistance lines, where I felt fresh selling might come into the market and dampen any upward move, at $53.60, $53.90 and $54. When

DOI: 10.4324/9781003144335-44

prices easily pushed through those levels and breached the $54 mark, well, that sent me a very clear signal to buy.

As it turned out, I was absolutely right. WTI went on a bull run throughout February and it ended up breaking $60 for the first time in a long while. Identifying the start of that move and establishing a long position worked out great for me. You only get a few of these opportunities in a year, where the signals are so strong. When you spot them, you have to take full advantage.

COVID rebound

After I'd established my position, I did happen to check around. I saw that OPEC and its partners were maintaining production restraint, and obviously, people were becoming much more optimistic about the economic recovery from COVID-19. Vaccines were getting rolled out in the U.S. and in Europe, while China was buying commodities heavily.

I also looked into the technicals a little more. I was hearing that there was more investment interest in oil, particularly from hedge funds. Well, I still have friends at hedge funds, so I made a few calls to see if the funds were really buying. From what I gathered, they certainly were.

When I heard that and I saw all of the positive news about the potential recovery from the pandemic, it reassured me about my long position, but, to tell you the truth, even if I had heard something different, I still would have been comfortable with the signal from the charts.

When we broke over $54 that was good enough for me, whatever anyone else might say. Of course, it's always nice when the tale from the chart coincides with the general sentiment.

Typically, I try not to hold positions for too long. I like to make a trade and then take my profits within a day or two. But the signal was so strong in February that I held my position and kept adding to it. It's not too often you see a market like that, and when you do, you need to do what I did and ride the trend.

Even when it's going your way, though, you need to watch the charts for signals that it might break again to the downside. I always look to establish points where I would cover my position. That might be because I am suffering losses and I feel they are getting too expensive, or because the signals are showing the market moving against me and unlikely to flip back my way.

On the downside, $49 was a big number for me. I saw that as a key turning point. If oil had dipped down to $48.50 temporarily in February, I wouldn't have necessarily worried, but if it had got down under $48 and there was no sign of a return to $49, then I would have started to reconsider.

After we broke $49, I think I established $48.40 as the point at which I'd sell if we retraced to those levels. You always need a level in your mind where you'd get out because it's starting to look ugly. In this case, it didn't, the oil price just kept popping right around me.

A lot of non-professionals won't buy if the oil price has been rising a lot because they figure it looks expensive and they don't want to get in and pay higher prices. That doesn't make any sense. If you think the market is going to keep moving higher, then you need to get right in, whatever the price you pay on entry. Your aim should be to keep buying until the market pulls back. In my case, I want to hold my position until I get the signal that the trend is breaking.

Studying the charters

I used to watch guys chart when I was on the NYMEX trading floor many years ago. Some of the biggest traders were charters, and I'd ask them what they were doing. By talking to those guys, I came to understand the various ways they used a point-and-figure chart, a day chart or a week chart.

Some big traders had their pencils out the whole day, marking 'x up' or 'x down' all day long. At first, to be honest with you, I'd be wondering what they were doing all that for, but once I realized that a lot of those guys were making some serious money, I figured that technical analysis was something I should look into.

Once the activity levels slowed down on the trading floor and the market was clearly moving electronic, I got deeper into charting and I was able to pick it up quite quickly. I've been trading based on price signals for several years now, and it's worked out pretty well for me.

Trading on charts is obviously 100% different from how I used to trade on the floor. When you were around the pits, and you were doing pretty decent business like I was, then you could usually get a feel from the flow of activity where the market should be going or wanted to go.

Back then, information was key. You might want to switch your position based on what the big traders on the floor were doing because some of them could move a market easily. Back in the day, if I was stood next to J Aron in an energy pit and if I saw them coming in hard when I was short, then I might have wanted to re-evaluate.

Family heritage

Trading is in my blood. My father was a stockbroker on the floor in New York all his life, one of my brothers is a bond broker and the other is an oil guy that ended up on the banking side. It was family that brought me to the trading floor in the first place: my uncle was chairman of a commodity trader, and he ended up getting me into the gold market on COMEX, and I wound up moving across to NYMEX when the energy markets started to really take off in the late 1980s.

I got out of NYMEX a year or two before the pits finally closed. I could see the writing on the wall. It was getting really thin because everyone was going electronic. Trading there was drying up, so I figured it was time for a change.

I worked for a number of firms after leaving the floor, but in terms of trading, charting started to look like a very good option to me. Obviously, you had to change your strategy when you left the floor and the key was to come up with a strategy that you felt comfortable with, and which had the potential to be profitable.

Despite my heritage, I can't honestly say I miss the trading floor. I actually think I sleep better now than I used to when I was trading on the floor because in those days you'd be so wound up from a day of trading – being in the pits was physically draining. Then, even after a busy day, I would like to go work out or have a couple of beers. Actually, I'd usually sleep better with a couple of beers in me!

It's also easier now when you can pop on the internet and see where the price is at 11 o'clock at night. If you have a position on, you can get out if you want to. But back then, once the pits were closed for the day, there wasn't much you could do about your position unless you could find an overnight desk to get you out.

Calmer style

It's easy to be nostalgic, but it was brutal on the floor. You might think the guy next to you is your friend, and, yeah, he's your friend, but not when you're taking 20 grand out of his pocket that day. It was a very competitive environment.

Maybe one of the reasons that I like charting as a strategy is that it is technical and mathematical, and so it takes all of the emotion out of trading. I guess I must have had enough emotion on the trading floor to last me a lifetime.

It's also a disciplined style of trading. In the past, when I traded, I had to make a judgment call, based on my information and my read of the floor and the flow, whereas right now I really don't need to consider too much information beyond the chart.

My responsibility is initially to set up a strategy, to figure out which charts to follow and where to set my entry and exit points. But after that, my role is just to execute the trades based on the signals that the charts generate.

Of course, there are no guaranteed profits to be made from charting – nothing is a certainty in trading – and sometimes the signals are mixed. But when the indications are as strong as they were in February 2021, well, then that's the time when you have to take full advantage.

Trading crude oil options

Crude oil options are option contracts in which the underlying asset is a crude oil futures contract, and which provide a form of insurance against rising or falling crude oil prices.

Option buyers pay an upfront premium to option sellers, similar to an insurance premium. In exchange, they acquire the right (but not the obligation) to take a specific position in the underlying crude oil futures at the strike price that both have agreed.

One of the most attractive features of options is that the premium payable is typically lower than the margin requirement needed to trade crude oil futures. This makes options cheaper to trade, and so some traders prefer options to futures as they can build up larger positions for the same initial investment.

As we will see, the flexible nature of options, where strategies can be built around specific strike prices and time periods, also allows traders to employ a variety of different trading and hedging approaches.

DOI: 10.4324/9781003144335-45

38 Trading on behalf of a nation

Gerardo Rodríguez joined Mexico's Ministry of Finance in 1996 after graduating in economics from the University of Puebla. After leaving in 1998 to study financial engineering at Stanford University and to take a role in the private sector, Gerardo returned to the Ministry in 2001 as assistant director general of domestic borrowing. He was promoted to head of public credit in 2005 and then to undersecretary of finance in 2011. In 2013, Gerardo moved to New York to join global asset manager Blackrock as a managing director and portfolio manager.

The Mexican government relies heavily on the taxable income from crude oil sales by our national oil company PEMEX. That makes Mexico's national budget very dependent on the price of crude, which is obviously extremely volatile.

Falling oil prices in the late 1990s led to unplanned budget cuts, which caused hardship in our country. Mexico had used derivatives opportunistically to try to 'insure' ourselves against oil price declines throughout the 1990s, but the government decided in 2000 to formalize the programme by formally establishing the Oil Stabilization Fund.

The fund was designed to reduce the impact on public finances of changes in the level of oil revenues derived from sudden variations in international oil prices. The fund was provided with funding from oil-related revenue windfalls, under an agreed formula, that it could use to execute hedges to try to protect the Mexican budget from any decline in oil prices.

When I joined the programme a couple of years after that, our aim was to develop something that would be strategic, that would be non-discretionary, and that would be based on strict rules. We wanted to make sure that there would be discipline in every aspect.

The aim of the programme was to protect the budget for the following calendar year, given the annual nature of the government's budget. Clearly, if the oil price falls and stays low, eventually the government will need to adjust its budgetary spending, but at least with proper risk management of the oil price, we would be able to protect strategic spending priorities and programmes that had been agreed for the next calendar year.

DOI: 10.4324/9781003144335-46

Strategic and systematic

We thought about our hedging programme on two levels: strategic and tactical. From a strategic standpoint, we would know the shape and timing of the annual budget and what resources it will require. That required us to be disciplined and to provide the budget with the necessary coverage.

The second element was tactical. That encompasses questions such as what hedging instruments we should use; what underlying security we should provide or require; what is the right timing to execute the hedges; with which counterparts should we hedge; how should we oversee and manage our positions on a day-to-day basis?

The tactical element required government officials to think like oil traders. We would spend a lot of time debating the state of the oil markets. We would discuss what was happening in the producer countries; OPEC's strategy; what was happening with China and demand growth; what was happening in the broader financial and commodity markets. Later on, we also had to add the development of U.S. shale oil into our analysis.

We did most of the research in-house and by the time we came to hedge we knew exactly what we wanted and what we needed. The problem in the early years was that the hedges that we needed were not available.

If you look at the crude oil that Mexico produces, the main grade is Maya, which is a heavy oil. Mexican production was steadily getting heavier and sourer, and so we needed to structure a hedge that would reflect that quality of crude oil, rather than just using the WTI and Brent futures markets, which reflect light sweet crude oil.

Our counterparts were sell-side banks for the most part, and we were always pushing the frontier of what kind of derivative instruments they were comfortable to quote to us. It was a process of interaction over a few years to get them to provide more exact hedges.

Keeping options open

Our programme was designed to cover the risk of the following calendar year to match the budgetary process. The fund was not allowed to share the upside in the event that oil prices rose, our mandate was solely to hedge against oil prices falling.

We decided that the best way to achieve our ends was to use options on the average oil price throughout the year. Options seemed like the ideal way of preserving Mexico's upside. The only downside was that we would need to spend money to buy premiums.

We relied on the central bank to execute the option hedges with our banking counterparts, although it was the team at the ministry that determined the rhythm and timing of their execution. When we saw a hedging opportunity, the central bank would call two or more of the trading desks of the banks, get a firm quote from them, and then select the most competitive quote on which to execute.

We would have four or five trading counterparts in place and would try to rotate our calls between them. We had put a lot of thought into designing a process that would hopefully limit how much the market would see us coming into the market and 'front run' us, which is when parties with inside knowledge of a future transaction make a trade before a larger trade comes in that will affect the price.

Over the years, it became harder for Mexico to be discreet about our programme. That was in part because local regulation that was designed to enhance transparency obliged us to reveal some of the details of our programme, such as around amounts and timings.

The success of the programme in 2008–09 also generated some additional publicity for the programme, which contributed to making our hedging more visible to the broader market.

Placing hedges

Going back to the tactical side of our programme, the officials involved had to decide the timing of our hedges based on our views of the oil market.

The Mexican government typically presents its annual budget for the following calendar year in September, and it has to be approved by November, so we would execute our hedging trades between September and November.

The 2008–09 period was unique. The first signs of the global financial crisis emerged in late 2007, and then, in early 2008, certain hedge funds as well as banks like Bear Stearns and UBS all started to face some issues. The crisis started to become more widespread.

During the summer of 2008, we were scratching our heads that, despite all of the disruption in the financial sector, oil prices had not reacted. In fact, the opposite was happening. All through the summer of 2008, the oil price continued to rise, and actually broke through $100 per barrel.

The rising oil price might look like good news for Mexico, but we were really concerned about the Mexican economy in general. We found out that our corporate sector was heavily exposed to foreign exchange rate risk and that created an important source of macro vulnerability for the country as a whole. When the foreign exchange markets had been stable, several firms had sold option premiums on peso volatility as a way to generate additional revenue. The higher volatility during the financial crisis meant that all of those options went against the local players, which created a big financial shock that they had to absorb.

It was clear that the financial crisis would create some significant challenges for Mexico, and this difficult environment made it all the more important that the ministry should get the oil hedging programme right. We discussed the situation in depth, and eventually, we made the decision to execute our hedges for 2009 early.

Our strategy hadn't changed, but our tactics had to respond to the evolving situation. In all my tenure, this was the earliest that we ever executed. Instead of September to November, we first went to the market in June 2008 and we had completed our programme by August, a good three months ahead of our normal timings.

Reaping rewards

As the financial crisis intensified, the oil price collapsed, and our options moved heavily into the money.

At one point, our options were a good $30–40 dollars in the money, and we had hedged around 300 million barrels. Probably at its peak, our mark-to-market assessment showed a positive variance of $15–16 billion dollars.

Because we had hedged so early, even before the 2009 budget was approved, we had actually ended up over-hedging, that is to say, we had locked in a higher price than we would need to cover the 2009 budget. That allowed us to unwind some of our 2009 hedges as early as October and November 2008 when they were already very profitable. This allowed our 2009 hedges to also support the 2008 budget, which was by then under water.

Clearly, our tactical decision to hedge early turned out extremely well for Mexico, but it was not an easy call to make. If you go to the market early, you have to pay more for your hedges. The additional cost of the premiums was probably 20–25% above what we would normally spend.

We had to make the business case that with so much uncertainty going on in the world, it was worth paying the additional premium, and luckily the approving committee agreed.

The hedging programme had proved to be incredibly effective. The profit from our hedges helped to carry the national budget through the first two years of the financial crisis. But there was no time to stop and take a bow. At that time, we were just too busy at the ministry dealing with the impact of the crisis.

This was a time when every day we had the feeling that the whole economic system could collapse. There was never a time where we could relax, so beyond a couple of pats on the back, there was no time for us to take a pause and to enjoy the success of the oil hedging programme.

I'm not sure at the time that any of us fully realized the implications of the performance of the hedging programme.

Several years later, when I had already moved to New York and joined the asset management giant Blackrock, I bumped into an old counterpart from one of the sell-side banks with whom we used to hedge. He pointed me to an article that described our 2009 hedging programme as the greatest single oil trade of all time.

I think that was only then that it truly struck me, just how significant and how sizeable our transactions had been. At the time, there was too much going on to really think about the scale of the numbers involved and to absorb all of the implications.

Mexican singularity

I stayed on as head of public debt management until 2011, after which I was promoted to deputy finance minister. I held that responsibility for almost two years, and then at the end of 2012, I finally left the government. I had spent a fantastic 15 years at the Mexican treasury department. I had started there as an entry-level analyst fresh out of college, and I finally left as deputy minister of finance.

When I left government, I had the clear idea that whatever I did afterwards, it was going to be difficult to find a job that I enjoyed as much as that one. Working within the government can be very fulfilling, and I was lucky enough to be given some significant responsibilities early in my career.

Working on areas like the oil hedging programme was extremely exciting: it involved a lot of technical challenges that were intellectually stimulating, but it was also very relevant, in that the decisions we made had a direct impact on our country.

Mexico's sovereign hedging programme is unique among major oil-producing nations, which is perhaps surprising when you consider the positive results that the programme has delivered over the years.

Mexico is certainly unique in the way it makes use of derivatives. In my mind, there are two reasons why Mexico is different. One is a positive reason, and the other is a negative reason.

If we start with the good reason, Mexico has always benefited from very competent technocratic teams within the finance ministry and the Central Bank that think deeply and that managed to find the political space that allowed them to construct the systematic and tactical components that are needed to get a well-constructed hedging programme in place.

Mexico has a long tradition of effective macroeconomic management, and our oil hedging programme is a good reflection of that. Some of the other oil producers in emerging countries do not necessarily benefit from that institutional know-how.

That's the good side, but the bad side is that if you look at some other oil producers, such as Norway, they confirm that the best way to manage a country's exposure to the oil price is for the country in question to save more and to prepare for when the bad years come when they can make use of some of those savings.

Focusing on saving rather than hedging would represent better value because it eliminates the transaction costs that Mexico has to pay for its hedging programme. This superior strategy requires budgetary discipline, and for a country to put away all of its oil-related revenue windfall, which over the years could reach many points of GDP.

The success of that strategy is dependent on politicians not being tempted to dip into the savings every year. Unfortunately, in a country like Mexico, where politics are a big part of economic discussions and where tax revenues are low, adopting a strategy based on savings has not to date been possible.

We have proved that we are good at designing and implementing an oil hedging programme, and in 2008 and 2009 we delivered truly exceptional results, but I would argue that we are hedging for the wrong reasons.

The more difficult conversation would be to discuss why Mexico needs such a programme. As a former official, I am extremely proud of what we achieved, but as an economist I have mixed feelings about our hedging. There is a superior strategy out there, but as a country we have not been able to construct the institutional framework to implement it.

39 The invention of synthetic storage

Dr Ilia Bouchouev is the former president of Koch Global Partners where he launched and managed the global derivatives trading business for over 20 years. Over the years, he introduced several energy derivatives products and was recognized as one of the pioneers in energy options trading. He is currently managing partner at Pentathlon Investments and adjunct professor at New York University where he teaches energy trading. He has a Ph.D. in applied mathematics and has published in academic journals on derivatives pricing and energy markets. Dr Bouchouev serves on the editorial board of Quantitative Finance and is a research associate at the Oxford Institute for Energy Studies (OIES).

I only really became an oil trader to get my U.S. Green Card.

I was a mathematician by training and when I was finishing up my Ph.D., I started applying to the big Wall Street banks. I had a vision of myself as a quant on an equities desk at Goldman Sachs or some role like that.

Then, one day I was introduced to someone from Koch Industries. He told me that it would be a waste to go to Wall Street and that I would be one of a hundred quants at Goldman, and that I would have more opportunities and stand out more at an industrial firm like Koch.

Then, he produced the clincher – Koch would sponsor me for permanent resident status and get me a Green Card.

Well, that was me sold. I couldn't turn down the offer of a Green Card, and so I started straight away at Koch on the options side.

During my Ph.D., I had been working on various options models but I always liked the practical side, and so I was very interested in applying my models to real-life situations to see if they would work and if they could generate any real value.

I started to think deeply about the optionality that a position in storage gives a firm. If you own storage or the rights to storage, then you always have the option to buy oil from the market when prices are cheap, store it, and sell futures to lock in the profits. Then later, when the contango narrows, you can deliver that oil back into the market from your storage and buy back your short futures position.

Or if you have an option over some storage capacity, then you can sell that option to another firm for a profit at times when storage is in higher demand.

DOI: 10.4324/9781003144335-47

If storage is in low demand, at least the only loss you have to book is the premium that you paid for the option to store.

Valuing optionality

Koch always liked to monetize optionality. They liked to have real options by holding physical assets, whether it was a refinery, a pipeline or any other asset. The oil traders at Koch instinctively understood that they had some value inherent in their storage options but they didn't know how to value it properly so that became my first project.

At that time, in the late 1990s, there was nothing much oil specific out there that would help you value the option on storage. I looked at one of the most popular commercially available models and it was showing a much lower value for storage than my own model was indicating.

The model was showing 20 cents per barrel when my models were coming up with at least 30 cents. I just couldn't understand the discrepancy but when I started to dig into the third-party pricing model, it turned out that whoever built the software put a cap of 400 iterations on its software. That was a hard-coded maximum. But if you allowed the model to iterate more, say 4,000 times, then the value increased significantly, and it ended up at around my level of 30 cents.

I realized at that point that all of the models that the industry was using were totally wrong and were massively undervaluing what storage options were worth.

So I went to my physical oil desk and I told them that if they and the market were valuing their optionality at 20 cents, then I would buy it from them and see if I could turn it into the 30 cents that I thought it was actually worth.

They were intrigued, and they thought I might be onto something. But instead of selling me their own optionality, they told me to go and buy that optionality from the market.

You have to give Koch huge credit here. There I was, this young immigrant scientist six months out of academia, with an idea that I thought was a good one, and they gave me the backing to explore it. They put trust in me and gave me a portfolio to run with no experience whatsoever.

Koch sat me next to the physical oil traders who told me they'd help if I had questions and also warned the brokers not to screw over this young quant. Management gave me a contact list, a phone and a risk remit and then they wished me good luck and left me to get on with it.

Acquiring inventory

I went out to the market and started calling all the oil storage companies, like Plains. Their asset was their tanks and so my pitch was that I would buy the option to make use of their storage capacity for 20 cents per barrel per month.

I called my strategy synthetic storage. The benefit to the storage companies was that they were going to get cash upfront from Koch that they could then use to build more tanks or other assets to develop their businesses further.

Some of the storage firms really liked the idea. They loved the idea of getting some cash up front and they liked the longer-term commitment that I was offering. I started small with three-month deals, but as the strategy began to prove itself, we expanded the tenor of our deals into one-year contracts, three-year contracts, and we were even able to look at five-year contracts later on.

In the world of physical storage, it's generally true that the longer the commitment you offer, the cheaper the storage rates. Storage providers really want certainty that their tanks will get used, and so they are prepared to offer lower rates if they know that the firm will be there for a couple of years or so. You might find if the market is, say, 40 cents per barrel per month for a three-month commitment, then that might drop to 35 cents for a six-month commitment, and then to 30 or so for a year or a multi-year commitment.

The storage firms really appreciated the longer-term commitment that I was offering and so they were happy to take Koch's cash. Many of them used our upfront payments to build more storage at the oil hub of Cushing, Oklahoma. I would guess that a lot of Cushing was built on Koch's cash – in fact, that might well be my greatest contribution to the oil market!

It was brave of Koch to let some inexperienced guy make these bets but ultimately the storage options I was buying didn't typically lose any value: they just sat there, and the only cost was the premium that I had paid upfront, which represented foregone interest on the cash.

You could see it as a warehouse strategy. We were buying ever longer-dated storage, holding it as inventory, and then once the optionality moved closer to the three- to six-month window that brought it more into demand in the spot physical market, I was selling it.

You could see what we were doing as providing a connection between the physical and financial markets. The storage company owns the physical storage, and Koch owns the financial storage. We were risking our capital against the longer-term value of storage.

The strategy of buying longer-dated storage optionality, holding it and then reselling it proved successful. It made money every year from the late 1990s onwards and by 2003–04, everyone at Koch was very comfortable with the strategy and was prepared to put more money at risk and do longer and longer-dated deals.

We were buying options on inter-month spreads from storage firms for very large volumes and for very long periods. I was paying out Koch's cash upfront for three-year strips of calendar spread options, and because of the three-year commitment, the firms were happy to sell to me relatively cheaply.

Taking profit

By 2007–08, I was getting cheap optionality in large volumes for a really long period of time and then trying to delta hedge the position. But the volumes were very large, and it was becoming harder to offset time decay by delta hedging. At the same time, the positions were showing very good profits, so my management started to ask how I was going to exit my position and book all of the profits that I was showing on paper.

The options that we had bought at 30 cents per barrel had already doubled in price because oil was on its run-up to 100 dollars per barrel. By then, it's fair to say that we were pretty much the main market in storage options, we had bought optionality from everyone because we had built such a good long-term relationship with all of the storage firms.

The play on timing that we had developed – buy long-dated, hold and then sell once the options were three to six months away – was working fine but we now had much larger volumes to move.

I realized that we needed to diversify our pool of buyers, and I suggested to the marketing folks on my team that we should go out to the pension funds.

In 2007/08, the contango had reached the oil market and the banks that were pushing passing commodity indexes to investors, such as the S&P GSCI index, were finding that the negative rolls during contango were having a massive impact on their results.

We realized that if investors were getting badly affected by the monthly roll in oil, then they ought to be interested in taking some protection against the difference between the front month and the second month. And because we had so much optionality on storage, we were in a great position to supply that insurance.

We went on a marketing mission to offer our optionality to everyone that was exposed to the GSCI – banks, pension funds, hedge funds. Of course, they loved it because it was exactly what they needed, and we signed up quite a few of them.

We started to unwind the book. You could call it a wholesale strategy. It was like some big grocery chain. I was buying my three-year strips in bulk, and so I was paying wholesale prices, but then when the optionality was closer to expiry, say three to six months, the funds would buy it from me at retail prices.

We were effectively connecting the storage firms that needed money upfront to build out infrastructure to pension funds that wanted exposure to commodities but needed insurance against the contango affecting their investments.

Listed options

We unwound some more of the position to funds, but not everything because we were still constrained. Koch is a private company, and some of the pension funds we wanted to trade with required more disclosure and statements than a private company would be willing to provide.

I was limited because I couldn't access all of the customers that I needed to in order to unwind the book so we had another idea: we could work with the exchange.

We went to the New York Mercantile Exchange (NYMEX), now part of CME Group, and we encouraged them to list calendar spread options on their trading floor.

This was really the ultimate in terms of market access. The exchange offered clearing services, which meant that there was no credit risk or need for disclosure between counterparties. With clearing, we could effectively trade with anyone anywhere that also had access to clearing at NYMEX.

By that point, we thought our optionality was worth maybe 50–60 cents, but we found that some of the participants on NYMEX were willing to pay up to 70 cents. It took us about a year to unwind all of the positions through the exchange but eventually we had successfully booked all of our profit.

Win–win

I'm proud of our synthetic storage strategy because it was a trade that worked for everyone. Of course, Koch made a lot of money, but we also provided the finance that was needed to help the U.S. storage firms expand.

When the value of options had already moved up from 30 to 60 cents, I went for a drink with a guy from one of the storage companies who sold me a lot of relatively cheap options. He knew he had given me a discount but he hadn't sold me everything so he was selling the rest of his position at high prices and he was making a lot of money and even more from renting out the tanks that they had built with Koch's upfront payments.

He patted me on the back, and he wouldn't even let me pay for the drinks. It's a great strategy when you make money, but your customer also makes money.

We also provided a useful service to investors that needed insurance against major moves in oil from one calendar month to another, and we played a role in connecting parts of the market that would never have found each other otherwise.

The trade also worked out for me personally. Koch Trading encouraged me to build out a global derivatives desk with a much broader mandate than our virtual storage strategy and I ran that desk for many years.

Not many companies would have backed me in the way that Koch did. And I eventually received the Green Card as well and I went on to become a U.S. citizen.

40 Making a major shift

After studying banking and finance at Australia's Monash University, Richard Fullarton joined Bankers Trust in Sydney as an equity derivatives trader. He moved to London in 1998 and joined Caisse des Dépôts and subsequently Crédit Lyonnais, where he was senior energy options trader. In 2001, Richard moved to Shell, where he spent 13 years, rising to be team leader for global crude oil derivatives. He had a spell at Glencore and as an independent hedging consultant, before founding commodity derivatives fund Matilda Capital Management in 2016.

In the eyes of an options trader like myself, a major oil company is essentially a huge book of options.

An integrated major produces crude oil; it buys and sells different grades of crude oil; and its refineries process crude oil and turn it into consumer products. This exposure throughout the crude oil value chain provides a major with tremendous optionality.

An oil major aims to build long and short positions everywhere to maximize its optionality. Producing multiple grades of crude oil in different regions, actively trading cargoes or pipeline parcels, operating refineries in different regions, all provide a major with different options to try to maximize its profitability.

A major with global operations has an almost inconceivable number of options that it can choose to either trade, manage or ignore. For the most part, though, these are real physical options that have real-life constraints attached to them rather than the pure paper options that a bank's options desk might trade.

Even something as huge as a refinery is essentially a billion-dollar options play. A major will spend huge sums to generate a long exposure to refinery margins, even knowing that the option comes with time decay because the structure is slowly going to rust away.

As a derivatives trader from an investment bank background who joined an oil major, one of the first tasks I wanted to investigate was which elements of the firm's tremendous optionality could actually be monetized profitably, and after that to help my colleagues unlock the value of their options. Shell

DOI: 10.4324/9781003144335-48

initially had other plans for me, and it was a journey of discovery for both sides to awaken the true potential of Shell Trading.

Banks to majors

I moved to London from Australia in 1998 when the Asian economic crisis hit, and I was approached by Crédit Lyonnais to work on their oil desk. I had traded oil equities in Australia, but I quickly realized that I didn't know anything about the actual oil markets. It was a tremendous learning curve, but I quickly realized that there were huge opportunities in the energy sector.

Shell asked me to join them in 2001 to work in a new business area they were developing with the Dutch bank ABN-AMRO. The concept was that ABN would bring those customers that needed to manage energy exposure to Shell, who would provide risk management expertise and derivatives execution.

This partnership was a good concept and was ahead of its time in many ways, but it meant that Shell needed to bring in some outside derivative traders and hedging experts to service ABN's customer flow. Shell essentially needed to build a bank derivatives desk or a small hedge fund operation within Shell Trading.

That was where I came in, and well, you can imagine how the sudden arrival of a bunch of bankers went down with some of the guys that were already in Shell Trading...

At that time, the Royal Dutch Shell board put much less emphasis on trading. There were many extremely smart people working there and Shell Trading was a hugely successful trading and customer management operation, but within Royal Dutch Shell, the trading business at the time was almost treated like a dirty secret.

Management did not report the results from Shell Trading because they did not want the shareholders to realize just how much money was being made out of trading compared with the core business. As a result, a lot of people were simply not aware of how active Shell Trading was. I remember counterparts back in the day that would laugh at Shell Trading and wouldn't hire Shell traders because they were not considered to be top tier.

As well as the company's relative silence around trading, the culture at Shell at that time was not conducive to the creation of a world-class trading operation. The career risk of doing something different was huge. In those days, it only took one blight on your record, and you wouldn't get promoted, meaning your career was effectively stalled.

Management was not incentivized to take on risk. I remember that instead of being applauded for implementing a successful risk management programme, traders would sometimes get questioned why their hedges had lost money, even if their underlying trades had performed spectacularly.

The mantra at the time was that 'investors buy Shell shares for exposure to the oil price', which was Shell-speak for 'do not rock the boat'. Somebody had to rock the boat!

Cultural changes

The turning point in changing the corporate view of trading at Shell was when they brought in external people like myself. But that cultural change took a long time – as the saying goes, you don't turn a supertanker around overnight – and at first, it generated a lot of animosity.

I also had to change my attitude; investment banking is very different to an oil major. In a bank, you are the asset, and in an oil major, the oil is the asset. Oil majors are rightly conservative about risk because getting something wrong on an oil rig causes deaths and environmental carnage, not a rap over the knuckles from a regulator. Other oil majors have crossed this risk line the wrong way at great cost. This was a learning experience and a culture change for all involved.

In retrospect, it was inevitable that our new desk was not going to be popular. By exclusively hiring externally, Shell was effectively saying that they did not believe that anyone internal had the skills to match the derivative traders working at the banks, or at firms like Enron, etc. That was not a recipe for a warm welcome.

A lot of the initial ill-feeling was summed up by the outrage over our trading screens. When we joined, flat screens for computer monitors were just coming in. Our desks were being fitted out from scratch, so we all got flat screens. Those were the only flat screens on the whole trading floor.

Picture it from a long-time employee's perspective. They saw a bunch of guys sitting there doing something with derivatives that they didn't fully understand. They also knew that we had come into Shell on higher external-style salaries. Then, to make the whole thing worse, we even had better equipment...

There was a lot of understandable scepticism about what we were trying to do. I remember hearing that making a few million here or there by trading derivatives was not really worth the effort, given that some Shell physical desks were making hundreds of millions each year without really trying.

What was interesting, though, was that many of the leaders in Shell Trading today are the people that walked over to us and asked us questions about what we were working on. Those guys that looked beyond the cultural prejudice against derivatives and against ex-bankers often went on to become senior figures in Shell or elsewhere, and many built important new businesses, such as Shell's LNG trading desk.

The prejudices slowly dissolved as we started to prove our worth. We were seen as part of the team and as adding value to both the crude oil and products trading teams. We were also able to demonstrate to senior management that we could price and hedge risk internally and add value to the core business which then makes you part of the core business.

Our desk began to analyze our trading business through the lens of an options trader, which meant that we could show traders when they were giving away optionality to customers.

We also won business for Shell because of our derivative capacity. We brought to Shell what I liked to call a 'McDonalds mentality': we started to ask always if the customer would like to upsize their order or would like to add a side order of some built-in risk management.

Trading convexity

My personal proprietary trading book was based on the energy options markets. I started by arbitraging options and later moved into developing our convexity trading strategy, which is where I made my name and most of my trading profits.

The focus of my options trading strategy was always to look for any potential mispricing due to the way trades flowed into the market and were absorbed.

At the time I joined Shell, energy options were still voice broked, by which I mean we did all of our trading via over-the-counter brokers who told us about bids and offers verbally over the phone or via a direct line to the desk.

Back then, the voice broker had enormous power because the broker decided whom they were going to call first with the juiciest bids and offers. Shell was a significant player in options, but we were never as large as some of the banks. Our relative size and importance meant we were unlikely to be first on the A-list for the brokers to call.

Unlike some of our competitors on the bank options desks, we clearly couldn't just rely on trading the order flow from the brokers, so we had to look at more innovative trading strategies.

The first thing that we spotted was that there were clearly opportunities to trade the difference between the different prices – the arbitrage – that various voice brokers were showing us. Each broker had different customers who were showing slightly different bids and offers so there were sometimes brief discrepancies in options prices that we could exploit.

There were also frequently arbitrages between the prices traded in the open outcry pits of the exchanges – then the NYMEX and IPE, later CME and ICE – and the over-the-counter markets that were handled by the voice brokers.

The OTC market was generally for Asian options, which are based on average pricing, but which we hedged with exchange options. There was good money to be made by trading with the OTC customers via the brokers and then offloading that risk onto the exchange trading floor. It just required us to monitor the performance of the single-strike options traded on the exchange against the average that we had bought or sold via the brokers.

This strategy became more significant as the Mexican sovereign hedging programme grew in importance (see Chapter 38). The Mexicans tended to hedge with Asian options and those banks that had sold Mexico the hedges, and then had to offload at least part of that exposure into the wider market.

Mexico would not talk to Shell Trading about their hedge even though the majority of Maya oil was actually bought by Shell. This was frustrating but the silver lining for me was that it meant that I knew that the banks had even more of the Mexico risk on their books and the opportunities for convexity option trades were even greater.

Finding pinch points

Over the longer term, where I made my profits and my reputation within Shell was by being able to correctly understand where the banks and flow providers were at maximum stress points from an options perspective.

Oil is unique among financial markets, in that the size of the customers is so huge and their risk management requirements can be so large that there are times when customer hedges are larger than the market's ability to absorb them.

One of the factors that first brought the banks into oil options is this sheer size of the market. There is always significant two-way business between producers and consumers, but sometimes there will be periods when the market is imbalanced, perhaps because all of the producers want to hedge at a time when it is hard to match them with consumers.

For example, when the Mexicans came in to hedge, sometimes people were prepared to pay abnormally high levels to hedge their options exposure. There would be short-term opportunities from the dislocation of pricing created by the sheer size of the Mexican trade, which was bigger than the market could easily absorb.

At times when the market is imbalanced between consumers and producers, the banks would step in and hold one side of the options, at least until they could pass some of that risk on to the other side at a later date. This created 'pinch points' in the market: times when the banks were sitting on substantial numbers of options in certain parts of the curve.

The banks' role in intermediating the risk worked most of the time. But when they got it wrong, they got it really wrong, which obviously created some significant opportunities.

With my banking derivatives experience, it was obvious to me that whenever the price of oil gapped up or gapped down, perhaps because of geopolitics, financial collapses, or even just changes in OPEC policy, the sharp moves would catch out some of the banks.

Banks that were sitting on substantial option risk, at a time when volatility was increasing sharply, would need to re-hedge their option deltas or even get out of some of their option risk in order to reduce their risk profiles.

As a firm, we benefited tremendously from these temporary dislocations in the markets. We acted almost like a hedge fund, in that we could see opportunities where the market would be under extreme amounts of stress and we would to a certain degree effectively step in and take an opposite view, based on where the flows were moving.

We called it 'trading on the wings'. Our skill was to capture the impact of sharp moves in volatility at times when the market was responding to a shock. We would try to step in whenever we felt the market was underpricing the impact of a potential change in volatility that, for example, would move the market towards an area where the banks were sitting on large numbers of short options.

Our ability to execute these convexity trades changed over time, as more market makers got involved in energy options and the number of players increased. The pinch points were more obvious back in the day when there were a smaller number of key banks that held all of the risks.

The dominance of a few banks was probably one of the Achilles heels of the oil market in those days, but being aware of the potential impact of that concentration of risk provided us with some significant trading opportunities.

Powering on

Shell's derivatives business started to become very profitable, and the year that I made more money than the North Sea physical trading desk really helped to get management to sit up and take notice.

There was also a changing of the guard in Shell. The global head of crude oil trading at the time, Mike Muller, had always been a big supporter of what we were doing, but now other senior figures also saw the value.

Within a few years, Shell had caught onto derivatives in a big way. Our desk, which had originally been viewed with such great suspicion, was now fully part of the mainstream of Shell Trading. The risk management excellence we had developed initially for crude oil and refined products soon spread wider throughout the business to create new derivatives businesses in areas as diverse as LNG, carbon or European gas and electricity.

In my view, the oil majors are now on par with the banks in terms of risk management capacity and are likely better than most. Shell, in particular, has become a true trading powerhouse and has rightly got the recognition internally and externally that it always deserved. The trading operation I left in 2014 was a world away from the one I came into in 2001, and it has only been powering on since then.

Shell Trading evolved when they brought in outsiders, but it was a slow process. Like all traders entering a new area, the key was that we were able to demonstrate our worth to the business. It was trading success that brought us credibility and influence.

After all, you can't turn a supertanker around by standing in front of it and pushing back. The only way to effect change is to get invited up onto the command deck where you can start to help with the steering.

Further reading and bibliography

There is a substantial amount of academic literature available that discusses oil prices and how they are formed, and many of the strongest papers are published by the Oxford Institute of Energy Studies (OIES).

There are also a lot of 'how to' guides to oil trading that are mostly aimed at individual traders that wish to speculate in the oil futures market.

Works that deal with real oil traders and their professional lives are less common. The following represent some personal recommendations:

Further reading on oil traders

- Ammann, D. (2011) *The King of Oil: The Secret Lives of Marc Rich*, St Martin's Press. The stranger-than-fiction tale of how Marc Rich virtually invented modern oil trading.
- Blas, J. and Farchy, J. (2021) *The World for Sale: Money, Power and the Traders Who Barter the Earth's Resources*, London: Random House Business. A history of the trading houses that are so integral to the commodity markets and especially to oil trading.
- Bower, T. (2009) *The Squeeze: Oil, Money & Greed in the 21st Century*, London: HarperPress. A compelling romp through the oil industry in the 2000s.

Further reading on the oil markets

- Bossley, E. (2013) *Trading Crude Oil: The Consilience Guide*, Consilience Energy Advisory Group Ltd.
- Horsnell, P. and Mabro, R. (1993) *Oil Markets and Prices, The Brent Market and the Formation of World Oil Prices*, Oxford: Oxford University Press. The first guide to how the Brent market developed.
- Imsirovic, A. (2021) *Trading and Price Discovery for Crude Oils: Growth and Development of International Oil Markets*, London: Palgrave Macmillan. The definitive analysis of the various oil benchmarks, such as Brent, WTI, Oman and Dubai.

- Johnson, O. (2018) *The Price Reporters: A Guide to PRAs and Commodity Benchmarks*, London: Routledge. A personal favourite: the history and background of Platts, Argus and other crude oil benchmark providers.
- Yergin, D. (2009) *The Prize: The Epic Quest for Oil, Money & Power*, Simon & Schuster. A masterpiece that provides the classic account of the development of the modern energy industry.

Index